Scott Wellinger

Juror

a Warren Dennihan Novel

Juror

A Warren Dennihan Novel

by Scott Wellinger

World Wide Publishing Group
New York   Los Angeles   London   Toronto
www.WWPGroupInc.com

For information, address: World Wide Publishing Group.

Jacket design by Jason Goodchild

Jacket photo by Ken Wasolinsky

Printed in the United States of America

10 9 8 7 6 5 4 3 2 1

ISBN: 978-0-9861514-2-2   (Ebook)
ISBN: 978-0-9861154-3-9   (print)

For SL

If only the page did you justice.

Epigraph

"The trust of the innocent is the liar's most
useful tool."

~ Stephen King

Prologue

I WISH HE WOULD JUST KILL ME. Please, just get it over with. I would beg him if he'd let me, but I can't speak. All I can do is wish and hope that this will all end, and that whatever happens, whatever is on the other side will be better than this.

It has to be.

Lying here on my own floor, in my own apartment, I welcome death—because I cannot take anymore punishment. More is coming to be sure, but I can't bear the thought, let alone the actual torture. I'm not sure how long this is going to continue, how long he is going to let this abuse drag out, but I need it to stop. Please. I'm a dead woman, I know it and he damn sure knows it. He has full control of me, he's had it since he walked through my front door. Has it been hours? Days? For all I know, he's been administering intolerable amounts of pain for a week.

What I do know is that I will never see the age of twenty-seven, and at this point I don't care. These are my last moments alive, from now until the torment stops, which I hope are few.

Pain and death are all that are left. Nothing more.

I'm blindfolded, so I cannot tell time. I have no idea how long I've been beaten and raped, only to have the process start all over again. I can't look him in the eye. I can't plead. Can't see light of any kind, natural or artificial.

Everything started from the knock on the door which now seems like days ago. I'd been trying to put him off, trying to keep him at bay, but he found me. I've been in and out of consciousness since then, every assault a fresh hell. And now I'm ready for the real thing.

I must deserve this, right? How could this much pain and torture not be justified? I've brought this upon myself, asked for it without using the words. Not like this. The words I used were 'dominated' and 'S & M' in the profiles I set up. I was looking for a good time and the grim reaper is who came calling. I opened the door, literally and figuratively, and I knew this day would come. Deep down in my heart of hearts I knew this would happen if I wasn't careful. It was just a matter of time.

My name is Sloane Nichols, and I've never been religious, but I'm praying now. I'm praying for it to end. No formal prayers—nothing as elaborate as a quote from the Bible or Torah or Koran or anything like that—primarily because I don't know any. I'm speaking from the heart to whatever creator I've offended. I'm crying out to Him or Her from the inside, from the depths of my soul, because the gag shoved into my mouth won't let me be heard by anyone else. I'm willing my testimony to whomever will hear me, whomever will hasten the end.

Maybe Connie from next door will get me some help. Those thoughts have come sporadically between my muffled screams of pain, but help hasn't come. Prayers have gone unanswered and are becoming futile. If she was coming, wouldn't she have already stopped this? Or would she just think this another night of loud sex? Every time I see her, I can see her judging me. She is one of those 'straight' people who has the same routine every day, probably the exact same routine sexually as well. First a few kisses, then maybe some oral if it's a birthday or high holiday, otherwise it's the same missionary position with Connie staring at the ceiling from under the same man. How boring.

I'm proud of my sex life, or I was. Maybe she was jealous. Maybe she was right to silently judge me. Maybe I am a whore or a slut or whatever other word she uses to describe me to her prude friends. We've been friendly since I soundproofed my apartment. The sex was loud and she complained to the landlord one too many times, so I had the work done. Paid for with sex. What can I say? The guy was hot.

Anyway, we've been friendly since. Friendly in a way that neighbors are.

Can I borrow some coffee? I'm out of K-cups.

Sure.

I'll be out of town for the weekend, can you keep an eye on my apartment?

Why not?

That kind of thing.

But she always had an air of being better than me since the day I moved in, even after I ensured that she would never hear another moan of ecstasy, or playful scream. Maybe she is better than me. And maybe she will see my death as proof that her lifestyle choice is the correct one.

No matter what I've done, though, no matter which choices I've made, this is too much to pay. Far too draconian. I want this to end. I want to die. No more pain. Please. I would beg, if only I didn't have this fucking gag in my mouth.

Everyone who knows me, sexually or otherwise, thinks of me as a fighter. As feisty. A wild cat on the prowl. All the fight has left me now, there is nothing left to fight for. All I can do is ask. Ask and hope and pray that my wish is granted. One desire weaves through my mind, and that is that I want this torture end. Please just kill me, I want to die. I welcome it.

My head has been hit so many times, it's a wonder that I can think at all. That's probably why I'm rambling. Why my thoughts are all jumbled. My brain is destroyed. My body is destroyed.

That's how it started. He came to the door, looking to hook up. He wanted a piece of ass, and it's not the first time he's been after me to give him some. I didn't want to at first, but I didn't have any plans, so why not let him in? He's wanted me for some time and been tracking me down to see where I'm living now. I put him off and teased him, but he found me. And he wants me. So Why not? At least that's what I thought at the time—what I was thinking when I opened the door and before it felt like the back of my head exploded and everything went black.

When I came to, It was still dark because I was blindfolded. My hands were bound, though the constraints didn't feel like my handcuffs, nor does it now. My fuzzy, pink handcuffs do the job but are much more forgiving. Soft yet sturdy. Sex should involve a little pain, but what's happening now, what has been happening for seemingly years is unbearable. These handcuffs are deeply cutting into my skin. My hands and wrists are wet and excruciating and are bound so tight that it feels like metal is cutting into my bones.

When I regained consciousness the first time, I tried to get up from the floor when I heard him coming toward me and lashed out at him in a futile attempt to get away. I made contact but I don't know if I hurt him. Probably not. I only know how much pain that I was in. I long for that pain now. That was nothing compared to what came after, and what has happened since.

I tried to scream in both pain and fear, but I've got a big wad of what feels and tastes like cotton in my mouth, so it sounds like a muffled nothing, even to me. I can barely breath and I cannot expel the gag. The fucking thing must be tied or taped to my head.

Blindly running was a stupid idea. I ran into a wall and took another blow to the head for my efforts. I'm still in my apartment, on the floor between my living room and kitchen I think I smell the Pine Sol. This was in the beginning, when my floor was clean. Also, I can tell where I am by the soundproofed echo. When he calmly tells me to stop trying to escape, his voice whispers throughout the high ceiling and chills me to the bone.

He informed me of how much it would hurt. What he was going to do to me, detail by detail, of how much it was going to hurt. He undersold it.

I felt him tear my clothes off, he wanted me conscious for the rape. I don't understand why he thinks he needs to rape me, I was going to give him what he wanted. *Is this some kind of game?* That's what I thought at first. But this is no game. Not for me.

Kicking and struggling to break free was a waste of energy, he is far too powerful. I am his play-thing and he again warned me that fighting is only going to bring me more pain than he already had in store.

If only I'd listened. But I didn't. He struck my left knee with something solid, I felt the thud of the object—and heard it—just before I blacked out from the pain.

Only he knows how long I was unconscious. Again. Only he knows what he did to me while I was comatose. But I do know what he did to me when I regained what was left of my senses. The muffled silence of my screams; the putrid smell of my eliminated bladder and bowels; the taste of wet cotton from my vomit; and the immense pain were the prevalent senses on overload. My head was throbbing. My knee was throbbing. My hands felt like they were being cut off from the restraints.

But this was still the beginning.

I long for that amount of pain. I long for it to end.

Something was shoved inside me. Not one of my vibrators or toys, this was much bigger and not meant for the job. I've never given birth, but that is what it must feel like in reverse. I kicked him and the blunt object away with my right leg, my good leg, but he quickly grew tired of the struggle and shattered my right knee. There was nothing I could do but take it and continue to scream into the soaked gag. He kept ramming it into me, feeling it deeper inside of me, and I thought I was going to be impaled.

My tears wet the blindfold. My entire body was wet. I was covered in everything I smelled; blood, shit, piss, vomit and whatever bodily function he's performed.

After being raped with what felt as big as a football, I was given a rest. Rest came in the form of another blow to the head.

I was roused to another invasion. This time anally. I was face-down on my own hardwood floor, lying in my own blood and piss and shit and tears. I tried to knock myself out by head-butting the floor, but failed.

And on it went. Over and over and over again. I don't know how many times, I don't know how long. Does it matter? Even once is the most heinous and horrifying thing that can happen to a person. I just want this to end. I will happily take a bullet, though I think that is too much to ask for. He seems keen on making my suffering last as long as possible, so death won't come quick.

There is no recovery from this. I try to stay positive. Sanguine. I Fantasize about being saved. I can change. I will change if I am spared, if someone will just come through my door and and save me. But what is left of me for someone to save? I only know that the pain is excruciating and has been for hours. Possibly days.

I hear him coming back. He still has his shoes on. His thick, heavy footfalls are approaching and the floor is vibrating on my face.

Is that bleach I smell? Or chlorine? What else can this sick bastard do to me? Why is this happening? No more. I don't deserve any more.

He's pouring it all over me. I didn't think I could hurt any worse, but the liquid is covering all of my wounds. It feels like I'm being burned alive. I no longer have the strength to scream, not that anyone would hear me anyway. Please let this be the end.

And then he tells me that it is. Have my prayers been answered? Does he finally take pity on me?

No.

He tells me that I'm no longer amusing him. He's through with me. I'm not making him hard anymore. I'm useless and irrelevant and I'm going to die.

Stop talking about it and just do it. I'm ready. Please. No more.

He lifts me up from behind and whispers into my ear.

"I don't think there's anything left for me to do to you. You can't even make me hard anymore. I didn't think it was possible for you to be more useless, but here you are. You're a worthless carcass, everything is empty about you. Everything but your gaping cunt is hollow. Vapid. But it's all over now. After this ..... After this ..... Hell is gonna be a breeze for you. I'll see you soon."

Fuck you, asshole. Just do it.

I feel a burn to my throat. My wet chest has a warmer fluid running down it. Somehow black is getting blacker.

I'm dying at long last.

Finally I can be without pain.

1

COFFEE WAS ALWAYS MADE AND READY FOR HIM IN THE morning. It was a routine they had shared since Ani had moved in. She was an early riser, her body accustom to only five or six hours of sleep since her freshman year as an undergrad. She'd worked her way through her bachelor's degree with little sleep, attaining even less during graduate school.

Ani worked at least one job to pay her way through school, sometimes more than one to make ends meet. When she wasn't studying, developing her thesis, or working, she volunteered what precious little time she had left. Sleep was a luxury afforded to people with less ambition and more spare time.

It was amidst one of these odd jobs—her hosting duties at Blue Ginger, a trendy restaurant in the Metro-West region of Boston, Massachusetts—where she'd met Warren Dennihan. He'd come in for fine-dining while on an investigation, his investigative services had been hired to find a missing girl. During his meal, he not only attained a table, but Ani's services as an informant about a restaurant regular in the process. She'd corrected his pronunciation of her name—Ah-knee—and promised to provide the investigator information when he said he would 'make it worth her while'. Her payment for said valuable information was a subsequent dinner date, the two had been an exclusive couple since.

Ani Chan had moved into Warren's South Boston three-decker less than three months after meeting him. She'd been quick to move forward with every step in their relationship, which was unlike her. She had a plan for her life, her career, and certainly how a man would fit into it prior to meeting 'Deni'. The meeting had taken them both by surprise. Everything that had taken place after the encounter in the restaurant was a first for her each step along the way. She'd gone to bed with him at the conclusion of their first date. She didn't date substantially older men, yet Deni was older than her by more than twelve years. She didn't date men who couldn't pronounce words properly, which pretty much eliminated men from 'Southie'—let alone live there herself. Not only did he win her over, she'd decided to move in with him relatively quickly. He never asked, but he didn't 'not ask' either. Within three months, she moved out of the affluent suburb of Wellesley and into gentrified Irish South Boston.

Ani abandoned her life-plan, her commitment to independence, even the type of man whom she planned to mate with. The heart wants what the heart wants, she reckoned. Even best-laid plans are foiled by love.

And she did love him. Ani Chan was all-in. She wanted the house, the picket fence, the two-point-five kids. She wanted to live the American dream with Deni. They had the house, they both had careers. It was time for a ring. But thus far, there hadn't been a proposal.

It took her six months just to persuade him to get a dog. Deni still hadn't fully agreed when a three year old Boston Terrier that she'd already picked up from the shelter arrived. He couldn't let the poor animal be put down, which is the story he was sold, so Hobey became their first pet, both together and individually.

Things were moving relatively fast. A year ago, both were single, lived alone and had a trajectory. Now, they shared everything, including a dog which over the past two weeks was still getting used to the new living environment. The trajectory had chosen them, Deni and Ani were along for the ride.

Ani rose every morning, made coffee, turned on Sportscenter if Deni was staying in Southie—the TV would stay off if her boyfriend was staying at his other house in Barstone, New Hampshire while working for an attorney there—then flip open her laptop. Feeding Hobey, the dog, was a new custom, one that sometimes was forgotten until after the laptop was open. This day was no different, coffee was brewing, the TV was on, Hobey's food poured, and she padding her way through the bottom floor of the three-decker in a satiny pink Teddy toward her computer.

"Dammit! Not again ..... DENI!"

Warren Dennihan slowly rolled out of bed without saying a word, sleep still in his eyes and whiskey on his breath, lumbering toward the coffee pot in the kitchen.

When Ani saw him in the kitchen from her stool at the breakfast bar—which doubled as an actual bar—she continued, "That bitch did it again. She corrupted my hard drive. AGAIN. You said that you were going to talk to her."

Deni just pointed to his coffee cup, then made the Shhhh sound with his finger to his lips. It was another routine and house rule that words weren't spoken until at least one cup of coffee was consumed. Even Hobey knew not to be underfoot until the caffeine had begun to pulse through his male master's veins.

Of course Ani knew the rule as well, and usually adhered to it for the sake of heated arguments, but this reoccurring situation was beyond ridiculous. Deni's ex, his on-again-off-again lover and computer genius, Althea Milonas, was not taking the loss of him well. She had considered him to be the love of her life, while Deni considered her to be a lover of convenience. She provided much needed computer skills, which Deni often needed for his private investigations business, but didn't possess. In return, he provided her with the male companionship she needed. It had been a little over a year and Althea was still installing viruses onto Ani's computer, no matter what type of anti-virus software she installed.

Despite her agitation, her disbelief and anger, Ani waited.

Deni was already in a bad mood about what the day would knowingly unfurl, throwing him a curve-ball before her boyfriend had a chance to adjust to being awake and caffeinated would not help her cause.

He made way toward the bar after pouring his second cup of Joe, Linda Cohn was on Sportscenter anchoring topics ranging from the Aaron Hernandez trial to NBA and NHL playoffs to highlights from the early baseball season. Despite the predictions, the Redsox were terrible so far.

"Okay. Calmly and slowly …. What are you ranting about?"

She took a deep breath before responding, "Althea. You said that you were going to talk to her. Did you?"

"I didn't have a chance yet," he said.

"C'mon, Bae. I specifically asked you to do this for me. Everything I have for work is on this laptop. Do you know how frustrating it is to have to go get this fixed before I can get any work done? What is this, like, the tenth time?"

"And do you know how hard it is to talk to that woman? There has not been one time that I've gone to see her and it not end up with us in bed? I haven't seen her, or talked to her in a year. For you." In addition to the morning cracking in his voice, his thick Bostonian accent made it impossible for anybody but those who knew him well to understand him. His accent was harsh even by Southie standards. The stereotypical, *Pahk tha cah in Havah-d yahd,* just doesn't quite illustrate it.

"For *ME?* You don't go see her for *ME?* Really? Really right now?"

"You know what I mean."

"You can't fuck her through a phone. Call the bitch."

"Do we have to do this? I'll call her. Okay?"

"You've said that before," Ani said. She calmed herself before continuing. "I know you're going to have a rough day, so I'm going to let this go for now. But we aren't finished talking about his, okay? Not by a long-shot." She leaned in and kissed him on the mouth.

"Ooooh," she winced. "Morning breath. How can you drink coffee without brushing your teeth first?"

"What's the point? I'd just have to brush them again after."

"Are you still in a bad mood? You drank yourself to sleep again last night."

"I ain't lookin' forward to today. This is the first time that I haven't gotten outta jury duty. Former cops slash current private investigators don't get jury duty. Instead of just makin' a phone call and gettin' the waiver, now they got a computer questionnaire that you fill out ahead of time and it says I still gotta show up."

"I know, Bae. I was there to help you fill it out, remember?"

"I remember, smart-ass. So I called the courthouse and everybody under the sun to get out of it, but I still gotta go downtown and sit in a room all day until they figure out that there was a screw-up."

"Mmmm. Sorry. How tough for you," she said in a patronizing tone. The couple was equally as supportive to one another as they were about giving each other healthy doses of ribbing.

"Colossal waste of time. I don't wanna talk about it. So what have you got going on today?"

"Well, I have to go get my computer de-bugged, for starters," she said with dripping sarcasm. "Then I have two office meetings before heading out to three shelters."

By shelters, she meant safe-houses for women who were victims of domestic violence. Ani worked for a privately funded non-profit dedicated to removing abused women—and often their children—out of their current situations. She ensured them a safe environment as well as getting them needed counseling, education, and back on their feet. The non-profit was one of the places she volunteered during grad-school and was extended a not-to-be-refused compensation package post-graduate degree. Ani was dedicated to her work and was well-paid for it.

Deni knew better than to compare work days with his girlfriend. He had seen horrors when he was a Massachusetts State Police Detective, and continued to since going out on his own as an investigator. The amount of human suffering Ani saw on a daily basis, however, was enough to make a person question the existence of humanity among those that called themselves human. She would often tell him of the horrific violence that was inflicted on the women and children that these men supposedly loved, and it would make Deni want to go out and show these aggressors some of his own brand of violence.

While he no longer fought amateur and sometimes the odd MMA fight, Deni still sparred at the same Brazilian Jiu-Jitsu gym four to five days a week. The sessions were not only therapeutic, but kept his skills intact for when he needed them on investigations.

The added benefit of keeping him in remarkable shape, which maintained Ani's physical attraction to him, was another reason to maintain his fighting ability.

Ani often had to refrain from giving her boyfriend all of the gory details about the men who abused her clients because Deni would most certainly offer as much punishment or worse once he got ahold of them.

Comparing days with Ani was never a good idea, so Deni decided to change the subject.

"Want to share a shower?"

A seductive grin came over her face as she pulled a pink spaghetti strap off her shoulder.

"If you brush your teeth first."

After making love in the shower and then cleaning themselves in readying for their respective days, the couple separately dressed for the business ahead of them.

Ani donned a form-fitting business jacket and dress; a size two, pearled, ivory/gold/metallic, Arthur S. Levine from the Lord & Taylor in the Copley Mall downtown. Her dark, brown skin contrasted the light colored garments, partially from her natural skin tone and the rest from soaking in the unseasonable early May sunshine Boston had been enjoying.

Deni put on his daily uniform, which consisted of a varying t-shirt, jeans, one of his ten sport jackets to conceal his .45 caliber Taurus PT1911 semi-auto pistol, and a pair of Converse, Chuck Taylor All-stars to match the blazer. While his closet was full, the hangers were lined with the same type of clothing. He never wore suits or even a collared shirt unless attending a funeral, though there were several tucked neatly in the back of the closet. His Irish skin was pale under his tapestry of tattoos, which a short-sleeved shirt and boxer shorts would cover.

"Whoa. You're really going to wear that shirt to jury duty?" Ani was laughing and yet somehow shocked at the same time. After a year of being with him, a year of his antics, he still had the ability to surprise her sometimes.

"Why not? There's no specific dress code," Deni explained.

"A t-shirt, maybe, but *that* t-shirt? You're going to get in big trouble."

"Maybe they'll toss me."

"Ah. So there was some thought put into it," she said as she closed the interval between them and pecked him on the mouth.

"Give me a call if I have to bail you out of jail," she continued with a chuckle. "I've got to go to the IT Department before I go up to my first meeting, thanks to your ex, so I've gotta run. Good luck."

"Thanks. Hopefully I won't need it."

"Oh, and take Hobey out for a walk please," she said as she exited the front door. "And he's probably going to do a number two, so bring a bag."

Deni looked down at his feet, the three year old dog wagging his tail.

Shitty start to the day, as expected.

2

THE SUFFOLK COUNTY SUPERIOR COURTHOUSE IN DOWNTOWN Boston, at 3 Pemberton Square to be precise, was built in 1893 utilizing second empire architecture. The building had an open floor-plan inside, with balconies looking down onto the main level from each floor above. The people needing to conduct business therein were mandated to go through the emptying of pockets and pass through a metal-detector, of course, then free to wander about looking for where and on which floor that business was to take place.

Warren Dennihan's business of checking in for his mandated jury duty was in a gargantuan room on the first floor. The room was set up as a cross between a town meeting and the DMV. A long line formed to check in at one of the many windows where a courthouse employee was waiting. Once ID was shown, and a number given along with another questionnaire on a clipboard, those reporting for jury duty were told to take one of the seats in the sea of rows set up in the remainder of the gymnasium-sized room.

It seemed like hundreds of people were there for the same purpose as Deni, all with the same set of characteristics which afford them the right to sit on one jury or another. Being chosen for such an honor was as arbitrary as choosing lottery numbers. Only a small criteria need be met from the pool of names gathered from the City Residents List to qualify for such a drawing.

The first of said criteria is residency. As one might imagine by the name of the list from which the juror names are pulled, the potentials are randomly selected from those that have a lease or mortgage in Suffolk County.

A big misconception among those chosen to fulfill their civic duty is that social security numbers are attained through the DMV. If the first three digits, which indicate the state in which the number was issued, aren't '010', that number is supposedly red-flagged for consideration. The involvement of the Department of Motor Vehicles —in Massachusetts the Registry of Motor Vehicles—is a complete myth since first, as in most cities, many residents don't own cars for myriad of logistical reasons.

In a city like Boston, where a sizable percentage of the population go to one of the 26 major colleges and universities therein, very few have a vehicle and use the T system to get around. Attaining a jury pool from the Massachusetts RMV would also mean that those who cannot or do not drive would be exempt from jury duty. While refraining from getting a driver's license might make the traffic a bit lighter, it would drastically thin the pool of potential jurors.

The second criterion for residents of Suffolk County to become a possible juror is simply by being a legal adult. Over the age of eighteen. Most of twenty-six colleges and universities within Boston do not have dormitories for reasons of building space and cost, forcing students to get leases and roommates, thereby making 'out-of-state' college students fair game.

Another on the short list of criteria required attain a jury duty 'notice for appearance' is the recipient being notified not have served on a jury within the last three years.

Deni was caught in that wide net, received a notice, which then told him to fill out the online questionnaire to see if he met one of the ten possible early disqualifications. Warren Dennihan was well over the age of eighteen, had a mortgage in Suffolk County on his three-decker in Southie, and hadn't served on a jury ever before in his life. Qualified as a potential juror, he was forced to go to the courthouse on that Thursday, May 8.

The second questionnaire, the one handed to him on several pieces of paper at the courthouse check-in, was nothing like the first. The online form simply made sure that he was a citizen, that he lived in Boston for more than 50% of the year, that he was between the ages of 18 and 70, that he spoke english, that he wasn't a live-in care provider for a disabled person, that he hadn't been convicted of a felony in the last 10 years, and finally that he was mentally capable. The paper questionnaire was much more detailed and seemed to indicate that he had already been preselected for one jury or another.

He had never made it to this step before. When he was a cop, he had gotten a notice to appear and his lieutenant at the time, Manny Titanitaukis, took care of getting him out of it. But that was a long time ago. He'd assumed that cops, past and present were excused from jury duty, a fact that was untrue and told to him when he called the courthouse when he received this current notice to appear.

A mid-forties lady was seated next to him in the row amidst a sea of chairs he had chosen to sit in. Unlike Deni, the woman didn't have a thick stack of papers in her hand.

"Excuse me. Did you get one of these?" Deni showed her the long list of questions.

"No. I was selected for a Grand Jury, lucky me," she said with a roll of her eyes.

"Oh shit. That sucks."

"Yep, I get a whole year of this, starting today. Forty bucks a day, how am I supposed to live on that? Or keep my job? My 'civic duty' is going to make me homeless."

Deni knew better than to say anything else. It appeared that he was on the hook for a single trial, being selected for a Grand Jury meant that you were on a panel to determine whether or not to indict each suspect over the course of an entire year. The poor woman next to him would have to listen to testimony from prosecutors regarding countless allegations for two or three days a week, for fifty-two weeks, deciding whether or not the Commonwealth had enough evidence to support bringing the accused to trial. She would be paid a total of $120 a week for her efforts, maximum, which is difficult if not impossible to live on, definitely out of the question living in the city of Boston.

"I'm gonna try to get out of it for hardship reasons, but my sister said that judges usually don't go for it," she added.

"I'll keep that in mind. Good luck."

"You too."

Deni went back to his questionnaire. The top portion of the paper on his lap said it was confidential and designed to expedite the process for jury selection. It gave further instructions on how to answer—truthfully and to the best of the recipient's ability—and that follow up questions would be administered once empaneled.

Under the general instructions, someone had hand-written in his full name and juror number, 05-0204. He was to fill in the rest of the forty questions, legibly, prior to being called into the courtroom.

1. What is your age? *41*

2. Sex: *MALE*

3. Do you have any problems with hearing or vision that would make it difficult for you to serve on a jury?

Deni thought about answering 'yes' in order to get out of being on whatever jury he'd been selected for; however, he also knew from having to testify at numerous trials as both a detective and as an investigator that lying on this form was the same as lying to the judge himself under oath, which would get him a felony perjury charge.

So he answered truthfully.

NO

4. Do you have any medical conditions that would prevent you from serving as a juror on this case?

I don't know what case this is, but I don't have any medical conditions, he thought. *NO*

5. Marital status: *SINGLE*

6. Do you have any children? If so, list their ages: *N/A*

7. In what section of Boston do you reside?

24

SOUTH BOSTON

8. Is english your first language? YES

9. What other languages do you speak, read, or understand? N/A

10. State your ethnic background/nationality (if not born in the U.S.): IRISH-CATHOLIC

He wasn't sure if that it what they were looking for, but it was true. Born and raised a Catholic in Southie, though he hadn't been to church since the last funeral. Or maybe it had been a wedding. He couldn't remember, but in either case it'd been a while.

11. Are you employed? If so, what is your status? YES. FULL-TIME. SELF-EMPLOYED

12. What kind of work do you do?

Yes! Here we go. I'm going to get out of this malarkey right here and now.

PRIVATE INVESTIGATOR - FORMER STATE POLICE DETECTIVE

13. Highest school grade completed: 10. G.E.D.

14. The Judge in this case will be The Honorable Emile Wallace, Commonwealth Criminal Court for Suffolk County. Do you or anyone close to you know or have any connection with Judge Wallace or any of his staff?
YES. TESTIFIED BEFORE HIM IN A CASE TEN YEARS AGO (ROUGHLY)

There. Another reason I can go home.

15. Have you or anyone in your family ever been a victim of rape?
NO. BUT I'VE KNOWN PEOPLE

16. Have you or anyone in your family ever been a victim of murder? *NO. - BUT I'VE KNOWN PEOPLE WHO HAVE BEEN MURDERED*

17. The case you have been selected for has received media attention that is likely to continue. You will be asked to abstain from television, newspapers, radio, the internet, or any other source with regard to this case. Would these requirements pose any difficulty for you?

Jesus Christ, what case have I been chosen for? Aaron Hernandez? No, that's in Connecticut. The Marathon Bombing? I gotta get outta this.

NO

18. Have you seen or heard anything about the following people with regard to the case; Chase Bromley, Sloane Nichols, Alexandria Pratt, or Justin Albright?

Shit. Now I know what this case is. The Sloane Nichols rape/ murder. I know the ADA, the cops that investigated it, the lab techs in Maynard. Yeah, I'm definitely getting outta this.

YES

Deni didn't bother filling out the rest of the questionnaire. It was pointless. He waited until his name and juror number was called, along with the names and numbers of the rest of the potential jurors for the trial, and entered into the hallway. Each questionnaire was collected as the fifty or so of the people called were then led down the hall, to an elevator and into a courtroom up on the third floor.

The court officer led them into Courtroom 1, the largest in Suffolk County Superior, and asked them to sit in the jury pit. The group of potential jurors waited for a great deal of time before the judge and lawyers from both sides of the table finally entered.

During the long wait, answers from the questionnaires were being analyzed by the Assistant District Attorneys and the defense team to determine if any potential juror should be eliminated for cause. Additionally, the defense team jury consultant was gathering as much data about each and every potential juror in an effort to compile the twelve members they thought best to render a not-guilty verdict.

When the voire dire session came to order, the ADA, Justin Albright, and his second-chair, ADA Amy Walsh were seated closest to the jury pit. The defense team was further away, at the other table. Alexandria Pratt, of the well-known and largest Boston law firm of Taylor, Higgs & Pratt, and her immense team were conferring with their client, Chase Bromley. Judge Wallace took his elevated place above the fray, ready to preside over the mess to come. A court officer stood ready in case His Honor failed, and a stenographer typed the play-by-play for posterity.

The case had been all over the news. The affluent son of New England's wealthiest property developer, Kenneth Bromley, had been accused of raping and murdering his former girlfriend the previous fall. Every gruesome detail of the crime was illustrated by the media for weeks after the crime, during the police investigation, finally relenting just after Thanksgiving. Deni could only imagine how much coverage was going to recommence now that the actual trial was about to begin.

He was also relieved that he wasn't going to have any part of it.

3

ALEXANDRIA PRATT, LEAD COUNSEL FOR THE DEFENSE AND the only female partner in Boston's largest and prestigious law firm, leaned in to speak with her team sitting behind the large table on the far side of the courtroom from the jury's perspective. Jury selection is a tough business. Twelve people who don't have the wherewithal to get out of their civic duty, sit in judgement, deciding the fate of those accused of crimes both large and small. While Alex had keen instincts on which of the fifty-five people preselected for jury members for her client, she would consult with; Max Courtland, the firm's expensive jury consultant; Kevin Bishop, her second chair; and to a lesser extent, Jack Elders, the firm's twenty-something attorney who passed the Bar Exam not yet one year prior—the irony of his name was a constant source of amusement around the five hundred offices of Taylor, Higgs & Pratt.

For the case at hand, Chase Bromley, son of the infamous Kenneth Bromley, would either leave the trial a free man or spend the rest of his days behind bars. Massachusetts doesn't have the death penalty, else the District Attorney would likely be seeking it; however, if Chase was sent to prison for rape and murder, he may just prefer the needle over what would be in store from his fellow inmates.

Alex worked exhaustive hours to get to her current position at the firm and status throughout the legal community. She started with the fledgling firm when it was just Brandon Taylor in his crappy two-room office near Dorchester. She'd been passed over for partnership when Taylor decided to merger with Higgs. Both Taylor and Higgs had separately been eking out their legal existences in the city despite their talent, the merger consolidated expenses while doubling their client pool. It would have been easy to add Pratt to the partnership back then, since they were changing the letterhead anyway, but her promotion came years later when the two founders could no longer ignore her contributions and acquittals.

She was at least ten years younger than the youngest of her co-partners, spending a good deal of her vast disposable income and vacation time to magnify the physical manifestation of that difference. Her plastic surgeon, stylist, and personal shopper were all within a touch of a button on her cell phone, all at the ready to go to work. Anyone with eyes would assume that some work had been done to keep father time at bay, but not even a carny could guess her actual age with accuracy. Early forties? Late forties? Late thirties? Fifty? Only the Mass RMV knew for sure.

Certainly not Max Courtland, who was well-paid for his ability to read people, seeing each and every peccadillo a person carries with them from the other side of a courtroom. And when his ability fails him, his team of investigators dug up what he'd missed. Court clerks were paid to divulge the list of potential jurors to Max, who then disseminated the list to his team to dig up reasons both for and against the individuals remaining empaneled. Jury selection is also big business.

Whispers from the defense table abound as the judge gave them time to confer. Each potential juror is asked follow-up questions from their questionnaires with regard to their fitness for the trial.

The prosecution gets first crack at them, asking questions that may eliminate them from eligibility, or prove that they were perfect for sending the accused to prison.

Then the defense has the opportunity to do the same. If the potential juror isn't eliminated for cause—religious views, bias for any number of reasons, or familiarity with anyone involved with the trial as examples—either side presenting their case can use one of their peremptory challenges. According to Massachusetts General

Laws c.234a, §71, each side can send four potential jurors home without giving a reason.

Alex Pratt turned to the judge after another in a long line of brief conferences, "We would eliminate this juror for cause, your Honor. He is seventy-one, which is over the maximum age allowed by law."

Age is one of the reasons a potential juror can be dismissed for cause, which would not count against one of the four peremptory challenges each side is provided without cause.

Judge Emile Wallace, nearing the age of seventy himself, took umbrage.

"Counselor, we've been over this. Unlike most people who try to get out of jury duty, he hasn't asserted his right to be freed from serving," he said as if the potential juror wasn't in the room. "I detect no mental capacity issue and you've asked him a litany of questions which he has answered to the court's satisfaction. I am not inclined to dismiss him based upon his age. If you'd like to use once of your remaining peremptory challenges, that is up to you, but he will not be eliminated for cause."

That is how the seventy-one year old, Jewish man, Oscar Brenowitz, became juror number one.

Juror number two, Renaldo Ramos Gomez, was the only other potential juror that didn't strive to get out of serving on the case. He had become a citizen within the last year, at the ripe old age of forty, and was looking forward to performing his civic duty as an American. His eagerness may also have had something to do with his being a Catholic, who always feel they are being judged and look forward to doing the same to others. He was asked a slew of questions from both sides and was confirmed in relatively short order.

A number of other jurors were confirmed as well; Paul Weist, a thirty-two year old non-practicing Jew became number three; Regan Avery, a single mother of two female teenagers made it through to become juror number four; Cherelle Garrison, a twenty-seven year old black woman from Roxbury couldn't get out being juror number five; and Jordan Raines was Cherelle's white counterpart as juror number six.

The two sides were getting closer. The prosecution and defense teams were nearly halfway to their twelve jurors—plus two alternates—confirmed into service, one by one, when another one was kicked.

The lead prosecutor, Assistant District Attorney Justin Albright, asked his usual question, "Is there any reason, not mentioned on the written questionnaire you filled out, that you think would interfere with your ability to fairly render a judgement on this case?"

Three of the previous six had all given a reason, none of them rendering a decision to eliminate them. Twenty-one year old Page Dolan now had her shot.

"I'm in the middle of final exams at Northeastern. Even if I could concentrate on the trial, I'd miss my exams."

"We've had other jurors in college," Albright said. "We can send your professors written notification which would allow you to take your exams in two or three weeks when this trial is finished."

"But I don't even live here when I'm not in school. I sublet my apartment during the summer, so I won't have any place to live. This is a nightmare."

"Your duty as a citizen is a nightmare? You live in Boston for more than six months out of the year, yes?"

"Yeah."

"Then you have an obligation to participate in our legal sys—"

"—Stop right there, Mister Albright," Judge Wallace interrupted. "Young lady, are you saying that this trial presents an immense hardship which would drastically interfere with your impartiality to the process of jurisprudence?"

"Yessir."

"I am absolving this juror from service," Wallace said to the courtroom. "Young lady, thank you for your time here today. Good luck with your final examinations."

He didn't have to dismiss her twice. Page practically jumped over the partition separating the jury from the courtroom gallery as she double-timed it out the large double doors at the front of the immense room, leaving the rest of the jury in her rearview.

Albright then moved on to the next person in the jury pit, asking the same open-ended question.

"Yeah. I'm a former state cop. Detective in Troop H."

"Police officers aren't always eliminated from jury duty, sir."

"Detective."

"Excuse me?"

"I was promoted to Detective."

"My apologies. You are no longer an officer or a detective, is that correct?"

"That's true. I work for myself as an investigator now."

"I don't see how that disqualifies you," Albright said.

"I know all of these people. The detectives you're going to call, the lab geek from Maynard …. I thought that was a no-no."

"Not necessarily." Albright went to his desk, retrieved the questionnaire from the hand of his second chair, ADA Amy Walsh.

"You didn't complete the rest of the form because you felt that you would automatically be disqualified?"

"Yeah."

"As a former detective, have you investigated rapes and murders?"

"Yeah. And I've dealt with some since."

"As an investigator," Albright clarified.

"Yeah."

"And in those cases, were you able to keep an open mind until your investigation had run its course?"

"Well …. Yeah."

"Have you made your mind up about this case?"

"I've seen a lot of coverage, especially when it first happened. Seems like there's a lot of smoke."

"Smoke. You mean when there is smoke there tends to be a fire," Albright said as a statement.

"I didn't say that exactly."

Albright went back to the prosecutor's desk not four feet away. He leaned in to Amy Walsh.

"I like him. A former cop is not going to let this guy walk."

"I agree," she said.

Albright turned to the judge. "We are fine with him, if it please the court."

"So noted," Judge Wallace said as he nodded toward the defense table.

Alex Pratt, stood from her seat behind the large table, pressed out the non-existent wrinkles on her Armani Collezioni jacket and skirt by hand before making her way toward the jury pit. Her team remained seated next to the accused, Chase Bromley.

"Let's put our cards on the table, you don't like my client and have already decided that he's guilty, correct?"

"And let's not put words in my mouth. I didn't say that or anything like it. I said, 'there's smoke,' meaning that there is enough evidence to bring this to trial."

"Meaning that you think he's guilty?"

"From what was in the news? If that's all of it? Yeah."

Alex went back to her table, taking a report from the desk, a report that was provided by Max Courtland's team of investigators.

"Your number on you questionnaire says 05-0204. Your name is Warren B. Dennihan, correct?"

"You obviously know that's true. I go by Deni," he said, knowing how she knew his name from doing the same exact investigative work for Ryan Wells, his attorney-friend in New Hampshire.

"This doesn't have to be adversarial, Sir. I just have a few questions for you, like if you hadn't left the employ of the State Police, you would have been fired. Is that not true?"

"I don't know that for a fact, but the writing was on the wall."

"I'll take that as a yes. Since then you have worked for a defense attorney, a Ryan Wells of Grantes, Wells & Associates in Southern New Hampshire, correct?"

"I've been hired by him on occasion to investigate for his clients, yes."

"So people that have been accused of crimes, go see this law firm," Pratt said as she looked at a piece of paper, "Or the one in

South Carolina, who you also sometimes conduct work for. These firms hire you to find evidence of their innocence, correct?"

"Jacob Grantes is in South Carolina now, and that was only one time—"

"—Yes or no, Mr. Dennihan?"

"Yes."

"And the fact that each client was arrested and in need of a defense attorney for a trial didn't bother you in any of those cases correct? You sought the truth regardless of the fact that there was, as you call it, 'smoke'. True or false?"

"True."

Alex walked back to her table, speaking to her team in a low voice as not to be heard by others.

"I'm not sure about this guy. He's a wild card. Do you see the way he's dressed?"

Max whispered, "I know. That's why I like him. He doesn't go with the status quo. He's an authority misanthrope, anti-police— especially given his past with them. He works for a defense attorney for Christ's sake. I wouldn't just abstain from using a peremptory, I would actively want him on the jury to nullify. I love this guy."

Kevin Bishop, Alex's second chair, and the inexperienced Jack Elders were both nodding their heads in agreement with the jury professional.

Chase Bromley, the accused, interjected in a louder whisper.

"Are you fucking kidding me? You're all thinking about keeping this guy? He's a cop."

"A *former* cop. A disenfranchised detective which could work in our favor. Yes, Chase. He stays."

"It's my money paying all you fuckers. I say kick him."

"It's your father's money, Chase. And he is paying top dollar for the best legal team Boston has to offer," Alex reminded him.

"He's buying me a walk-away. This guy is going to burn me."

"Like it or not, he stays."

Alex then turned to Judge Wallace.

"If it please the court, your Honor, this juror is accepted."

"So noted. Will you please stand sir?"

Nobody moved.

"Sir ...." Wallace shifted some paperwork around his desk. "Mister Dennihan is it?"

"Yeah."

"Mister Dennihan, will you please stand up for me."

Deni did as asked.

"Will you open your blazer please."

Deni again did as instructed, though hesitantly. The shoulder harness and pistol he normally wore under his jacket had been removed per instruction when he tried to enter the courthouse with them.

"Was this your idea of a joke, or did you wear that shirt as a means of being discounted as a juror?"

"Whatever do you mean, Judge?"

Everyone was staring at Deni's black t-shirt with a graphic from the band *TOOL* emblazoned on the front. The image depicted a dark figure standing over a legless child with the words 'Prison

Sex' below it. The shirt was merchandised from a song of the same

name on the band's *Undertow* album and tour.

"What I mean, is that while we don't have a specific dress code for jurors, if you wear anything like that to court again you'll be found in contempt and may insert yourself into a trial of your own. Am I clear?"

"Does that mean that I'm coming back?"

"It does indeed. You are juror number seven. We will now break for lunch. Everybody back here in one hour, both jurors and potential jurors. Mister Dennihan, I would recommend that I not see that shirt on your person when you return."

The gavel came down, everyone stood while Judge Wallace rose and went into his chambers.

On Thursday, May 8, Warren Dennihan thusly went from being potential juror 05-0204 to actual juror number 7.

4

JURY SELECTION RECONVENED AFTER A ONE HOUR LUNCH, AND both sides again went through the remaining potential jurors, posing their questions.

Sixty-three year old Evelyn Rocher was the first to answer ADA Albright's ambiguous question of what, if any, reason she would have for being an unfit juror. Her assertion being that if she missed two or three weeks of work, her boss would fire her. She claimed that because of her age, her boss was looking for any excuse to fire her, a prolonged absence would seal the deal. She then asked the Assistant District Attorney if he would hire her if she got fired, because she doubted that anyone would be lining up to hire a sixty-three year old woman who was looking to retire within a few years.

Judge Wallace informed her that she couldn't legally be fired from her job because she was selected for jury duty, and to contact the office of the District Attorney directly if that should happen.

The widow Rocher didn't contend that she'd already made a decision about the case or would be impartial, so when Alex Pratt was finished asking her questions, Evelyn became juror eight.

Next up was Gina Fung, a mid-thirties racist who thought that everyone secretly thought just like her. Blacks were underachievers who stole what they couldn't hustle out of some sucker. Hispanics, like juror number two, Gomez, were wet-backs who snuck into the US in order to steal a job from some poor schmuck because he was willing to do more work for less money, under the table. Yellow people, like her, were smarter than the whites who kept them down and segregated into their own section of the city; white women only ventured into Chinatown to get their nails done, white men to get a hand-job at one of the massage parlors. She was brazen about her views, because she said that everybody saw things the same way only it wasn't polite to say so outright. If she was being provocative for the purpose of getting out of jury duty, it worked. She was released from service in less than a minute of her racist tirade.

In her place was Ben Post, who turned thirty the week prior and was as gay as anything that had ever been called gay. Ballerinas were less gay than Ben Post. He was 'out' about it, not that there was any fathomable way that he could be 'in'. Flamboyant Ben became juror number nine, despite his dramatic protestations.

Unemployed Jamar Dubone, a twenty-four year old black man, was excited to learn that he would be getting forty dollars a day, until he learned that he couldn't double-dip by collecting unemployment for the days he served. He too would lose money by being on the jury, and despite trying to get out of it once he realized the financial ramifications, became juror number ten.

Sherlie Lovett, a forty-three year old Executive Director of Human Resources for City Sports, a national activewear chain, became number eleven.

Rounding out the dirty dozen was Denai Moshe, a fifty-six year old black man who drove the T commuter train on the Purple Line.

Two alternates were selected from the remaining people from the original twenty-five.

A man was let go because english was remotely considered a second language.

Another because she had moved outside of Suffolk County — the resident list was outdated, as was her driver's license, according to her — and was told that criminal charges would be filed against her if she was lying.

A woman who wanted to be a part of sending Chase Bromley to prison wasn't allowed to do so, a peremptory challenge was used by the defense because Max Courtland had dug up an old allegation of being raped while she was in college, though Alex didn't officially express why one of her challenges was used to the court.

Still another potential was dismissed because the man was borderline retarded, and the prosecution felt that he didn't have the requisite skill to decide on what he wanted for lunch, let alone guilt or innocence.

One alternate, Marissa Gantse—a thirty-eight year old housewife—caused quite the scene. She was determined not to be empaneled, one way or another.

She had made it through ADA Albright's questions and was cleared to remain on as an alternate jury member, in the event that something should happen to one of the twelve and therefore need to serve. Mrs. Gantse had done her best to be eliminated but obviously had to step up her game. When Alex Pratt began her subsequent questioning, it got interesting.

"Good afternoon, as you've heard me say all day, I'm Alex Pratt, the lead counsel for the defendant, Chase Bromley. And as I've done all day, I would like to follow up with some questions that you've given both on the questionnaire and to ADA Albright's inquiries.

You indicated that there were some facts that you wanted the court to know when you were speaking to Mister Albright. Could you elaborate please?"

"As I said to him, my sister was a victim of domestic violence from her then husband. I had to live with her calling me at all hours of the night, staying in my home when she left him only to go right back and take more abuse .... It was a terrible few years. From what I've seen on the news, your client had been abusive to the woman who was killed for some time before he killed her—"

"—Allegedly. Allegedly killed her," Pratt interrupted.

"Well, that's what I'm saying. He abused her so she left and he tracked her down and I think he did it."

"You think that from what you've seen on the news?"

"Yes. And I don't think that I could be objective," Gantse said.

"Even before any witnesses have been called or any testimony has been rendered, you think that he's guilty before he's had the opportunity to present the facts?"

"Yes. Honestly, yes. Is that so wrong?"

"There are no right and wrong answers here, Misses Gantse. Your full name is Marissa Elizabeth Gantse, yes?"

"Yes, but how do you—"

"—Public records, Misses Gantse. You live in Jamaica Plain, correct?"

"Yes, but—"

"—Great. As I was saying, there are no right and wrong answers here, just the truth. And I think that while you seem to think that you know the truth, and have come to a supposed decision, you've not been telling the truth."

"What are you talking about? I'm not on trial here, your client is," Marissa said.

"If you fail to tell the truth, or answer verbal or written questions dishonestly, then you will also eventually be on trial for perjury and contempt of court. So before you say another word, I want to take you back to question thirty-eight on your questionnaire. When asked if you, or anyone close to you, have been a victim of rape or domestic abuse. To that question, you answered 'no'. Now, in an obvious attempt to get out of jury duty, you answered a question posed to you by Assistant District Attorney Albright, that you did, indeed, have someone close to you suffer domestic abuse. Which is it?"

"I did. Yes."

"Your sister you just said?"

"Yes."

"According to independent information that we've gathered," Alex said waiving a piece of paper, "you have one brother and no sisters. You grew up in Brookline, Massachusetts, correct?"

"How in the hell—"

"—Freedom of Information Act, Misses Gantse. But what's important now is that you discontinue lying during a court proceeding."

"She is my best friend, so she's like my sister."

"Let's just stick to the facts, not what is or isn't 'like' something else, okay?"

Marissa Gantse hesitated as she looked around the courtroom.

"Fine."

"Why don't we take a step back? To before you lied. You have opinions, we all have opinions in this country. That's one of the things that make it so great. Another reason is that everyone is entitled to a fair trial, where they can confront those that accuse them and ask that their accusers prove before a panel of their peers that what they are accused of is true, not the other way around. You know that, yes?"

"Yes. And in my opinion, as I've said, is that I think he's guilty."

"And my question to you, Marissa, is how could you possibly have that opinion when you've not heard one person testify or seen one piece of actual evidence? I normally wouldn't take this much time with a potential juror, as long as we are all being honest here, I would use one of my challenges and send you home. But that's what you want, isn't it? That's why you're saying what you're saying. You don't really know for sure if my client did what he is accused of. How could you?"

"So what? I don't want to be here. Two weeks, three? A month? No, I don't want to be here."

Judge Wallace stepped in.

"Want? Mrs. Gantse, we don't want to get into *want*, Because nobody *wants* to be here for a lengthy trial. Nobody *wants* to hear the gory details of what the victim went through in her final hours of life. You're not any different from everyone else. What the attorneys have asked you—what *I'm* now asking you—is if you are eventually called upon to be a juror, because one of the selected twelve cannot complete their duties for some unforeseen reason, that you could commit to giving the defendant a fair trial based solely on what is presented in the courtroom and following the law as I give to you and the other selected jurors."

Marissa Gantse looked deflated.

"I guess so."

"Miss Pratt, do you have any further questions for Misses Gantse?"

"I do, your Honor."

"Then carry on."

"Thank you. You said that you have an opinion about my client based upon what your friend, who you called your sister, went through. That person's husband or boyfriend wasn't my client, correct?"

"Husband, and no, he wasn't."

"And your husband isn't like that, is he?"

"No, of course not."

"Neither of your two sons are violent, are they?"

"Wait just a second, how do you know so much about me?"

Ten seconds went by which felt like an hour. The two women stared at each other as if they were in a contest to see which one would flinch first.

Alex did.

"They aren't, correct?"

Another few seconds passed. Alex didn't receive an answer to her question, nor did it appear that one was forthcoming no matter how much time passed.

Marissa finally answered the defense attorney's question with reluctance.

"No. My boys are kind and decent and loving."

"So you agree that not all men are like your friend's husband and shouldn't be lumped in with men who would do those horrible things to women, correct?"

"Correct."

"So you, of all people, would have the ability to step back and listen to facts, and make a judgement based upon those facts. Not what is presented on the TV, or in a newspaper, or radio .... But what occurs right here in the courtroom, yes? You seem like an intelligent woman who can separate those things. You are that woman, yes?"

Marissa hemmed and hawed.

"Yes. But I still don't think I'm ..... Uh ....." She looked at the judge, "*Qualified* to be on this jury."

"Be that as it may, you are further aware, that in our system of justice, the prosecution has to prove beyond a reasonable doubt that the person accused of the crime actually committed the crime? That the person accused doesn't even have to take the stand in his defense, and if he chooses not to, that that fact alone is not a basis for finding him guilty?"

"Yes, I know those things. I'm not an idiot."

"Then I think you would be perfect for our jury and more than qualified," Pratt said as she walked back to her table.

"May I say one more thing?"

Judge Wallace spoke up.

"No, Misses Gantse. That is all. You are the first alternate, and as such will be present for all testimony and adhere to the same schedule and instructions as the empaneled twelve. Thank you."

"This is bullshit!"

"Excuse me? Did you say something?" Judge Wallace faced her, she had his full attention.

"Yeah. This is bullshit. There is no way that I should have to —"

"—Let me stop you right there," he said. "You have two choices, you can sit down and be quiet or you can be found in contempt of court and you can be carted out of her in handcuffs while having your Miranda rights read to you. One of those rights is to remain silent. Choose wisely Misses Gantse."

Marissa Gantse slowly took her seat without issuing another word in protest or otherwise.

When Alex returned to her seat after the outburst, Max Courtland, who was consulting the jury profiles crafted from his investigators, whispered to the lead counselor.

"Good job. The rest of this jury pool is no good. We can't have any of them on our jury. We needed her."

"I'm not so sure, Max. She hates us."

"So what? She wanted out of this trial, and the longer she's in it, the more distain she'll have for the system. By the end of this trial, even if she gets on the jury, she will hate the ADAs and the judge and anyone else who represents government."

"I don't know, Max, the friend of hers .... "

"There is no friend. She was lying, believe me. She's a damn good liar, but make no mistake ..... She *is* a liar. Liars try to get away with lies. Good liars have worked to perfect their craft over time. They've been caught and they know what it's like to be judged. She'll be on our side, trust me."

"We still have to choose one more alternate from that pool that you despise," she whispered, pointing to the reports as if the people the reports represented weren't sitting a few feet away.

"I know. Just let the first one that Albright likes go through and hope that it doesn't come back to bite us in the ass."

5

DENI WENT DIRECTLY HOME AFTER COURT THURSDAY
evening, ready to drink himself into oblivion. And he would have if
Ani had let him get away with it. After six Redbreast Irish Whiskies,
that she counted, she decided to hide the bottles.

Ani knew better than to apply logic and reason to the
situation. She knew why he was getting 'blotto', and why he had
been for the past few nights. Of course he didn't want to get jury
duty, nobody does. But he had cases to investigate, a business to
run. Now to actually get empaneled on a jury, one where the
defendant was accused of a brutal rape and murder—not that any
rape and murders are tame—was added need for inebriation. He
drank nightly, but not to such excess.

Her boyfriend had seen the worst deeds man had to offer,
and heard daily from her cases what was happening to so many
women who had run to shelters to escape those men. This was the
last thing he needed, and yet there was nothing he could do about it.
Except to get drunk.

When Deni was bent to get bent, she gaslighted.
Psychological warfare at its finest. She'd dealt with her boyfriend
enough to realize that confrontation was not in either of their best
interest. He would never harm her physically, though he had more
than enough strength to do so, even if he wasn't a third degree
blackbelt in Brazilian Jiu-Jitsu. But he did sometimes say some
things that he would later regret, things that he would never say if he
was sober. Words can often hurt more deeply than physical pain
which can heal and be somewhat undone over time.

She too could dish out harsh truths when provoked. Ani was no pushover. She had the ability to save hurtful, verbal jabs—the ones that cut the deepest—until the time when they made the biggest impact. Her Master's degree in psychology was at times more impactful than Deni's mastery of martial arts and prepared her well for verbal altercations, not that she ever truly wanted to be invested in any.

Both parties in the couple were strong-minded and strong-willed. They gave each other jabs in humor, each keeping the other on their toes. It was only when alcohol was plied to the situation that things were often taken to offense and feelings were hurt.

And so Ani simply hid the whiskey bottles, poured herself a tall glass of wine after a long day of dealing with victims of domestic abuse, and waited for Deni to start digging through the cabinets of his bar when he needed another refill.

When he finally succumbed to the fact that he was out of whiskey, he would ask her if she was sober enough to go out and get him a bottle at the package store. Thus, the glass of wine she'd poured herself but taken nary a sip of. She would tell him that she'd been drinking, and therefore shouldn't drive. The packie was just far enough away where walking was not worth the effort over a bottle of booze, definitely not worth getting a DUI, so he would begin the process of sobering up.

"Bae, why don't we just go to bed. Maybe tomorrow you won't hate the idea of being on a jury so much," Ani said.

"Bae, bae, bae. Why do you always use tween words? I don't even know what that means. You're almost thirty years old for fuck sake, you're 'literally' too old to say shit like 'yolo' and 'swag' and the other shit you say. Drives me nuts. You're supposed to be smart."

"I am *Smaht,* asshole. *Wicked smaht."*

"Well ya talk like a Taylor Swift wannabee. Everything is 'blessed' and 'totally'. You're 'obsessed' with sounding like a jackoff."

"Okay *Bae*, whatevs. I can't even with you right now," she said in the parlance of a tween on purpose. "At least I know how to dress myself. Are you wearing that t-shirt inside-out because of court today? I told you ....."

"You're tryin' to fuck with me aren't ya?"

"Do you want to fight? Is that what's going to make your night? You've had a shitty day, I get that. Well, I've had a shittier day, believe me. Have you ever seen what a wife and three kids look like after years of getting cigars put out on them like they're an astray? Well I have. And that was after the amazing start of my day, having to go to get my hard-drive fixed because of your ex fuck-buddy. So the last thing I want to do is fight with you as a finale. Me getting pissed and throwing things isn't going to solve anything, and you'll feel even worse tomorrow."

Time passed as Deni's sluggish brain processed Ani's statement.

"Trial starts Monday. I gotta tell She that's she's on her own for the length of the trial starting Monday. Probably three weeks. Maybe a month. FUCK!"

"Lisa is a big girl, she can handle whatever it is that you've got going on. Just come to bed and get a full night of sleep. You'll have a better head about it tomorrow."

"Okay."

He started walking down the hall behind Ani, her hand extended back searching for his.

"You know I'm a pretty lucky to have you," he said.

"I know it."

"You want to talk about your day? Who is this cigar asshole? Maybe I can pay him a visit."

"No I do not, and no you won't."

After the morning ritual of coffee, silence, petting Hobey, then getting ready for work, Deni got into his Land Rover and headed to his office. It was going to be a rougher Friday than usual. Ani had been cool this morning. The lack of sex made for a dismal start. The verbal altercation the night before was the undoubted yet unspoken reason.   The things he'd said seemed to have been forgotten, but Deni knew better. Ani, like most women, often forgive but never forget.

Now he would have to tell his semi-disgruntled employee, Lisa Sheed, that she would be juggling all the balls they had in air for the foreseeable future. A lot can happen to investigations and to a business in a month.

Blink 182 was on the twenty speaker stereo system in his Range Rover on the drive in. *'What's my age again?'* was playing on Pandora, forcing Deni to be reminded of the mini-fight he'd had with Ani. He vowed to get her some flowers on the way home that night.

The drive to his office took less than fifteen minutes despite the traffic.

Lisa Sheed, the only other employee of DIS, Dennihan Investigation Services, was already in the office as usual. She was also a former State Police Detective from Troop H, but had been a detective at a different time than Deni. Immediately after he left the Crimes Against Persons detective squad in fact, having inherited Deni's old partner, Rick Hobbs. She sat at Deni's old desk, listening to his old partner spout off about former Massachusetts State Police Detective Warren Dennihan.

Deni had left in part because of Hobbs, Sheed was dismissed in large part because of Hobbs. The two shared a hatred for the man and common denominator for their dismissals. They also now shared Deni's current office space because he felt partly responsible for her dismissal. He'd injected himself into one of her murder investigations, the case which ultimately led to her being sacked, so he offered her a job at DIS.

That was a little over a year ago, the same time and same investigation which birthed the relationship with Ani. What started as giving her part-time work while she figured out her next move, begat clients and investigations that she brought to DIS. Within a few months, Lisa Sheed was a full-time employee, garnering full-time wages, and has been bucking to be made a full partner since. Sheed was always the first one in the office in the morning, and the last to leave at night. Thus far her efforts have not been rewarded.

"Hey boss," Sheed said when Deni arrived.

"Hey She."

"How was jury duty? I didn't hear from you at all yesterday."

"We'll talk about it later. What do we have on the books for today?"

"I was just looking at that. We've got four background checks, one hunt for a deadbeat who owes over $70k in alimony, and Ryan just called about a new case he picked up in New Hampster. All that should keep us busy for a couple of weeks and the keep the coffers full."

"Great," Deni said plopping down behind his desk next to hers.

"You look like shit. Do a little boozing again last night?"

"What's it you ya?"

"Ooh. Grumpy. That means you didn't get laid. You and Ani have a fight?"

Deni just stared at her.

"When are you going to give her what she wants?"

"And what is that?"

"For an investigator, you can be a fuck-tard."

"Insulting your boss. Great way to get what *YOU* want, huh?"

"Funny. She wants a ring, idiot."

"Lemme ask you a question. When did my love life become the primary topic of conversation in this office?"

"Do you want to know about Reggie? I can talk about her all day long. She's great. October is just around the corner, we can make it a double wedding. It's not too late."

"I'll keep that in mind, She."

"Seriously. It wouldn't be a big deal. We've already got the venue and everything. You've known Ani for about the same amount of time that I've known Reggie. Ani wants to get married, I don't know how she feels about a double-wedding, or a lesbian wedding for that matter, but I know that Reggie wouldn't care."

"I get enough of this conversation at home, I don't need it here too," Deni said.

"You two talk about lesbian weddings?"

"Fuck ya-self."

"Oh-kay. But let me just say that you shouldn't string her along. She moved in, she picked out a dog, and now the next step is to get hitched. If you dangle the carrot too long, she will eventually resent you for wasting some of her best years on something that never happened."

"And I thought she had the degree in psycho-babble."

"You're hysterical this morning, Deni. If this PI thing doesn't work out you can always go into comedy."

"My plate is already full. Let's change the subject."

"Fine with me. Want to talk about making me a full partner?"

"Jesus, She. Broken record. It's all fun and games until you're on the hook for all the bills too. This place is a big nut to carry."

"Is that a balls joke? You don't think a woman can handle it? I've been right next to you for—"

"—This has nothin' to do with male or female."

"I don't pull my weight?"

"Did I say that?"

"Because I'm a dyke?"

"You know better."

"Then what?"

"I've been at this a long time, She. You were a relatively new detective for the staties and you've been with me only about a year. You're young and smart and talented and who knows if this is what you wanna do for the rest of your career? This shit is dangerous. What does your future wife or husband or whatever you call yourselves think?"

"You know she supports me. This is what I want, so it's what she wants for me."

"She's not afraid of, ya know, somethin' not goin' right?"

"Of course, but she hates the hours worse. Is that why? All these times I've been hounding you? This isn't about me, it's about you. All of it. The marriage, the partnership ..... It's the Carina thing. Ani. Me. You don't want to relive that cop you knew down in Charleston. You think letting Ani in, or partnering with me, that you could lose somebody again. Let me be the first to burst your bubble, Guy, you don't have control over everything that happens to those that are close to you. What's in the cards, is in the cards. You can't live the rest of your life without getting close to anyone, Deni. That's no way to live."

"I'll keep that in mind. Now let's talk jury duty."

"How long did it take them to kick you?"

"They didn't."

Sheed gave an exaggerated nod. "And that's why you didn't come back to the office .... "

"And why I won't be in the office for three weeks, probably more like a month," he said.

"Ha. You got roped into a trial? Sucka. Which one?"

"You ain't gonna like it."

"Why, because I'm going to be doing all the work around here for a while? I'm used to it."

"It's the Chase Bromley trial," he blurted. "I'm lucky juror number seven."

Anyone with eyes would be able to see the look of shock and horror on Sheed's face. Not much phased her. Lisa Sheed was tough, strong, and calloused from investigating crimes against persons. Domestic abuse and rape, however, hit close to home. Once a prolonged victim herself, tormented by a man she convinced herself she loved, her tolerance level for men who abuse women is very low. She had once convinced herself that she was attracted to men, convinced herself that she was to blame when the last of those men beat the shit out of her for the slightest of whims, and has since come to the belief that all abusers should die a painful death with the same conviction.

"No shit?"

"No shit."

"That guy needs to fry, Deni. Massachusetts should bring back the death penalty just for that piece of shit."

"We'll see."

"Deni, you know my past with domestic violence. With rape. I'm willing to hold down the fort here if you promise to send that asshole to hell."

"I'll do my best."

"Not good enough. I want you to promise."

"How can I promise, She? That's why they have trials."

"They should skip the trial and just shoot him in the dick. Publicly. We can all watch him die. Slowly. His father should be forced to watch it happen and pay for all the spectator's drinks."

"This ain't China."

"Just put him down, Deni."

"Like I said, I'll do my best."

6

THE TRIAL STARTED ON THE MORNING OF MONDAY, MAY 12, with assistant District Attorney Justin Albright's opening statement. With voire dire completed, the selected jury was in their place by juror number in courtroom one, within the Suffolk County Superior Courthouse. Each seat in the box was filled, the twelve members and the two alternates, a captive audience in virtually every respect.

Criminal court cases in the Commonwealth of Massachusetts have specific procedures and formulae for getting to the truth, as does every other state in the union. Once an arrest takes place, the accused pleas either guilty or not-guilty at an arraignment. If the accused claims to be innocent, or uses a justification defense, the attorneys on both sides commence with the evidentiary dance. The Commonwealth is a reciprocity state, meaning that both sides have to 'show you theirs' in terms of evidence. Next comes the onslaught of omnibus motions which run the gamut of seeking a complete dismissal to throwing out a piece of evidence. Once all cards are on the table, a deal is either struck for a reduced prison sentence in exchange for forgoing a trial, or the two sides get set for said trial. The process of 'taking it to the hoop' is what takes time. That is why the horrific crimes that took place with respect to Commonwealth v. Bromley happened in the fall of one year, and the trial is now commencing nearly halfway through the next.

For the trial, and every other criminal matter in Massachusetts, the prosecutor states their case first and rests their case last. They are allowed to bookmark their case against the accused because they have the more arduous task of having to prove guilt beyond a reasonable doubt.

The defense attorney goes second, and second to last respectively. The defendant and his or her representatives are also the furthest in terms of distance away from the jury. This is deemed fair not only because of the burden of proof standard, but also because, psychologically, it decreases the chance of a jury member being intimidated by being slightly more removed.

Assistant District Attorneys Albright and Walsh stood from behind their long table closest to the box, as the jury walked into the criminal courtroom on the third floor to take their seat inside it. Two tables were moved together on the opposite side of the courtroom where Pratt, her client Chase Bromley, and her team consisting of Courtland, Bishop, and Elders sat. Judge Wallace sat upon his elevated place of control on the bench, ready to preside over Bromley's fate. The words *In God We Trust* were tattooed on the wall behind His Honor.

Once everyone was seated, Judge Wallace gave his instructions and outlined what could be expected during the trial. The court stenographer hammered away on what looked like an outdated mini-typewriter, ensuring that every word was saved for posterity. Some of the jurors were likewise hand-writing on their pads of paper which were given to them when arriving for trial that morning, some appeared to be exhausted at the outset.

" …. And therefore anything that I instruct to be ignored, as a matter of law, cannot be taken into account when deliberating over your eventual verdict. These proceedings are scheduled to take place over the course of three weeks, possibly more, or less though less likely. The media has been all over this case, and there is no reason to suspect that the coverage will diminish—especially since there are reporters and cameras in this very courtroom."

Several members of the jury took in the standing room only crowd, noticing reporters and cameras and artists in attendance.

"Members of the jury, you are prohibited from speaking to any member of the media, or anyone else for that matter with regard to this trial. Not your spouses, not your friends, not with any of the lawyers, not with me, not even your pets."

There were a few light chuckles, more out of politeness than the fact that the judge's comment was funny.

"You are furthermore prohibited from taking in any information other than what is provided to you during the trial. No newspapers, no television, no internet, no radio or any other format with which people get their news in this day and age. I want to be clear about this, because any information discussed during deliberations that was not presented at trial is considered jury tampering, and is a felony punishable by a prison sentence of up to ten years. One last instruction before we begin with the Commonwealth's opening statement—your deliberations are to commence at the completion of the trial, not before. You may not discuss your feelings with other members of the jury about guilt or innocence until you are instructed to do so by me. If there are no questions, we will begin."

Nobody on the jury panel budged, nor behind either table.

"Very well. I assume Mister Albright will be speaking to the jury?"

Assistant District Attorney Albright stood while his second chair, Amy Walsh, remained seated.

"That is correct your honor."

Justin Albright donned a dark blue suit, a crisp white shirt, and a red tie with paisley on it hung from his neck. He'd chosen the ensemble on purpose, red white and blue instilled confidence. Patriotism. He was the law, and the law could be trusted. The law was going to rid Boston of a monster.

Stress from the job had him prematurely graying, his hair was more salt than pepper though his scalp was completely covered. He'd spent his career in the District Attorney's office, prosecuted trials big and small for fifteen years. But this was the big one. This was the one that would get him elected to District Attorney next year. His boss was retiring, he was the air apparent. As long as he didn't screw this up.

Albright walked around the table, straightened his jacket before buttoning it closed.

"Ladies and gentlemen of the jury, I would like to first thank you for your service. It is a cornerstone of our legal system that twelve citizens, like yourselves, sit in judgement over the accused. Crimes against the people, must be judged by the people. The process is necessary in the business of justice. The business of putting the most violent and the most predatory behind bars. Criminals who would do us harm cannot and must not be allowed to live freely among us, they must be locked away. They must be kept away from civilized people like yourselves.

We are here today, and over the course of this trial, because Chase Bromley is one of those predators. He mustn't be allowed to continue his terror on the people of Boston. No woman will be safe if he once again escapes justice. Another family will have to suffer the same loss as Sloane Nichols' family.

Chase Bromley, the defendant, has led a life of privilege. His wealthy father has ensured that people who were wronged by his son, kept their grievances out of the light. The defendant has never been punished for any wrongdoing, and so he thinks that he can get away with the brutal rape and murder of his former girlfriend, Sloane Nichols.

The Commonwealth will prove, without any doubt whatsoever, that the crimes against the victim not only occurred, but happened at the hands of the defendant. None of the facts that we will present are going to be argued. Because these facts are indisputable, the defense will try to spin them, saying that they mean something that they do not. But at the end of the trial, when you add up all of the evidence, the evidence that is not going to be disputed, there will be only one conclusion."

Albright went back to his table to consult his yellow legal pad. He then turned back to the jury to finish his opening statement.

"Chase Bromley, the defendant, has a long history of domestic violence. Boston PD has been to his address on numerous occasions, responding to 9-1-1 calls when his then girlfriend, Sloane Nichols, lived with him. But because of his father and his connections, Chase Bromley was never arrested. He was allowed to continue to repeatedly beat her until she couldn't take any more. She left him. She moved out and managed to get a TRO, a Temporary Restraining Order, against him. There was nothing 'daddy' could do to stop that. No way to make that go away.

Sloane's leaving him infuriated the defendant. Nobody gets away with telling him 'no'. So he found out where she lived. Over the course of months he sought her out, giving the victim a false sense of security. We have a witness who put him at the victim's apartment the day of the murder. The fact that he was there, that he violated the restraining order, is not in dispute.

You will hear both our medical examiner and our forensic scientist tell you about the horrors that occurred to the victim, over a long period of time. You will hear from the detectives who investigated the crimes. You will hear evidence of the horrific violence that fell upon the victim at the hands of the defendant. You will hear that semen, belonging to Chase Bromley, was found in Sloane Nichols' dead body. You will hear how a sock, also belonging to the defendant, was shoved into her mouth to muffle the screams while these horrors happened to her. You will hear testimony that the defendant's fingerprints were identified in an apartment that he wasn't allowed within five-hundred feet of. Again, none of these facts are disputed.

The defendant has no alibi over the course of time that these atrocities occurred. He claims to have been in his home," Albright once again looked at his yellow legal pad, "playing video games — according to the statement he gave the police.

Over that span of time, which you will hear took in approximately twelve to fifteen hours, Chase Bromley cannot account for his whereabouts. How is that possible? Nobody can corroborate seeing him over the course of a fifteen hour time period? That is a long time, ladies and gentlemen. Nobody can testify to seeing him somewhere other than where the victim was brutalized over that span of time, because he was there. You will hear from our witness who says so. His DNA says so. He was the perpetrator of these atrocities.

The top count of Murder in the First Degree, is what we are asking you to find the defendant guilty of. Murder one. Murder in conjunction with one or more Class A Felonies, which in this case were; Breaking and Entering, Assault, Forceable Imprisonment, and Rape. We are also asking that you find him guilty of the lesser included charges of; violating a restraining order, Evidence Tampering, and Hindering Prosecution.

Because he did it.

He did all of those things you are going to hear about and it wasn't because he snapped. Nor was it a crime of passion. He raped and tortured the victim for as many as fifteen hours before killing her."

Albright paused for effect.

"*Fif-teen* hours, ladies and gentlemen. It's difficult to even imagine.

Chase Bromley planned what he was going to do, and did it slowly and painfully. And then he tried to cover up any trace of DNA by pouring bleach all over the victim and the apartment."

Albright took yet another break to consult his notes. He looked to his second chair, ADA Amy Walsh who nodded, then turned back to the jury.

"The defendant before you is guilty. As I've said, none of the facts that we will present over the course of this trial are going to be argued. The talented defense attorney, Alexandria Pratt and her team, will try to spin those facts—but they are *FACTS*. Chase Bromley committed the crimes of Breaking and Entering, Violating a TRO, Assault, Forceable Imprisonment, Rape, Murder in the First Degree, and a slew of other related misdemeanors."

Albright read all the charges again to impress upon the jury the number and severity of the crimes Chase Bromley was charged with. He paused after the second reading to attain his desired effect.

"He needs to be put away ladies and gentlemen. Boston cannot and will not be safe unless you find him guilty. Guilty of the crimes that he committed. At the conclusion of this trial, we will be asking that you find the defendant, Chase Bromley, Guilty. Thank You."

Albright took his seat. Judge Wallace allowed the silence to linger a beat before letting the defense, Alex Pratt, stand to give her opening statement.

"Miss Pratt. The floor is yours."

"I would like to postpone my opening statement for when I begin to present my case, your Honor," she said.

"Objection," Albright stood.

"M-G-L 234 sub 71, your Honor," Pratt argued, referring to Massachusetts General Law 234A §71. "I have the right to waive the opening until I commence with my case."

"Standard litigation format, your Honor, as outlined in the Mass Criminal Procedure Manual," Albright defended. "Opening statements occur at the opening of the trial."

"That's not how seventy-one reads, Judge. I have the option to either give an opening statement or waive it until the, quote 'opening of the case'. I haven't opened my case, nor will I until I begin to call defense witnesses."

"You are correct, Miss Pratt. Overruled. The defense will render her opening at the conclusion of the Commonwealth's case," Wallace said. He looked at his watch. Albright's lengthy opening statement after the judge's instructions took them to almost noon.

"Since I'm sure the prosecution's first witness is not here to testify, as he is slated to testify tomorrow, we can adjourn for the day. If the jury is willing to work through what would normally be a lunch break in order to pick a foreperson, they can be excused for the day," Wallace said in the jury's direction.

He received a sea of nods in return. Getting out early on the first day was a welcomed surprise.

"Very well. The jury will retire to the deliberation room to determine a foreperson, and *only* to determine a foreperson. Once that has been determined and forwarded to me via the court officer, you will be free to leave until tomorrow."

Wallace banged his gavel and left the courtroom ahead of all other parties.

7

TWO HOURS BEFORE THE JURY LEFT THE COURTHOUSE, AS
they were selecting their foreperson, Chase Bromley left to go home
for the day. His $1 Million bail had been continued, which in and of
itself was a public outrage. The arraignment judge who originally
issued the bail amount and mandated that an ankle monitor be worn
at all times, had taken some flack in the press about the decision,
but argued that he was well within his discretion and that a public
figure such as Bromley would want to appear at trial to clear his
name.

     Kenneth Bromley, Chase's father, a well-known real estate
developer, put up the bail money. Everyone in New England knew of
him if they didn't know him by sight. He helped Bob Kraft build
Gillette Stadium in Foxborough for the New England Patriots before
they built their dynasty, was the key instrument in the redevelopment
and beautification of both the Seaport District and Long Wharf in
Boston, revitalized downtown Providence, Rhode Island as well.
And those were only the most public of projects under his watchful
eye. When Kenneth Bromley put up his assets for his son and
promised that Chase would be present for every court appearance,
the judge at the arraignment believed him.

     Chase Bromley's movements had been tracked by the
Department of Probation as he freely moved about the city, with the
use of the ankle monitor by the Department of Probation, for every
minute of every day since.

     The tiny red LED light blinked as he entered the chauffeured
Mercedes Maybach waiting for him, and continued to do so as he
was dropped off at his $9.5M Back Bay brownstone on Beacon

Street. Both the car and the brownstone were bought and paid for by none other than Kenneth Bromley, of course.

Within thirty minutes of Chase getting home, Kenneth walked through the front door like he owned the place, because he did, though he didn't live there. The brownstone with attached garage and basement was built in 1873, but had been completely modernized before Sloane moved into it with Chase. To the right, as the senior Bromley entered the 12-room home, was the first of the living rooms.   His son was slumped into a plush couch watching NECN coverage of his trial on the flatscreen.

"Just walk right in, Dad. Please. Don't knock or announce your intention to visit."

"I own this property, Chase. You seem to forget that along with the fact that the only reason you aren't in a cell with rotating bunk-mates is because of me," Kenneth said. He took a seat in the tufted barrel armchair next to his son. He pressed the power-off button on the touchscreen universal remote control.

"I wasn't watching that. So what did dear-old-dad expect to dig through while I wasn't here?"

"I came to speak with you."

"How'd you know I was here? I'm supposed to be in court right now," Chase said.

"Since I pay for your driver, and it's my million bucks I'll lose if you vanish, I have an interest in keeping track of you."

"So he dropped a dime that I was getting out early," Chase calculated out loud.

"I have some concerns that we need to discuss."

"Of course you do. What could be bothering my father today? What did I do this time? Should I hazard a guess?"

"You'd have plenty to pick from, wouldn't you? My son has a public trial where he's been accused of raping and murdering his ex-girlfriend, for starters—"

"—Here we go."

"Or how about he shows his father, the man who keeps a roof over his head, absolutely no respect."

"I have a job, Dad."

60

"Really? You call day-trading the money that I keep funneling into this scheme a job? What if I turn off the faucet?"

"Is that what this is about? You want your money back?"

"And where would this windfall come from? You're into me for millions—on top of this place, the Mercedes, your legal team .... Should I keep going?"

"No, that won't be necessary."

"You're far too old to still be suckling on the tit, Son. But you're all that I have left since your mom passed so I keep shoveling money toward you to keep you from falling into a cesspool of your own making. It's past time for you to get your shit together, but that's not what this is about. My concern is with your general demeanor, not just with me, but at the trial. With your legal team."

"As usual, I don't follow."

"You gave Alex some grief during jury selection. Over this cop that you didn't want on the jury."

"Former cop, as I've been told. I don't see how he's going to help win the jury over. And why am I even talking about this with you? She's MY lawyer. Isn't that shit supposed to be private?"

"Privilege is for the person paying for it, which is me," Kenneth said. "It's my money, and she's my friend through her partner Brandon Taylor—You know, as in Taylor, Higgs & Pratt? You may have seen the letterhead."

"I'm not sure that's how it works, Dad."

"Son, the things you're not sure 'how it works' could fill a room. She says that you sit there slumping like you are now, like you don't give a shit if you go away for consecutive life terms or not."

"And you believe what she says? It's not like you're there to see for yourself," Chase said.

"Not only do I believe her, but the cameras illustrate it. Even if I wanted to be in the courtroom, somebody has to make the money being thrown down this toilet." Kenneth looked around the well-appointed living room. "This all costs money you know. Alexandria may be a friend of a friend, but do you think her efforts here are pro-bono? Ten million is what you're little faux-pas is going to cost. The least you could do is act like your interested in the outcome."

"You think I did it, don't you?"

"With the evidence they have, Chase, I know damn well you did it. Add this colossal fuck-up to the long list over the course of your life? You sent your mother to an early grave over your nonsense."

"You can't blame that shit on me. I had nothing to do with it."

"You think all of the late-night phone calls and the police visits were helpful do you? That woman stayed up nights worrying about her only child. Celine may have died of cancer, but the stress is what gave her the cancer in the first place."

Chase shook his head. "That's bullshit and you know it."

"You've been overindulged your entire life, so maybe some of this is my fault. Your mother made sure that you had everything that you ever wanted, every whim was indulged. She coddled you and I allowed it. I even kept tradition alive when she passed. But this trial? This is not something that you can slide through like you usually do. This is the rest of your life we're talking about here. There is no way in hell that I'm going to sit idly by while you throw the opportunities you have away. Opportunities that most people would do anything for. For better or for worse, you're my only son. You're all I have left. You're going to sit there, shut up, and act like you didn't do all of the horrible things that happened to that poor girl. We are going to get you through this, together. You're thirty-two years old, you've got the rest of your life if we can straighten you out once and for all."

"A lifetime of abuse. Maybe prison isn't so bad."

"Look around you, Son. What is so horrible about where you live and the opportunities you have? Am I really that bad of a father where you'd go to prison just to spite me? I'm trying to save you from the rape you're going to have to endure in prison because of the rape and torture you inflicted on Sloane."

"I didn't rape her, Dad. For the thousandth time."

"She shoved a baseball bat into herself repeatedly and then committed suicide? I'm not stupid, Chase. Neither is Alexandria Pratt."

"It was a softball bat and she's never actually asked me outright if I did it or not."

"Of course not. She can't allow you to perjure yourself or provide false information at trial. Alex can propose alternate theories but not if she knows for a fact that they are false. You can lie to your lawyer, and that information is privileged, but she can't turnaround and spread that lie. She's an officer of the court. So she didn't directly ask you if you committed the crimes that you're accused of because she knows you did it. She spared you from having to lie to her, and from having to lie to the jury if and when she puts you on the stand to testify. She's a damn good lawyer. You need to do your part."

"My part is to tell her the truth. That I didn't do it," Chase said.

"Save your bullshit for those who will buy it. Your part is to sit there, shut up, and *pretend* like you didn't do it."

The day would have ended much earlier for the jury, as the judge indicated, had selecting a foreperson been as easy as the project sounds.

But it wasn't that simple. Human nature took over and the people that had tried so diligently and failed to get out of jury duty, now wanted to be in charge of it. Each seemed to have their own hidden reason for why they should be elected foreperson. Some, like Paul Weist, for alpha-male reasons. Some like Jamar Dubone, Denai Moshe, and Cherelle Garrison because they're all African-American and felt that this mini-society should mimic the milestone the nation had overcome with Obama. Renaldo Ramos Gomez, as a new American wanted to exercise his new rights to the fullest, and Ben Post because he was gay and why not? Oscar Brenowitz and

Evelyn Rocher because they were the most senior in terms of age. All but three and the alternates—neither of whom could obviously be a foreperson—contended that it should be they who were in charge for reasons spoken and hidden.

Warren Dennihan silently sat in his seat at the conference table, watching the human race devolve before his eyes.

As did Sherlie Lovett.

Thirty year old Jordan Raines didn't give a rat's ass who was in charge as long as it wasn't her.

The yelling and bickering went on for over an hour, through what would have been their lunch break before one of the alternates, Marissa Gantse, stood and spoke above the roar of the crowd.

"Can everyone just hold on for a minute!"

The room came to a reluctant silence.

"I know I'm only an alternate, but I have an idea of how to solve the foreperson problem," she announced.

Someone said, "Why do you give a shit?"

"I don't. I just want to get out of here. I can't be in charge since I'm an alternate, so I have no other agenda save for getting the hell out of here so I can go home to my husband and kids."

"What's your big idea, miss thang?" Ben Post offered in a huff.

"Let's take a vote. Who here thinks he did it? That Chase Bromley is guilty?"

Regan Avery spoke up. "We aren't supposed to do that. The judge told us not to come to any decisions until the end of the trial."

"Just humor me," Marissa said. "Come on. Show of hands. We don't need a formal ballot or anything. Just raise your hand if you already think he did it."

Everyone raised their hand with the exception of Warren Dennihan, Jordan Raines, and Sherlie Lovett. Ten people raised their preferred hand, including the other alternate who did so despite not being able to cast a vote, let alone be a foreperson.

"Okay. At least you're all being honest, that's a start. Does that mean that the three of you think he's innocent?"

Warren Dennihan spoke up.

"No, I think he probably did it. But since all I've heard so far is one opening statement—other than what I've seen on TV—I'll save my judgement for when it counts."

Jordan and Sherlie nodded their heads.

"That's what I thought. So in my humble opinion, that leaves only you three as a possible foreperson. You're the only ones that are even remotely objective at this point."

Oscar Brenowitz, the seventy-one year old Jewish man took exception.

"Now wait a minute, young lady. I never said that I wouldn't be objective. You just asked if I thought he was guilty."

"Which you're not supposed to have done yet, Sir. It's not a personal attack." Marissa turned to Warren. "You. What's your name?"

"Deni. Call me Deni."

"Okay, Deni. What do you think? Do you want to be the foreperson?"

"No."

"Maybe that's why you should be."

"No. Pick someone else." Deni turned to Jordan Raines. "You."

Soon-to-be-retired Evelyn Rocher spoke up.

"This infant should be in charge? How old are you? Eighteen?"

"It's not polite to ask someone's age you old battle-axe. And I'm in my thirties, but I guess everyone looks like a child to someone with one foot in the grave," Jordan replied.

"This is how you speak to elders," Oscar said in Evelyn's defense. "You should be ashamed."

Marissa pointed to Sherlie Lovett.

"You're next. What's your name and what's your deal?"

"Sherlie. My name is Sherlie and *my deal* is I'm an executive with a large company. City Sports, I'm sure you've heard of it."

A gaggle of nods affirmed her statement.

"I'm ultimately in charge of over a thousand employees. I'm in Human Resources so I do a lot of dispute resolution. I can do it. I can be the foreperson if everyone is amenable. I guess I'm qualified is what I'm saying."

"In the interest of time and aggravation, can we all agree that Sherlie is our foreperson?"

Paul Weist, the Jewish alpha-male said, "No."

"Of course not. Why should it be this easy? You've only been fighting over this all afternoon, why stop now?" Marissa sat down hard in her chair, defeated.

"I just don't think she should be in charge is all. Why not me?"

Deni stood up. "Anyone other than this prick who thinks he should be foreperson, raise their hand."

Nobody did.

"See? Not for nothin', but when you're a leader, and you look back and find that nobody's following you? You're alone," Deni said. He then looked around the room. "Anyone who thinks Sherlie is qualified and should be the foreperson, raise your hand."

Seven people, including Deni, raised their hands.

"That's a majority," he said after doing a rough count. "Congrats Sherl. You're in charge of this mess."

8

THE SECOND DAY OF THE TRIAL, TUESDAY, BEGAN WITH testimony from the Chief Medical Examiner, Doctor Mark Bowman. Normally, a prosecutor likes to present the case in the sequence of events as they occurred, like any story or movie. An easy-to-follow sequence makes it easier for a jury to determine how the crime or crimes took place, and therefore pass down the correct verdict. Confusion equates to doubt and doubt means that monsters are set free to roam the streets.

He or she therefore preferred to present the events and evidence of the crime or crimes as the police uncovered them. Often because of scheduling conflicts, however, experts and medical examiners and the like cannot appear in front of a jury at the exact date and time preferred by the prosecutor.

Such was the case in Commonwealth v. Bromley. Doctor Bowman, a busy medical examiner with a packed schedule, had all of the pressing demands that come with the job description, including other cases and other trials to give testimony in. Assistant District Attorney Albright would have liked for the two detectives assigned to the case, Leiman and Champagne, to testify first, but May 13 was Mark Bowman day whether ADA Albright liked it or not.

Nobody in the courtroom was looking forward to the vivid details of the how and the when Sloane Nichols was tortured and killed. The room was dripping with dread of the uncertain certainty of what was about to unfold. The television press had given the general public insight over the previous months as to how gruesome the acts upon the victim were, getting as graphic as possible for their viewership with warning statements like, "The images you are

about to see are disturbing and not intended for younger viewers."
The jury was about to see the human wreckage in much greater
detail.

Easels were set up in the center of the room, just in front of
the judge, yet strategically aligned for both the jury and the press in
the gallery. The court stenographer was hidden behind them but
could be seen through the skeleton of the easels, as nothing had
been set upon them as yet.

The defendant was upright and stoic, unlike the slumped
posture he'd been displaying through voire dire and the opening
statement. He seemed to be the only one who was interested in
what was to come. Bromley's team was conferring around him,
preparing for the ME's testimony.

Albright and Walsh were having a conference of their own,
discussing last minute strategies on how to inflict the most damage.
Bowman was going to tell more than the thousand words each of
the pictures supposedly told. The prosecution not only needed to
show that crimes had been committed, but also instill a lasting
impression with the jury about the horrific nature of said crimes.

The jury had taken their seats, Judge Wallace perched on
high, and all parties on both sides of the aisle had retaken their
seats. Wallace rapped the gavel.

"Commonwealth v. Bromley continues. Will the prosecution
call their first witness?"

"We will, your Honor," Albright said as he stood.
"Commonwealth calls Suffolk County Chief Medical Examiner,
Doctor Mark Bowman."

"Very well."

Court officers opened the large double doors at the entrance
of the room, a slight man with a full mustache and beard walked
through them toward the witness stand. He was wearing a gray suit
which exacted the color of the hair near his temples. He swore to
tell the truth, the whole truth, and nothing but to everyone present.
He then took his seat and stated his full name and occupation, the
reporters in the pews were already taking copious notes. Cameras
were capturing footage for the evening news and sketch artists were
putting a generous likeness to the page.

"Doctor Bowman, you have stated that you are the Chief Medical Examiner for Suffolk County, are you new to the position?" Albright began by laying the groundwork, solidifying that the doctor was the real deal and not some hack with a diploma.

"No. I've been in the Coroner's Office for over eleven years, the last four I've been Chief," Bowman said.

"And Chief means that you have several other examiners who report to you?"

"Yes. I'm ultimately responsible for all of the autopsies performed in Suffolk County, and I've been consulted on cases outside of my jurisdiction."

"Outside of your jurisdiction? In Massachusetts?"

"Yes, and nationally."

"Why do you suppose that is?"

"Objection," Alex Pratt stood. "He's leading, your Honor."

"Sustained. Move along, Mister Albright."

"Doctor Bowman, you've consulted on cases and were promoted four years ago to your current position because of your experience and expertise, correct?"

"Presumably, yes. I've either performed or examined over a thousand autopsies in my career. I have degrees in physiology, forensics and medicine. I've been published in the New England Journal of Medicine, and sit on boards for both Harvard and Tufts Universities."

"Did you perform the autopsy on Sloane Nichols last October?"

"I did," Bowman said.

"Were you assigned to the case by chance?"

"No. It was a high-profile death, I assigned the case to myself."

"And did you determine a cause of this high-profile death?"

"Yes. Sloane Nichols presented with broken bones, bruises, and violations of a sexual nature; however, her head was nearly taken off, which was the ultimate cause of death. Her assailant used a sharp blade, later determined to be a chef's knife from the victim's own kitchen. It was used to cut her throat from mandible to mandible, or just under her ear to ear." Bowman displayed the cut on his own throat, drawing the line with his forefinger from ear to ear.

"The knife was sharp enough to do the job; however, enough force was used to not only sever her carotid, but moved so deep into her neck from front to back that the person responsible nearly cut her head clean off. The killer stood behind the victim, and using upward pressure back toward himself, cut through the platysma muscles, the mastoid process, the thyroid gland and trachea, nicking the hyoid bone on the way to the posterior triangle. In layman's terms, the killer pulled the knife not only into the neck but upward towards himself from behind her with enough force to decapitate her."

"At this time, if it please the court, I'd like to offer a photograph into evidence and mark it Exhibit 1A. It's a crime scene photo of the victim's neck."

"We object, your Honor. It is the defense's understanding that Mister Albright is going to display several pictures of the victim on these easels, blown up to five hundred percent. The photos are going to be displayed for mere shock value, which will prejudice the jury and far outweigh their probative value. The witness has testified as to what killed the victim. For what reason—other than for shock value—could there be in revealing these photos and at the size he's blown them up to?"

"Miss Pratt, we went over this in pretrial motions. The prosecution has the responsibility of proving the crimes, these photos are proof of the crimes. Objection is noted but overruled."

Alex sat down. Jack Elders leaned across Kevin Bishop to softly ask why she hadn't created a bigger objection over the large photos. She whispered back to the eager, young attorney, "I wanted the objection noted in case of an appeal. We don't want the jury to think that we are afraid of the photos. We're not arguing that she was murdered, we're arguing that Chase didn't do it. You need to pick our battles with a jury."

The jury consultant, Max Courtland nodded in agreement, solidifying that the lesson was well-taught.

Albright had already leaned 1A up on the first easel, and turned back to the witness. The photo depicted a close-up of

Sloane Nichols' throat. The inside of the victim's neck was on display which caused gasps from not only the jury but the gallery as well.

"So her death was instantaneous?"

"The cut to her throat finished the job, but what was done to her was not instantaneous, no. The victim had been tortured for as few as twelve and as many as fifteen hours prior to the fatal wound."

"Can you expound on that, Doctor?"

"There was blunt-force trauma to her Occipital Fontanelle, or the back of her head, that had caused internal cerebral hemorrhaging, which had begun to heal. Based upon the amount of blood inside the victim's brain, how it pooled and coagulated, I determined that this was the oldest of her wounds. That specific evidence further leads me to conclude that this was the blow that initially incapacitated her which allowed the killer to inflict the numerous other wounds. Since the wound was the earliest and determined to be twelve to fifteen hours older than her fatal injury, it was the chief indicator of how long the victim was tortured."

"Meaning that the victim, Sloane Nichols, had regained consciousness at some point before the fatal cut?"

"Correct. Not only had she regained consciousness, but no other damage was inflicted until she was aware of what was happening to her. That was the killer's goal. Not only did he want to inflict as much pain as possible, he wanted her to feel it."

Alex Pratt stood. "Objection. Facts not in evidence. How does the doctor know what the murderer was thinking?"

"We're getting there, your Honor. If we could have some latitude?"

"Overruled. But get there quickly, Mister Albright."

"Yes, Judge."

Albright turned back to Dr. Bowman. ADA Amy Walsh, his second chair, put up more enlarged photos which were named Exhibits 1B and C. These were close-ups of her wrists and mouth.

"Doctor. What, if any, determining factors in your autopsy made you conclude that she had regained consciousness and that this was the goal of her assailant?"

"Several indicators. Her wrists were bound using wide, plastic zip-ties. She had tried to escape, noted by the deep cuts into her Flexor Carpi Ulnaris muscles. The killer ensured that his victim was bound very tightly toward the Tuberosity of the …. " Bowman was an experienced witness and sensed that he was loosing the jury already.

" ….. In layman's terms, he made sure that she was bound with the wide ties closer to the bottom of the hands instead of the meat of the wrist to avoid slicing across an artery, like someone might if they were trying to commit suicide. He inflicted immense pain over a long period of time and didn't want his victim to have the ability to end it herself."

"And what, if any, additional pain was inflicted upon her, Doctor?" Albright asked like he didn't know while motioning to Walsh to erect more pictures on the easels in advance of the answer.

She quickly responded, as was rehearsed, erecting more exhibits and were named 1D through H. One such photo depicted the victim's nearly decapitated head with eyes blindfolded and duct tape around her mouth.

"A tube sock was shoved into Sloane Nichols' mouth, which prohibited anyone from hearing her screams, which anyone would have done if the pain from what I'm about to describe was inflicted upon them. The killer was careful not to wedge the sock so far into her mouth that she would be asphyxiated, but far enough in where she didn't have the ability to spit it out. The sock was then duct taped to the victim to hold the sock in place. I sent the adhesive remnants to our laboratory in Maynard for testing."

Bowman paused to make sure that he hadn't lost anyone, that the jury was paying attention to him and understood. Several members of the jury were writing down notes on pads of paper.

Albright urged him on after entering the sock in an evidence bag into evidence as Exhibit 2.

"Please go on, Doctor."

"The killer then began systematically raping her, both vaginally and anally. We know it was rape for a variety of reasons, the most compelling because both of her knees were broken."

"And you conclude this why, Doctor?"

"She would have kicked at her assailant, trying to defend herself from being further violated. If the killer had bound her ankles, like he'd done to her wrists, he wouldn't have been able to enter her. Sloane Nichols' feet would have been bound together, thereby forcing her legs to be closer together. He was therefore forced to incapacitate her legs when she wouldn't stop kicking. She suffered another blow to the head, this time to her frontal bone or forehead, corresponding to damage done to the wall in her apartment, which indicates that, though blindfolded, she tried to escape. A willing participant in a sexual game doesn't try to escape her own apartment.

Furthermore, the large, aluminum softball bat that was later used to defile her vagina and anus was used to shatter her patellae and meniscuses. Her kneecaps. The pain would have been excruciating, and again, not something that one would willingly let happen to them."

Albright produced the bat from the prosecution table and walked it toward the medical examiner. He was sure to hold it so the jury could see it on the way. The evidence tag that was tied to handle fluttered in the air on the short trip.

"This bat?"

"Yes."

The makeshift weapon was then entered into evidence, Albright then proceeded with further questioning while bringing 'Exhibit 3' to the jury so they might inspect it closer.

"And these violations took place over time, Doctor?"

"Yes. The amount of pain would cause her to pass out, which didn't suit the killer."

"Objection. The witness is again making statements against facts not in evidence," Pratt said.

Judge Wallace responded before Albright had the opportunity to. He then spoke to the ME directly.

"Doctor, do you know that she passed out for a fact, or are you making certain assumptions?"

"Judge, I can state with a better than ninety-percent certainty that given the length of time and number of times that the victim was beaten and raped, that her brain would shut down her body. Even people with an abnormally high tolerance for pain would shut down with the amount of abuse the victim had to endure," Bowman said.

Judge Wallace turned back to Alex Pratt and her team. "Overruled."

Walsh had taken down all of the previous enlarged photos on the easels and replaced them yet more heinous images, marked Exhibits 1I through N. Sloane Nichols' dead body was lying in a pool of blood, her body was splayed out in the most unnatural of contortions.

Nearly everyone in the courtroom winced at the images.

Albright went back to his witness.

"Doctor, this wasn't some sex game that went out of control, was it?"

"No. No. No way. As I've said, the amount of damage was inhuman. Sex was a major part of the killer's dominance over the victim, but there was no way that anything that was done to her was consensual. None of it. I've heard of sex acts involving large objects, but with this amount of tearing? No way."

Albright again held up the large, purple, Easton aluminum softball bat.

"Is this the object of which you speak?"

"Objection. Asked and answered," Pratt bellowed without leaving her chair.

"Overruled. The witness can answer."

"Yes. As I said, the bat was used as a phallus. Her assailant was aroused by her violations."

"Can you elaborate, Doctor?"

Some of the female jurors were fidgeting in their seats. Several of them, male and female, averted their eyes from both the bat and the pictures that were still on display. The victim's struggle and damage was becoming real.

"There was semen found inside the victim. Again, both in her vagina and anus. Samples of the semen were also sent to our forensic lab for testing, along with the sock and adhesive sample I mentioned earlier. I can't testify to the processes of the various tests, since I wasn't involved, but I can say that the reports I received indicated that all of the semen came from the same person. One person entered her, on more than one occasion, and ejaculated. This took some time. Then the use of the softball bat, in this case with a barrel diameter of two and three-quarter inches, inserted into both orifices, caused tearing and stretching. The order in which the events occurred is clear, since trace amounts of said semen, according to the report, were found on the bat.

Additionally, this would make sense since in order for the male assailant to get tactile pleasure from being inside the victim, and therefore ejaculating, he would have had to insert himself before using the bat. The only conclusion is that when he was finished using her to pleasure himself, he tormented her and humiliated her with the softball bat. None of this was pleasurable, none of this was a consensual sex act. From the beginning to the fatal end, the events which took place were against her will. Further evidence of this was her broken fingernails."

Bowman pointed to one of the photos still erected on an easel. The photo depicted a close-up of Sloane Nichols' hands.

"Was there any evidence gained from under what was left of her fingernails?"

"Unfortunately, no. Her killer used bleach to sanitize the victim and the area around her. I say 'sanitize' but I really mean destroy evidence. The hardwood flooring, her fingernails, and the DNA that was beneath her were all destroyed. The bleach was poured all over the victim, tainting the blood, urine, vomit, and feces she was lying in. Only the DNA evidence deposited inside her vagina and anus were salvageable. Sloane Nichols fought off her killer as best she could, but over the course of time, after being blindfolded, bound and gagged—without the use of her legs—she was no match for her aggressor."

"Which, from your testimony, lasted roughly twelve to fifteen hours."

"Correct."

Tears were flowing from some of the female jurors. The nearest court officer to the jury had a box of tissues passed around. The judge looked around the courtroom, realizing from the faces therein that they were as weary from the photos and testimony as he.

"Now would be a good time to take a break."

9

DENI WASN'T HUNGRY AFTER SEEING AND HEARING the first witness for the prosecution in court. He knew the ME. In fact, he had known him for a long time. Deni had worked with him when he was a state police detective in Troop H, and had run into him since while investigating cases independently.

Mark Bowman was a no-nonsense kind of guy in his private life, let alone his duties as a Medical Examiner. He was all about facts, and nothing but the facts. He could have embellished his testimony in court, making every painful minute of what Sloane Nichols had gone through that much more horrific. But that wasn't his style, and Deni knew it. She'd gone through hell in her last day of life, no hyperbole or colorful flourishes were necessary for anyone to understand that hell.

And Deni had seen what hell looks like. He'd seen the worst in human nature, the most evil shit that a person could think of. And yet the testimony he'd heard as juror number seven sickened him. He could only imagine how the others felt and what they were thinking.

Each of the jurors had gone their separate ways for the lunch break. Some smoked cigarettes outside the courthouse as Deni passed. Some headed past Congress Street toward Faneuil Hall, while others seemed to wander off to a clandestine destination for their short reprieve.

Deni went across the street to the Kinsale Irish Pub & Restaurant. Many a non-Irish had called the establishment home when called to court for one type of refreshment or another. While juror number seven wasn't hungry, a belt of Irish would settle his nerves. The proprietor chose not to carry Redbreast—Deni's favorite true Irish Whiskey—for some ungodly reason, so he let the bartender pour whatever was handy. Two doubles later, he was ready to go back to court.

The line to get back into the courthouse after lunch was a long one. Each of the jurors waiting to get back inside to resume listening to the evidence in the trial began to talk amongst themselves.

Deni'd heard one too many 'the sonofabitch did it and should fry' to not get involved.

"We're not supposed to make any decisions until the end. It's only the first witness," Deni said.

Regan Avery, juror four, spoke in a loud whisper while in line. She was three people ahead of Deni. "You saw those photos. And the doctor told us what happened. The bat? That poor lady. You can't possibly think he's not-guilty?"

"I didn't say what I thought, one way or another," Deni said. "The ADA is gonna try and make this Bromley prick seem as guilty and savage as possible in order to get a conviction. Just keep that in mind when you're listenin' to the witnesses. Anyway, the defense attorney is gonna have a crack at him now. Let's see how many holes she punches into his testimony."

There were more comments from other jurors, but Deni couldn't hear what they were as everyone had turned forward. The line to get inside the courthouse was beginning to move at a more brisk pace.

Soon they would be back inside, listening to the good Doctor, Mark Bowman, defend his findings to the very talented defense attorney, Alexandria Pratt.

Once the courtroom had calmed down, everyone back into their assigned places, Judge Wallace informed Alex Pratt that she was free to cross-examine the witness.

She stood, straightened her Anne Klein Glen pant suit as she came from behind the defense table.

"I just have a few questions for you, Doctor Bowman. First, do you have any indication from the horrific damage that was inflicted upon the victim, what time the semen that you found inside Miss Nichols was ejaculated into her?"

"Not an exact time, no."

"Care to give us an educated guess?"

"Objection, your Honor," Albright said. "Asked and answered. He said 'no'. That should be that."

"Your Honor, I wasn't able to depose this witness, I would ask that the court bear with me. The reason for my insistence will become clear."

"Objection is overruled. The witness will answer to the best of his ability," Judge Wallace said.

"The victim was found within four hours of her murder, at 10:00 a.m., when she didn't show up for coffee with her colleague as was prearranged. The attacker took approximately twelve to fifteen hours to kill her …. If I *had* to guess, I would say within twenty hours of being found, or sometime between 2:00 p.m. and 5:00 a.m. on Sunday and Monday of October six and seven of last year. The semen was deposited into the victim during that span of time."

"And you're making your educated guess based upon the assumption that the person who tortured and held the victim captive, is the one who, in your words, 'deposited' the semen into her?"

"Yes."

"But couldn't she have had sex some time before her attack, and the semen been left over from the consensual sex earlier on that Sunday?"

"I suppose," Bowman said but without enthusiasm.

"What do you mean, 'you suppose', Doctor? Isn't it true that semen can last inside a vaginal or anal cavity for as many as seventy-two hours unless expelled?"

"That is true. However, in most cases semen wouldn't survive the high acidic levels inside the vagina or anus. Also, in most cases, the ejaculate will leak from either orifice, or be cleaned with one soap or another. No soap residue was found and the victim in this case wasn't afforded the luxury of being able to clean herself, nor was the ejaculate able to be expelled from her by being upright. Her broken legs more than indicate that she wasn't able to be upright."

"I understand, but I didn't ask you about most cases. I'm asking about this particular case. And I asked you if it was true that semen can last inside a woman's vagina or anus for as many as seventy-two hours, which you said was true. I can have the court stenographer read it back to you if you wish."

"There is no need for that. I stand by my statement, such fluid can last as many as seventy-two hours inside either cavity under the right conditions."

"So, would you care to revise your statement of 'I suppose'?"

"No."

"And why is that, Doctor?"

"Because the victim was held captive for so many hours, she was forced to eliminate her bladder and bowels where she lay. The deposited fluid would most likely be eliminated with it."

"If that is the case, then how is it possible that you found any semen at all?"

"There were trace amounts inside her and on the bat."

"Which could have been initially deposited up to seventy-two hours before and been present when the bat was later used to violate the victim. Isn't it possible, Doctor, that the she had consensual vaginal and anal sex—where the semen was deposited—and then later, her rapist-killer used a bat and possibly a condom? Is that possible?"

"Is it POSSIBLE? Anything is possible. But it's not likely."

Alex Pratt looked stunned.

"Why is that not likely? You testified, under oath, that the forensic evidence on her person and under her broken fingernails were destroyed by the application of bleach. That the killer poured said bleach all over Sloane Nichols to destroy such DNA evidence. Why would he then leave such an obvious DNA trail by not using a condom? Ejaculating into the victim, more than one time as you've testified, but only destroying the exterior evidence seems at odds, wouldn't you say?"

Bowman didn't respond. He looked at the prosecutor's table for help, but neither Albright nor Walsh could help him.

Alex let the time pass, watching the jury get confused by the contradiction. The thirty-seconds that passed felt like a year. The tension in the courtroom was palpable. A feather falling to the floor would have made a deafening sound.

"Well, Doctor? Doesn't that seem to be at odds? The killer didn't know that such semen existed, nor would he care because it didn't belong to him. He destroyed the only evidence that would link him to the victim by applying the external bleach. For the last time, doesn't that scenario seem more than possible, more than 'you suppose', but likely?"

Bowman shrugged and looked into his lap.

"Yes, it does."

"Can you repeat that, Sir?"

"Objection. Repetitive," Albright said.

Before Judge Wallace made a determination, Pratt withdrew the request.

"The witness doesn't have to repeat himself, I think we all clearly understand him."

Alex headed back toward her seat, then spun around, re-approaching the witness in an exaggerated display of having an afterthought.

"Oh, Doctor. Is there another piece of medical evidence at odds that you've failed to mention here today?"

"Objection. Leading."

"Ask a specific question, counselor," Judge Wallace warned Alex.

"You have a degree in internal medicine, yes?"

"Yes."

"Then you're undoubtedly familiar with the drug Benzodiazepine?"

"Yes. Valium."

"And did your examination of the victim indicate a history of use with this and other drugs?"

"Yes."

"I'm confused as to why you didn't mention that."

"I wasn't asked," Bowman said.

"Why wouldn't ADA Albright ask you about her drug use?"

"Objection," the prosecutor was on his feet and looked worried.

"Sustained."

"The victim was a habitual drug user, correct?"

"Objection. What does the victim's drug use have to do with her rape, torture, and murder, Judge?"

"Your Honor, the victim's lifestyle put her in significant risk, our defense posits the likelihood that one of her many relationships from said lifestyle committed these heinous acts, not my client," Pratt said to the judge but directed toward the jury.

"Overruled."

She turned back toward Bowman.

"Doctor?"

"Yes, she used many drugs."

"The biggest of which was Valium, yes?"

"It was the most predominant found in her system, yes."

"The drug can last in a person's system for nearly a month, correct?"

"Depending on the dosage and habitual use, Benzodiazepine can last in a person's system for up to twenty-three days."

"Why do people use the drug? Is it hallucinatory?"

"It can be if it's used in it's unintended forms such as crushed and snorted, or if the liquid from is injected. It is prescribed as a muscle relaxant, to treat anxiety or as a sedative for those who don't sleep well. Unfortunately the drug is highly addictive and often misused. Increasingly more doctors aren't prescribing it and have switched to Librium or other sedatives in lower, less addictive dosages."

"So her Valium wasn't prescribed?"

"The math suggests she was taking twenty milligram doses, so no. At least I wouldn't think so. No responsible doctor would provide a long-term prescription for that kind of dosage."

"So she likely attained that drug, among others, illegally?"

"Objection. Facts not in evidence."

"Withdrawn," Pratt said before the judge ruled.

"Was she on the drug when she was raped, tortured, and murdered?"

Albright stood. Wallace waved him back to his seat without saying word.

"Doctor?"

"No. She'd been on it earlier, but the effects had long worn off by the time her killer began his long, steady, torture."

"Meaning she used the drug, and others, recreationally, but hadn't during the twelve to fifteen hours before her murder?"

"Correct."

"Bringing us to the conclusion that she ingested recreational drugs, heightening her consensual sexual pleasure earlier on October six, prior to her drug dealer-rapist-killer arriving some time later."

"Objection, your Honor."

"That I'll sustain."

"Then I have nothing further, your Honor." Alex went back to her seat.

Judge Wallace turned to the ADAs. "Care to redirect?"

Albright and Walsh whispered to one another for a few seconds, not responding to the judge.

"Hello? Mister Albright?"

"Quickly, Judge," he said before turning to the witness. "Doctor, Benzodiazepine, the active drug in Valium, would deaden the pain inflicted upon the victim, correct?"

"Correct."

"And therefore the drug would negate the intended pain the person who tortured Sloane Nichols was seeking for his own pleasure, correct?"

"Objection." It was Alex's turn to object. "How could the doctor know what the killer intended unless he, himself was the killer?"

"Sustained."

"Then I have nothing further," Albright said.

10

THE MEDIA CIRCUS SURROUNDING THE TRIAL OF Commonwealth v. Bromley was purified bedlam from the beginning. If the news coverage hadn't been widespread enough when the body of Sloane Nichols was originally found the previous October, the subsequent trial was certainly going to fill the void. Seemingly every news organization sought to provide the public with the latest and biggest single-murder trial since Jodi Arias.

Throughout jury selection, opening argument, and the first day of testimony from Dr. Bowman, the media was either inside the courtroom, outside the courthouse on the steps lying in wait, or both. No matter how a person garnered their news—newspapers, television, the internet, or applications on their smartphones—at least one representative from that outlet was on sight to bring the latest developments in the Bromley trial. The Boston Herald, The Globe, NECN, and local affiliates from CBS, NBC, ABC, Fox, and the ilk were mixed in with national news sources like CNN and alternative news sources like AlterNet and The Huffington Post. Even hacks like USA Today was represented.

The early end of the day in which the Medical Examiner took the stand was no different. Bowman was expected to fill the day between examination and cross, but Alex Pratt had finished with him earlier than scheduled. There were two hours to spare before the four o'clock hour, not enough time to begin testimony from any of the next witnesses, even if either of the detectives from Troop H or the CSU supervisor, Chantal Trudeau, was present. Witnesses aren't allowed to be inside the courtroom until after they have testified—and may not be allowed to watch after they testify if one of the attorneys notifies the court of their intention to recall a witness later in the trial—in an effort to achieve unbiased testimony. Most witnesses have better things to do than loiter about outside the courtroom while waiting to testify, nor do they like to be accosted by the media, so they arrive at the scheduled time to perform their function. The detectives and the Crime Scene Unit supervisor was slated for Wednesday into Thursday, and therefore weren't on hand to testify.

Court business may have ended earlier than expected on Tuesday, but the media was there regardless. Jurors went out the rear entrance to leave for the day while the attorneys on both sides were subjected to the gauntlet outside the main entrance. Both ADA Albright and Alex Pratt gave brief interviews with their respective entourages behind them to the various cameras, microphones, and recording devices.

Albright stood on the steps next to Amy Walsh speaking about the District Attorney's office's commitment to justice for Sloane Nichols and her surviving family. He reiterated Chase Bromley's guilt, and made a blanket statement of the 'overwhelming evidence' supporting that the correct defendant was on trial.

Not fifty feet away, near the bottom of the steps, Alex Pratt also spoke about justice. She said that it wasn't being served by bringing Chase Bromley to trial, professing that the real rapist-murderer was still at large. She assured all those that were listening that justice would prevail and that her client would prove his innocence by the conclusion of the trial.

Chase Bromley, like the rest of his defense team, was in front of the cameras, though in presence only. He was told to remain stoic, not to say or do anything unless specifically told to do so by Alex and Alex alone. Her client did as he was told, standing next to his legal team who stood in front of the media like the dream-team that it was.

His conduct, both in court and on the steps in front of the courthouse, was a minor miracle.

While one set of reporters recorded the pontifications of the prosecutor, another set from the same news sources were listening to sermonizing about the miscarriage of justice by the camera-friendly defense attorney. News teams from the same source split up to get sound bites from all sides, then piece together a supposedly unbiased report for those at home. Each brand claimed to have a slant that no other news source had, though the various takes came from the exact same speeches, using the exact same sound bites.

Just another day in the salt-mines of the American Legal System.

"How did it go today, Bae?" Ani had just come home from her day, counseling women who had been beaten down into former shells of themselves by the men they once loved.

She tossed her keys into the bowl, which lived on a narrow stand by the front door, before petting Hobey.

"Okay, I guess," Deni said as he sat at his bar watching the news coverage of the trial on the elevated flatscreen. The wilted remnants of the dying floral arrangement Deni had given his girlfriend on Friday was in a vase on the end of the countertop. "I'm not supposed to talk about it, you know that."

"You're also not supposed to be watching it on TV."

He took a sip of his Redbreast in lieu of a response, though his eyes said all that needed to be.

Ani ignored the look and came up behind him, kissing him on neck after Hobey had his greeting. The dog returned to his chew-toy when he realized that his brief belly rub was over.

"I don't know how you can listen to it all day and then come home and have it rehashed before your very eyes, whether you're supposed to or not."

"The media coverage on this is relentless," Deni said. "If the guy slumps in his chair, he's guilty. If he sits upright and keeps his poker face on all day, he's guilty. Anyone who says that news is unbiased has their head up their ass. They're trying this case on the courthouse steps. Period."

"From everything I've seen, which might be just as you say—biased—he *is* guilty. Who cares how he gets locked up and the key thrown away, as long as it gets done, right? Granted, I'm not in the courtroom, but it seems clear to me that he's a monster and this is just a formality."

Deni shook his head. "The point of a trial is to get the truth, and people already have their minds set on what that truth is. I'm all-for puttin' this prick down if he did it, but he can't get a fair shake the way things are now. He probably did do what he's accused of, or at least a portion of it, but why have a trial if everybody decides whats-what before it's all said and done?"

"He gets no sympathy from me," Ani said. "I deal with the handiwork of these assholes on a daily basis. These so-called men use their wives and girlfriends as a punching bag, then they want to stick their dicks in them like everything is fine. Maybe they say they're sorry and maybe they don't, but they expect them to stick around for another round. And these women, most of them with kids, think that they don't have choices, that they have to stick around and take more abuse. Just take your licks and then lie there until the master gets his rocks off. These women are left with no self-worth and told that they're nothing without the piece of shit that's holding them down."

"I know, I get it. I've seen some of that shit too, and I'm with ya. I don't know how you do it day in and day out, I really don't. But this is a little different, hun."

"How is it different? Because he's rich?"

"Seriously? What the fuck? You honestly think I give a shit if he's rich or poor?"

Ani took a deep breath.

"No. Not you. But from what I see on a daily basis? I think it does. Money makes it more difficult for abused women to leave, and it makes holding the bastard's feet to the fire more difficult as well. Look at all of the football players who've been in the news lately for beating up their girlfriends. Those women won't leave the sons of bitches. Why? Money. I'm sorry, but this hits home for me. Maybe we shouldn't talk about it."

Deni looked at the wilted make-up gift at the end of the bar and was reminded of the last verbal altercation he'd gotten into with Ani. He wanted to avoid another fight with all of his being. Instead of furthering his stance, he got up from his stool and gave Ani a hug.

"You're right, let's not talk about it."

He then kissed her on the lips.

"You wanna take it out on me?"

"I don't want to punch you, Bae."

He kissed her again, put his hand on her butt drawing her yet closer to him.

"That's not what I meant anyways."

"Oh," she said with a giggle. "I like it on top. You still have your old handcuffs?"

"From when I was a cop?"

"Mm-hmm. It might be fun to try it."

"I think I can dig them up," Deni said. "What's gotten into you?"

"Just spicing things up. But maybe we should come up with a safe-word?"

"Yeah? What's the fun in safe-words? I'm the one gettin' handcuffed."

She laughed at him again.

"But what if you don't like what I'm doing?"

"Then I'll tell ya to cut that shit out," he said as he ventured down the hall toward the bedroom. "What are you plannin' on doin' to me?"

"Find those handcuffs I'll show you. Just give me a minute, I'm going to shower and change."

Deni heard the water turned on in the shower.

"You don't need to shower, I like the way you smell."

"I want to shower. I'm knee deep in shit all day, I want to wash it off."

"You're just going to get dirty again."

"Then I'll shower again," she yelled from the bathroom while disrobing.

Deni was in the bedroom, rifling through his closet looking for handcuffs. He called back to her.

"Knee deep in shit?"

"Metaphorically. It'll make me feel better. Want to join?"

"If I get into the shower with you, we won't need these handcuffs," he said as he walked into the bathroom with them in hand.

Ani was inside the shower stall, Deni could make out her silhouette in the frosted glass from the other side. He opened the door, getting an unobstructed view of his wet, naked girlfriend.

"We could start in the shower .... "

Deni took off his more sensible t-shirt, a vintage Boston Braves circa 1941 t-shirt, the one he wore in court. His tattoos covered the skin where the short-sleeved shirt was. Ani loved the body-art and continued to be turned on by the tapestry of ink.

"I guess we're not going to need these," Deni said, putting the handcuffs and key on the vanity. "You're the boss, shower it is."

She grabbed the front of his jeans, bringing him close to her, pulling him into the shower. The denim was getting soaked and clinging to his body but he didn't care.

She kissed him below the ear and whispered into it.

"I like being the boss."

11

PRIOR TO THE COMMENCEMENT OF TRIAL ON WEDNESDAY,
Judge Wallace called all attorneys and the defendant into his
chambers. He was not wearing his black robe, nor was the top
button of his oxford shirt fastened. His sleeves were rolled up his
forearms, his necktie hung loosely and uncentered. Emile Wallace
looked disheveled and without sleep.

The judge's clerk, Seth Warner, had called both the
prosecution and the defense at the behest of his boss to be present
at the early hour. He currently sat behind a computer screen in the
corner with WestLaw was pulled up on the screen. Seth and the
search engine sat waiting for the judge to ask for relevant case files
he might need for the business at hand.

An abundance of chairs were set up, more chairs than were
necessary for; Alex Pratt; Max Courtland; Kevin Bishop; Jack Elders;
the defendant, Chase Bromley; Assistant District Attorneys Justin
Albright and Amy Walsh.

Everyone in the room had the same two thoughts running
through their minds.

Why the 8 a.m. meeting? And Judge Wallace looks terrible.

When everyone was present and seated, His Honor began.

"Thank you all for coming in so early. You're all probably
wondering why and also why I look like I didn't sleep last night. The
answer is because I didn't get any sleep last night."

He brushed back his thinning hair.

"I spent the night, excuse me, *WE* spent the night," he said
nodding to Seth in the corner, "trying to decide what to do about a
serious media coverage problem we have—"

"—Your Honor, the press has the right," Alex interrupted but was cut short herself by the judge.

"—Let me finish, Counselor. I'm well aware of the First Amendment protections afforded to the press. I've also been made aware of the absolute bedlam that has occurred with respect to this case, and it's nauseating. I watched video coverage on one channel showing a privileged communication between you and the rest of your defense team with the defendant, Miss Pratt. The reporter narrated over the exact communication, and I'm sure paraphrased in order to defray any civil action, but the breach was made nevertheless. Another channel was revealing the names and addresses of the jurors for God's sake. Have any of you seen or fostered this nonsense?"

"I've seen some of it, your Honor," Alex said.

"I made her aware of it, Judge," her second chair, Kevin Bishop, said. "I was taken aback by the coverage of that communication as well, which is why I brought it to her attention."

"I didn't see those particular news reports, your Honor, but we certainly wouldn't object to a gag order," ADA Albright added.

Prosecutors almost always want a closed courtroom and an order directing both parties not to speak to any member of the press because the media affects the jury. Jurists cannot help but be subjected to the coverage, large or small, that their particular trial gets.

Conversely, defense attorneys typically love the media and use it to manipulate, if not nullify, their jury. Nullification is illegal, but short of locking up each juror in a room with no electricity, nobody has found a way to completely stop it.

"Gag orders have been deemed unconstitutional," Alex said. "I can give you case after case where the higher courts have upheld the public's right to information. Waller v. Georgia, Rovinsky v. McKaskle, State v. Hauptmann, Commonwealth v. Bowker .... Just off the top of my head."

"I'm not issuing a gag order, Counselor. While the Commonwealth has a long tradition of erring toward the First Amendment versus the Sixth Amendment, it is ultimately my responsibility to properly and legally weight the rights of the defendant to a fair trial against the societal right to justice in a public trial. Thus my lack of sleep. Doing nothing, simply letting this circus continue, however, is not an option."

"Your Honor—"

"—Be quiet, Alex," Judge Wallace exclaimed. He rarely used first names in a business setting.

"Pursuant to CPL 360B, sub 90 ....," the judge continued as he began shuffling papers on his large desk. His clerk filled His Honor's void.

".... Quote, 'A four-part test must be utilized in determining whether the right to a public trial has been violated: (1) the party seeking to close the hearing must advance an overriding interest which is likely to be prejudiced; (2) the closure must be no broader than necessary to protect that interest; (3) the court must consider reasonable alternatives; and (4) the court must make findings adequate to support its action.' end quote," Seth recited from his computer screen.

"Thank you, Mister Warner. Sequestering is not only an unfair burden on the jury, but also an added and usually unnecessary expense to the Commonwealth. We only sequester the jury in the rarest of occasions. Gag orders, as the defense has already advised, have been ruled unconstitutional and those appeals have been granted on nearly every occasion. Therefore, I've decided to ban the media from the courtroom."

"Judge—"

"—Let me finish. Daily transcripts will be made available upon request to any member of the media, provided they have the appropriate credentials. I will not go so far as to establish a media room in the courthouse; however, if either the Commonwealth or the defense would like to speak to the press directly, or submit a press release, that is within the scope of public interest."

"I object, your Honor," Alex Pratt said. "I would like to file a motion for a hearing on the matter. The public interest and the right for that trial to be made public outweighs any damage that may or may not have been done to date. There simply isn't enough room in the courtroom for the number of people in Massachusetts who want to witness the actual trial, and depend on the media coverage to see the play by play."

"Objection noted, Counselor, and overruled. This is well within my discretion. As I said, the legislation on this, which I'm basing my decision on federal law, specifically with respect to capital cases—though Massachusetts doesn't have the death penalty—because *if* we sentenced people to lethal injection in this state, the people would likely be seeking it."

Seth again spoke up from his corner, reading WestLaw from his screen.

"Estes v. Texas, Chandler v. Florida, US. v. Gurney, US. v. McDougal. In all of these capital cases, the appellate courts reversed the guilty verdicts due to, quote, 'cameras and media coverage having an undue influence on not only the juries, but on the public which risked jeopardizing any retrial should the coverage nullify,' end quote."

"We are going to get this right the first time, counselors. I will not have the work of the jury, myself, and all present, be for nothing in the event that the defendant is found guilty and have that verdict reversed on appeal. The people of Suffolk County have the right to closure *and* the right to a fair and public trial. This order provides both."

Judge Wallace paused and looked at all in attendance on the other side of his desk. Nobody interrupted him, not even Alex Pratt who failed to see the point in it. The decision was made and he was correct in assessing that his decision was well within his discretion.

He then continued.

"Here are the ground rules." He again paused, this time so they could retrieve legal pads. Second chairs, ADA Walsh and Kevin Bishop, did the honors of transcription for their respective teams.

"I'm going to appoint a Court Information Officer to assist the media in obtaining accurate information and transcriptions. The person will be my clerk, Seth Warner, because he is impartial and can assist in any laws or procedural matters should any broadcast company decide to get litigious. He will not be allowed to give his

mccc

eft

opinion about the merits or demerits of the case, but simply assist interested media parties in getting accurate information to the public, as per their right. Questions on this point?"

There were none.

"Good. Next, seating in the courtroom will be closed to all but artists for said interested parties in the media. He or she will not be allowed any recording devices, as again, transcripts will be made available. Are we clear?"

"Yes."

"Yes, Judge."

"Okay. Any and all witnesses going forward will be kept in a witness ready-room, as I'm sure the media will be just outside the doors of the courtroom and waiting in either the third floor lobby or by the elevator. Witnesses will wait in that ready-room until they are called into the court to render their testimony. Only those witnesses who are scheduled to appear on any given day need wait in the witness ready-room."

Judge Wallace looked around his chambers again, all within remained silent.

"Finally, the jury deliberation room will also be the area designated for jury breaks. They will no longer be able to leave the courthouse until the completion of court on that day. The jury will continue to enter and exit through the back of the courthouse on Somerset Street before and after each trial day. If they haven't been doing so up to this point, they need to be made aware that they are now mandated to do so.

Any questions? No? Excellent. We might have done this at the start of the trial, but I had no idea the lengths that the media would go to for this trial. With the Boston Marathon trial and the Hernandez trial happening virtually simultaneously to this one, who could foresee not only the local but *national* attention this would get? At any rate, we are going to get ahead of it before we end up with a mistrial. As of now, there is no harm since the jury isn't supposed to be watching any coverage of the trial anyway. If I get the sense that jury has been contaminated, I'll be forced to take additional measures if not do the unthinkable by declaring a mistrial."

Judge Wallace looked at his watch.

It was almost nine o'clock.

"Seth, will you advise the jury of the new procedures before we begin?"

"Sure thing, Judge."

"Excellent. Time to get some coffee. I'll see you all in court."

12

THE JURY COULDN'T HELP BUT NOTICE THAT THE courtroom was barren compared to previous days. The only thing missing was the stereotypical tumbleweed rolling down the aisle to complete the 'ghost-town' image.

However, this wasn't the only indication that something was awry Tuesday morning. The moment they entered the deliberation room prior to being called into the courtroom, each juror was handed two pieces of paper.

The first was a menu with ten items on it. There was a place for a first name and instructions to check one box for the corresponding meal and one box for a desired beverage. Any questions as to why a meal was offered on this day and not the previous were answered by the second and larger piece of paper.

A memorandum from Judge Emile Wallace explained that henceforth, jurors would be provided a meal for their break—free of charge—but the tradeoff was they were no longer allowed to leave the deliberation room for said break. Each trial day, the jurors would either be in the deliberation room or in the courtroom from the time they checked in until the time they were excused for the day. No explanation was given as to why the change was taking place, and the court officer who gathered and led them to the courtroom every day was of no help either.

The smokers were livid, and their complaints fell on deaf ears.

It wasn't until after the jury was in the courtroom and Judge Wallace took his place that any form of reason was given. His Honor spoke in vagaries about the need to make the gallery less congested and less noisy. He went on to say that the crowds in and around the courthouse made entry and exit to and from the building more obtrusive to those who had business in the trial, and the new procedure was implemented to make lunch breaks easier for all involved.

Juror number ten, Jamar Dubone, spoke out of turn, letting the judge know of his disagreement with the decision. Jamar stood and said he spoke for all smokers and that not being able to leave the courthouse meant that they weren't allowed to smoke cigarettes, which was an undue burden on those with the habit. The twenty-four year old went on to say in fragmented ebonics that he wanted off of the jury when Judge Wallace was unsympathetic to plight of the nicotine-addicted, to which His Honor remained steadfast.

The interruption to the daily itinerary took but a few minutes, tantrum included, and the trial pressed on with the prosecution calling the two Massachusetts State Crimes Against Persons investigators from Troop H who caught the case, Detectives Joshua Leiman and Martin Champagne.

Each took the stand and in short-order described the events of their investigation, which led to the arrest of Chase Bromley. There was no muss or fuss about it, simply how the scientific results from the Crime Scene Unit, the Medical Examiner, and the Forensics Lab had made their job easy. Add the science to the canvas of people who lived in the same building as the victim, one of whom had seen the defendant in the building within twenty-four hours of the murder, both detectives felt the case was a slam-dunk.

Chase Bromley's fingerprints and DNA exemplars had been on file from previous legal scrapes, all of which had never been taken to the hoop, meaning the defendant had not previously seen the inside of a courtroom. There were a few drug charges that never stuck, which the detectives attributed to his father's prominence. The defense objected to the attribution, which the judge sustained, but the damage had been done. The jury wasn't technically allowed to use the previous scrapes with the law and subsequent failures in prosecuting him, but they certainly couldn't un-hear it.

Nor could the testimony from the detectives be dismissed about the seven 'Double-D's'—Domestic Disputes—Boston PD had on file for Chase Bromley. Each arrest, fingerprinting, and DNA swab was catalogued and filed, but there was no need for the information since the charges themselves were never filed. Each time, the accused was held for cool-down periods of various lengths and released. The defendant freely walked out of the Boston Police Station at 40 Sudbury Street in each case, which is less than a five-minute walk from the very room where he was finally being brought to justice.

Alex Pratt's cross-examinations of the two detectives was strong, but not strong enough to unring the bells that rang true with the jury. Her client had done some bad things. He was privileged and had previously gotten away with everything up to allegedly murdering his former girlfriend.

There was no spinning that the former couple had used and abused copious amounts of drugs. Nor was there a way to disprove the history of domestic incidents the local cops had responded to, even if they were rough sex acts that went too far, as was the claim. All the defense could do with regard to the arrests was to beat the fact that the victim, Sloane Nichols, failed to file charges against her former boyfriend, in every instance. She had been on record saying that the two liked to have rough sex and that outside parties had called the authorities, which was why he'd been arrested.

Sloane Nichols would eventually leave Chase Bromley, a Temporary Restraining Order had been filed, prohibiting him from being within five hundred feet of her or her building. There was no way to spin that fact either, as much as Alex tried.

Delving into the previous legal indiscretions with the State Troopers was a waste of time for her. Alex didn't want to focus on those previous arrests in any event, but even if she could spin them in her client's favor, it was the local cops that responded to those complaints, not the staties. What was the point in cross-examining two men who couldn't testify to anything but what was in the local police reports?

So she focused on the current investigation and the crimes he was now defending himself against. In delving into the investigation by the two detectives, Alex exposed three big flaws.

Because the detectives had garnered evidence which tied her client to the victim within seventy-two hours, in the form of semen, and a witness's statement and later sworn affidavit saying that she had seen him in the apartment building, a place he was legally forbidden to be within five hundred feet of, they stopped investigating. When the Crimes Against Persons detectives, who were overworked with high caseloads, added the circumstantial scientific evidence to the previous double-d's on file with the local cops, they sent the case to the riding ADA and moved on to the next case. No other interviews were conducted, no other stones turned over. Chase Bromley was their man, period.

Flaw one.

The second was when Alex Pratt asked both detectives, who separately gave corroborating testimony, that no drugs were found in Sloane Nichols' apartment.

A habitual drug user, as the Medical Examiner testified that the victim was, didn't have said drugs in her possession. Meaning she was out of said drugs.

Probably time to call her dealer.

Albright objected, saying that maybe Sloane Nichols was trying to get clean.

The defense attorney reminded the jury that there was a lot of room in 'maybe'.

Flaw two.

Finally, Alex illuminated a fact that was largely skimmed over when the ADA questioned both detectives.

There was no forced entry.

Whomever killed Sloane Nichols, Alex separately dragged out of the detectives, walked through her front door.

Why would the victim voluntarily open the door for someone with whom she was hiding and had filed a TRO against?

Unless she wanted him to come in. Unless she'd invited him.

Neither Leiman nor Champagne had a good explanation.

Flaw number three.

Both Detectives were on and off the stand in short order. The jury was sent to the deliberation room to ponder the trial in silence over their previously selected lunches.

Chantal Trudeau, the CSU supervisor who worked the scene of the rape-murder, was the next witness to take the stand after the lunch break on Tuesday, May 13. Her testimony created much more drama and tension to the proceedings. Testimony from scientists of any kind, even from the Crime Scene Unit, can often be tedious and boring due to the uber-technical detail and vernacular that these individuals tend to use. Most CSU personnel aren't as riveting as the actors on television shows like *Bones*. This witness, this scientist, was very different.

The bulky woman who took the stand had purple hair, fire-engine red glasses a-la Sally Jessy Raphael, and mismatched clothing like she'd just walked out of a Salvation Army Surplus store. It took about ten seconds for the jury to determine that the thirty-something crime scene expert was a fire-cracker with a sense of humor.

ADA Albright had first crack at Trudeau after she took the stand and pledged to be honest.

"Misses Trudeau can you please state for the record your educational background and current position."

"Miss, please, I'm married but I use my maiden name."

"Very well, *Miss* Trudeau. Can you—"

"—I currently work for the Massachusetts State Police Crime Scene Unit as a level three supervisor. I hold multiple degrees from McGill University, including doctorates in both Microbiology and Molecular Biotechnology, as well as a bachelor's in both Odontology and Forensic Science. I am a fellow in both the American and Canadian Academies of Forensic Sciences." Trudeau then looked to the jury, "All of that just means that I'm a science geek. If someone commits a crime and there's a dead body left for me to examine, I'm pretty damn good at finding out who did it."

Several of the jury members chuckled silently.

"Objection," Pratt said without standing.

"Overruled, Counselor.   You can challenge the witness's statement on cross," Wallace said.

Albright continued with a rare smile. "And how long have you been a 'a science geek'?"

"I've been in my current position for about five years, I used to work for the Mounties in Montreal before moving to the states."

"Mounties?"

"Sorry. Royal Canadian Mounted Police. Our version of the FBI."

"Our? You're Canadian?"

"I'm a dual citizen because I married someone from the states. I took the position here in Boston because she wanted to move back to her hometown."

Alex Pratt stood behind the defense table.

"This is all very fascinating, your Honor.   What does the witness's marital status and sexual orientation have to do with the court case before you?"

"Sustained.   Move it along Mister Albright," Wallace said while rolling his finger, the international signal for forward movement.

Albright turned back to his witness.

"You were the point-person on the scene last year, correct? You were in charge of securing the apartment of Sloane Nichols and evidence management of the entire scene, yes?"

"Correct. I make sure that the scene of the crime remains as it was when the responding detectives found it, direct all CSU support personnel on evidence procurement, and ensure that all said evidence gets properly tagged and secured to be sent to the lab for further testing." She again turned to the jury panel. "I'm like the real-live version of Gary Sinise on that CSI show."

There was more grinning from the jury, they seemed to like Chantal Trudeau. Pratt again stood to object but His Honor waved her down before she spoke word.

"And were you successful in securing the scene? Meaning that neither the apartment nor the body of the victim at the scene were contaminated in any way?"

"I was successful in securing it, yes. I always ensure that my scenes are pristine or the people that screw up are in big trouble with me. I'm not always the sweetheart I am right now, I can get real nasty if I have to."

"So is it your testimony that the evidence collected from both the victim and the apartment are legitimate pieces of evidence from the crimes that took place there?"

"Yes."

"And what, if any, were those evidentiary findings?"

"There were several key pieces of evidence, some in the apartment and some on or inside the victim's body. Which do you want me to testify about?"

"All of it," Albright said.

"Then I'll start with the apartment. The entire place of residence was dusted for fingerprints, swabbed for trace DNA evidence, hair fibers collected. There were twenty-seven items tagged and bagged to be sent to our laboratory for testing."

"And were their any preliminary findings in the apartment prior to sending the evidence to the lab?"

"We determined from the hand-held AFIS device that a set of fingerprints, with a seven-point match, belonged to the defendant, Chase Bromley."

"Is that all?"

"In terms of preliminaries in the apartment, no. We retrieved two blood-types, A-positive and AB-negative from the bedroom, using a RamLab LIS. We matched type AB-neg to the victim, and it was later determined that the other was matched to the accused." She turned to the jury. " We have all the best toys."

Again, some of the jury members found Trudeau amusing.

"And for those of us that don't really understand blood types, what does that mean?"

"Blood type really means blood group. Each person has blood antibodies or blood antigens on or in their red blood cells. Each group; A, B, AB, or O have either antibodies in the plasma around the cell, or antigens inside the cell—indicating positive or negative respectively. While blood type isn't as identifying as DNA, it narrows down the possible number of people we are trying to identify into a select group," she explained to the jury.

"So if I hear you correctly, you're testifying that both the defendant and the victim were both in the victim's apartment, and both left trace amounts of blood at the scene. You can say this with a high degree of certainty because the blood types matched."

"Correct, yes. His blood, A-neg, had trace amounts, the victim's blood was much more substantial. Virtually all of Sloane Nichols' blood was outside of her body, near the living room."

ADA Amy Walsh put up a large floor-plan of the victim's apartment up on the easel for the jury while Albright continued to question the witness. The floor-plan was marked into evidence for the prosecution.

"Did you determine why the defendant's blood was in the bedroom while the victim's blood was in the main part of the apartment?"

"After the defendant was arrested, his body was searched which produced several fingernail cuts on his person which are consistent with the hands of Sloane Nichols. She scratched and clawed at him in the bedroom, where the rape must have begun."

"And that sums up the evidence you collected in the apartment?"

"No. We also swabbed the DNA evidence from the aluminum softball bat that was used to violate the victim in the living room area, which we later determined had both the defendant and the victim's DNA on it. On the body of Sloane Nichols, there was plenty of visual evidence to support our conclusion as to the manner in which she was attacked and killed; however, bleach had been used to contaminate any testing, rendering it unusable. I believe that the bleach was used to eliminate evidence of sweat, hair fibers, and DNA under her fingernails where she'd scratched him. Both vaginal and anal canals were swabbed for later testing, which lacked a chemical contaminant, and again matched DNA to Chase Bromley."

"From the semen?"

"Correct," Trudeau replied. "And lastly, the tube sock that was shoved into the victim's mouth had sweat and epithelial cells," she turned to the jury, "skin cells," then back to Albright, "which later was tested and matched to Chase Bromley."

"In using your education and vast international experience, did you make any determinations as to what occurred in the apartment of Sloane Nichols on October six and seven of last year?"

"I did. Chase Bromley entered the apartment and brutally raped the victim, Sloane Nichols, beginning in the bedroom, where he ejaculated inside her. He then continued to abuse her for many hours with an Easton bat, which he used both as a phallus to enter her, as well as a weapon to shatter both her knees. When he grew tired of it, the defendant sliced her throat which ultimately killed her. The defendant poured bleach on the victim in order to cover-up his crimes."

"Thank you," Albright said to Trudeau. He then turned to Judge Wallace, "I have no further questions for this witness but reserve the right to recall her at a later date if the need arises."

"Very well," the judge said as he turned to the defense team. "Your witness."

Alex Pratt stood and approached Chantal Trudeau who took a sip of water from the glass on the witness stand.

"*Miss* Trudeau, you collect evidence at the crime scene, and your only responsibility is the crime scene—correct?"

"I don't follow your question," Chantal said.

"No? Well, let me make it more clear. Once you investigate the scene and collect evidence, you make a couple of preliminary findings for the detectives to run with before sending it all off to the state crime lab in Maynard, Massachusetts. Yes?"

"Yes."

"So you have no control of the evidence once it's all 'tagged and bagged', as you said, and sent to the lab?"

"Well, no, but—"

"—Just yes or no will do, thanks. So all of the things you said here on the stand today are your best guesses but not really accurate, correct?"

"No. That's incorrect."

"Really," Alex said in an obvious and dramatic fashion. "So you know that my client raped the victim in the bedroom?"

"His DNA was left in the bedroom."

"No. His blood type was left in the bedroom."

"Which was later determined—"

"—Which you just said you had nothing to do with, *Miss* Trudeau. You know nothing about subsequent tests, because you didn't perform them. The lab technicians in the state facility did, and if a mistake happens down the line, those results might not be accurate."

"Was that a question?"

"No, it wasn't. Because we know that to be fact. Just as we know many other facts which you failed to get correct while testifying."

"Objection," Albright bellowed.

"Counselor—"

"—I'll illustrate my point if you'll allow me, Judge."

"Approach?" Albright wanted a mini-conference with Wallace without the jury hearing the details.

Everyone sitting behind both tables gathered in front of the judge's bench save for the defendant. Wallace covered his microphone with his hand.

"Your Honor, the defense is merely trying to smear the testimony of the witness in order to gain favor with the jury," Albright whispered loudly to illustrate his outrage.

"I'm allowed to discredit the witness. As far as gaining favor with the jury, I'm not sure how I can do that when the jury clearly likes the witness. If anything, Judge, I'm going to look like a big meanie."

"Get there quickly," Wallace whispered. "Overruled," he bellowed to the courtroom.

"*Miss* Trudeau," Alex said as she turned back to the witness before everyone had returned to their seats, "can you state for the record, *for a fact*, from the preliminary findings at the scene, and *only* from the preliminary findings at the scene, exactly when the blood the CSU team found in the bedroom was deposited there?"

"*EXACTLY*? No, however—"

"—So it is entirely possible that Sloane Nichols had sex, rough sex, with my client in the bedroom at some point prior to the events which led to her death? *OR*, she had sex with somebody else who happened to have type A-negative blood?"

"But the DNA later determined—"

"—You had nothing to do with later. You only had information about the blood type until you were given subsequent reports," Pratt interrupted. "How did you determine the A-neg blood type at the scene, anyway?"

"As I said, A RamLab LIS was used, the results linked to the Samsung tablet within five minutes. Like I said, we have some great gadgets."

"And this device is a portable prototype of the centrifuge equipment that is used in full laboratories, correct?"

"Correct."

"How long had the technology been used out in the field at that time?"

"Only a few months, but—"

"—So not really proven. In those few months, the on-scene results haven't been one hundred percent accurate, have they?"

"One hundred percent? No. About ninety-six percent," Trudeau admitted.

"So, you're ninety-six percent certain that the blood type found in the bedroom was A-negative?"

"At the scene, that's correct. But it was later confirmed—"

"—Again, *NOT BY YOU*."

"Be that as it may, your client's DNA was determined to be present at the scene," Trudeau said in an antagonistic tone.

"But *NOT BY YOU*. Let me ask you, was my client's blood or semen found on any of the bedding when you ran your preliminary tests?"

"No."

"And why do you suppose that is?"

"The bedding was taken off the bed and was found in the washing machine," Trudeau said.

"I'm confused. You're telling me, you're telling this court, that my client raped the victim in the bedroom, and when he was finished, he tossed the sheets in the washer before resuming the torture?"

"Yes. In order to cover up his crimes. He did pour bleach on the victim for the same purpose."

"Was there a tube sock in the wash?"

"No."

"Interesting. Was the other sock found?"

"No."

"He shoved one of his socks into her mouth and wore the other one when he left after murdering her?"

Trudeau shrugged. "How would I know that?"

"Fair enough. It just seems very odd, don't you think? Why go through all the trouble of a cover-up, just to leave a key piece of evidence linking him to the crimes right in the victim's mouth."

"Objection."

"Withdrawn. We'll come back to that, okay Miss Trudeau?"

"If you say so."

"You don't think it's possible that the victim had sex with my client or someone with the same blood type, rough sex, where each of the willing parties might have scratched one another, and was later raped and murdered by someone else?"

"You already asked me that. I don't believe so."

"I did not ask you that specific question, and you didn't answer it. Shall we go back to the court record to verify?"

"No. And no, I don't think that what you indicated is possible."

"It's not possible?"

"Objection, asked and answered. Repeatedly," Albright said.

"Overruled. The witness will answer."

"Anything is *possible*," Trudeau said in obvious frustration, "but I wouldn't bet on it."

"Uh huh. How about the front door? Was it kicked in or pried open or tampered with?"

"Not that we found, no."

"Meaning that Sloane Nichols knew her killer?"

"One would think, yes. And your client did have a history with the victim," Trudeau said sarcastically. "They used to live together, correct?"

"And why she might have a stray sock from my client in her possession which was then used to gag her by the real killer, but I'll ask the questions *Miss* Trudeau, thank you very much."

Pratt let her comment marinate throughout the room before continuing her questioning.

"You're medical findings at the scene match Doctor Bowman's medical report in that the victim had her head struck several times during her lengthy torture, correct?"

"Yes. Our findings corroborate the ME's."

"Which led your team to assume that she knew her assailant, let him in, and that person hit her on the back of the head upon entrance?"

"Yes."

"Where you *think*, because that's really all you can do since you only know first-hand what your team found at the scene, he took her into the bedroom and had unprotected sex, finished, washed the sheets, then resumed his heinous assaults with the aluminum bat in the living room?"

"Yes."

"Hmm," Pratt mumbled while feigning complete confusion. "Let's skip forward to the murder. After all of the things Sloane Nichols had to endure, her killer used a chef's knife—one of those twenty-seven items you 'tagged and bagged' you mention earlier—was from the victim's own kitchen, correct?"

"Yes. The knife was covered in blood and consistent with the deep cut to her throat, which nearly took her head off by-the-way."

"Were there any fingerprints on the knife?"

"No."

"Hmm again," Pratt said as she exaggeratedly scratched her head. "So to sum this all up, you're saying that you believe that the rapist and murderer of Sloane Nichols was so careful to cover up his crimes that he washed the sheets, poured bleach on the victim, and wiped off his fingerprints from the knife, but left one sock behind and didn't use a condom which left his DNA inside the victim for the forensics team to find?"

"Yes. Criminals often forget one or two pivotal pieces of evidence which lead to their apprehension."

"That would be one big oops, wouldn't you say?"

"Objection."

"Withdrawn."

"Miss Trudeau, you don't have anything to add to this case other than you used some new-fangled gadget to get a 'ninety-six percent sure' blood-type do you?"

"Objection."

"Withdrawn."

"You are coming dangerously close to a contempt fine, Counselor," the judge warned.

"My apologies to the court. Just one more question for you, Miss Trudeau. Did you find any evidence of drug use at the scene?"

"The ME's report—"

"—*AT THE SCENE*, Miss Trudeau. For someone so smart, you seem to be having trouble grasping what 'at the scene' means. Did you?"

"No."

"No vials. No prescriptions. No needles or accoutrements of any kind?"

"No."

"Because a drug dealer would want them and steal them for resale."

"Objection."

Alex raised her hands in surrender as she walked back to her seat.

"Withdrawn. I'm through with this witness."

13

ANI WALKED THROUGH THE FRONT DOOR TO THE THREE-
decker she shared with Deni in South Boston on Tuesday night, after
another long day of working with domestic abuse victims. Deni was
sitting in his living-room recliner with a highball of Redbreast in one
hand and petting Hobey, who was comfortably sitting on his lap,
with the other. The television was on, the nightly news on WBZ-TV
CBS channel 4 was covering the Chase Bromley trial.

"Wow. You just can't get enough of this trial can you?"

Deni didn't make a bid to get up, nor did the Boston Terrier.
The only indication Hobey gave that he was happy to see his other
master was the brief wagging of his tail. Both mildly irritated her.

"You're never gonna believe this shit, hun. Come look at
this."

"Really? I just walked in the door. My feet are killing me and
I all I want to do is shower and change, because apparently a kiss
from my boyfriend is too much to ask."

"I'll kiss ya face off in a minute, I promise. Come look at this.
Quick."

Katrina Brown, one of the television station's investigative
reporters, was larger than life on the sixty-inch screen. She wore
long, dirty-blonde hair with highlights, a light green blouse which
accented both her jade eyes and her ample bosom, while holding a

microphone with the station logo in front of the Suffolk County Superior Courthouse.

Deni turned the volume up while Ani moved into the house and seated herself on the riveted leather sofa.

> *"..... And while the press is no longer allowed inside the courtroom, we were able to get an exclusive interview with one of the jurors on the case. This unnamed source has told WBZ that while the case is still being heard, and will for next few weeks, the jury has already decided that the defendant, Chase Bromley, is guilty of the brutal rape and murder of his former live-in girlfriend, Sloane Nichols."*

Deni turned to Ani who was now deeply engrossed in what was being said on the television.

"Do you believe this shit? A Juror!"

"Ssssssh, Bae. Listen."

> *"..... Chase Bromley, son of Kenneth Bromley, the wealthy property developer, is facing consecutive life sentences in prison, without the possibility of parole, when he reportedly WILL be found guilty of his alleged crimes at the conclusion of his trial. Sloane Nichols, the victim, was found dead in her apartment last October, approximately six months after leaving Bromley. Our source has confirmed that the victim had a temporary restraining order against Bromley, though his fingerprints, blood, and DNA were found at the scene."*

A generous drawing of Chantal Trudeau sitting on the witness stand was posted on the television screen from an artist who was obviously allowed in the court gallery earlier in the day.

>"..... *The two detectives who were assigned to the case, Joshua Leiman and Martin Champagne, both testified earlier today before the lunch recess, but we're told that the real show stopper was the crime scene expert that finished the day's testimony. Chantal Trudeau, formerly with the Royal Canadian Mounted Police in Montreal, described in detail the blood evidence as well as the fingerprint analysis and other forensic evidence that has convinced this jury that the accused is guilty of his alleged crimes.*
>
>*While Chase Bromley has professed his innocence since being arrested, it would appear that his legal team, headed by none other than the preeminent attorney Alex Pratt of Taylor, Higgs & Pratt, should look to cut some sort of deal with the District Attorney's office in order to achieve a reduced sentence. Bromley is currently free and being closely monitored with the use of an electronic ankle bracelet, after his father, Kenneth Bromley, put up $1 million in bail money."*

The television cut to a split-screen, the nightly news anchor, Jack Adler on the left and Katrina Brown on the right. Jack began to interject questions to the live report from the courthouse. The annoying time-lapses between the completion of the questions from the news desk until when the reporter heard the questions in front of the courthouse and responded was maddening to Deni.

"….. Katrina, isn't it a bit early for the jury to have made up its collective mind?"

"It is, Jack. There is still a long list of witnesses the prosecution needs to call, for example Willow Bauer, the state lab technician that will take the stand tomorrow."

"I see. If the jury has already made up their minds, how is the trial going to be deemed fair? Doesn't the accused have the right to a fair trial?"

"I couldn't agree more, Jack, however it has come to our attention that, according to this unnamed juror that has given WBZ-TV the exclusive rights inside the story, the evidence that has been presented so far is damning enough for them to have made a decision. After only two days of testimony, the verdict in the Chase Bromley trial is already in."

"Thanks Katrina. Now on to our other Boston trial, where we will now go live to the John Joseph Moakley Courthouse for the Marathon Bombing trial ….."

Deni turned to Ani who appeared to be just as stunned as her boyfriend. Hobey left his comfortable position as the recliner was moved into the upright position.

"I think I just got out of jury duty."

Ani nodded.

"Isn't it illegal to speak to the press while you're currently on a jury?"

"Yep. This is a mistrial, no two ways about it," Deni said. "If they find out who this juror is, they'll be in a cell right next to

Bromley. Holy shit. Who would speak to that fuck-tard reporter? I'm tryin' to think who would do it."

"You think they'll investigate it?"

"No question, hun. Whoever it is just cost the taxpayers a pretty penny. They'll hang this fucker by his nuts."

"What if it's a girl?"

"Funny. You know what I mean. They'll probably go after Tits-McGee at the network too. There's no way this Bromley prick can get a fair trial in Boston now, thanks to her. No way in hell. The defense is gonna have to go venue shopping somewhere outside the city and even then .... Even with the Hernandez trial in Connecticut and the marathon trial here, who hasn't heard of this case? It's made national news, never-mind local and state."

"What will happen if they find out that they can't find a fair place to hold a trial?"

"That's a big if, but *if* that happens? He'll walk."

"Wow. That poor family," Ani said.

"Sloane's family?"

"Yeah."

"I hear ya. No justice. No closure. If the trial happened and came back not guilty, that's one thing. But to free the bastard because a juror screwed the pooch? I'd want both their heads on a plate."

A few moments passed in silence.

Ani broke the quietude.

"Now can I have my kiss?"

Deni smiled, his mood changed. Everything had changed. He would be off the jury and back to his normal life by end of day on Wednesday. He moved from his chair, laying on top of his girlfriend on the sofa.

"You can have more than a kiss."

"Seems like both our days just got better."

"Mm-Hmmm."

He kissed her like a man without a care. He kissed her like he hadn't in a week.

"Let me shower first," she whispered.

Deni moved away from her, kneeling on the sofa.

"But I'm ready. Look at me here ...."

"You better hide that thing when you take Hobey for a walk," Ani said while giggling.

"Noooo. Now?"

"I think he's ready too."

The Boston Terrier was doing circles by the door.

"Take him for a quick walk while I shower. I promise I'll get that thing back at full salute when you get back."

"I'm gonna hold you to that," Deni called to Ani as she padded down the hall to the bathroom.

He then looked to the dog who was still begging to go out by the door.

"Just because you're fixed doesn't mean you gotta cock-block me."

14

FOR THE SECOND DAY IN A ROW, ALL ATTORNEYS IN THE matter of Commonwealth v. Bromley met in Judge Emile Wallace's chambers before the commencement of the trial. Only on this day, Wednesday, May 14, there wouldn't be any testimony. Because there wasn't going to be a trial that day, and maybe not on any future day.

On Wednesday, just like Tuesday, His Honor looked terrible and without sleep. Unlike the previous day, the judge was spitting-tacks mad. He was going to seek sanctions against whomever was involved in the malfeasance that was likely going to derail his trial.

"....I don't see how there is any way we can move the trial forward, your Honor," Alex Pratt said while pacing in the judge's chambers. Everyone else, including Emile Wallace was seated.

"If I find out that you had anything to do with this in order to get a mistrial, Alex, I'll make you my personal cause. I'll have you in front of the ethics committee and disbarred, just for starters."

"I'm insulted that you would think that I would do something like this, Judge. I am an officer of the court, and my record speaks for itself. And why would I? How are we supposed to get a fair trial now? CBS is a national network. The AP press has already picked it up and running with it."

"I'm well aware. And sit down. I've already got a migraine, your pacing is not helping."

"We oppose a mistrial," Albright said on behalf of the DA's office. It was no shock that he wouldn't want to delay this trial or to start another, his side was winning, if the news report was to be believed. "Whatever juror was involved, we can dismiss and bring in an alternate. The jurors aren't supposed to be watching the news anyway. We can determine what, if any, harm was done before we make a decision about a mistrial."

"*We* make a decision, Justin? Last I checked it was my name on this docket as lead jurist, ergo this is *my* decision. Unfortunately."

"Your Honor, we've only had two days of testimony, why not just start the trial over? I'd be willing to explore the option of finding another impartial jury here in Boston before moving to change venue, if that makes your decision easier," Pratt said. "If we don't start over, you've created a reversible error if, and apparently when, my client is found guilty. You will have handed me an appeal on a platter, which means we'd have a new trial anyway."

"Watch your step, Alex. I don't like to be strong-armed." Judge Wallace turned to his clerk, who was again in his place in front of his computer in the corner of the judge's chambers and looking just as haggard as his boss. "Seth?"

"Press Shield Law, Emile ..... I mean Judge. It will be incredibly difficult to go after Katrina Brown or WBZ and win," his clerk said.

"I meant case law. I'm afraid of setting a precedent here. Any time a trial doesn't go in the way of the defendant, they can tamper with a jury through the press."

"I haven't been able to find a Commonwealth case directly on point," Seth said. "I found a federal case where there was actual, proven tampering. Capital case in Texas, southern district. A juror was sabotaging the trial at the behest of the defendant, was paid to leak information to the press, in fact. US v. Tierney. The judge in that case questioned the jurors individually, en seorsum, to determine who and how the jury had been affected."

"That sounds like the best course of action," Judge Wallace said.

"Your Honor."

"I don't want to hear it, Alex. I'm angry and tired and there is absolutely no harm in ascertaining the extent of the damage that has been done. I also want to determine who this 'unnamed source' is in the process. If, at the end of my individual questioning of each juror, where attorneys from both sides can be present, we either don't uncover the culprit or we find that the jury has been damaged beyond salvation, then you still get your mistrial. If it is at all possible to salvage this mess, then we will have saved the taxpayers about a half a million bucks and attained justice in the bargain."

Deni knew what was going on. He knew why the judge was calling each juror out of the deliberation room, individually. He was trying to find out who had derailed the trial by speaking to the press. Nobody was confirming it, but he knew all the same.

He watched and waited his turn, as each of the jurors was called upon, in order by number, and taken by a court officer into the judge's chambers.

Some of the other jurors were whispering among themselves, likely trying to determine why they hadn't been led into the courtroom for the Wednesday version of the trial. Something was amiss, and if any of the other jurors were aware of what that problem was, Deni didn't hear it explained.

"Juror number seven," was bellowed by a uniformed officer as Jordan Raines, number six, came back into the deliberation room with the look of exhaustion. She was in her late thirties but carried the fatigue of someone much older, which was not the way she'd looked at the start of the day.

Deni rose from his chair and followed the officer down a hallway and through a door which had 'The Honorable Judge Emile Wallace' etched into the clouded glass.

He was offered a seat in the center of the room.

Attorneys abound from both sides of the aisle around the perimeter of the room. Deni was surrounded by everyone he'd seen in the trial thus far, save for the witnesses and defendant himself. The man with the name on the door sat at his desk in front of him, without his black robe. He looked terrible. He stared into Deni's eyes for a few seconds before beginning his questioning.

"We're on the record," he said in the direction of the court stenographer who moved a few fingers on the keys of her machine.

"Mister Warren Dennihan, yes?"

"Ya know my name."

"There's no need for this meeting to be hostile, Mister Dennihan. Do you know why you're here?"

Deni feigned ignorance.

"No. And call me Deni."

"*Mister Dennihan*, none of the previous jurors have told you why we've called them in here?   Why we're calling every juror in here?"

"Nope."

"Honestly?"

"Yeah. Honestly. Were they supposed to? I don't think any of the others really like me very much. Nobody really talks to me."

"You strike me as the type to rub people the wrong way."

"Are you still pissed about the t-shirt thing?"

Judge Wallace ignored the question.

"Have you been watching the news coverage about this trial, Mister Dennihan?"

"I was instructed not to."

"That's not what I asked you.   I asked if you have been watching the news coverage of the trial in which you are currently a jury member of."

"No, I haven't."

"Have you spoken to the press about the trial or about any conversations you've had with the other jurors about this trial?"

"No. And as far as the jurors, as I said, nobody really talks to me."

"So if we pull your phone records, we won't find any phone calls to or from any member of the press?"

"Can I assume that you've already done that and know the answer to that question?"

"Is that supposed to be some kind of answer, Mister Dennihan? Because it's not. I'd like you to answer for the record," Judge Wallace said indignantly.

"No I haven't. Not recently, and not about this case. I'm a private investigator. I've had occasion to use the media during my investigations, but not since I got stuck with jury duty."

"You are aware, are you not, that jury tampering and jury nullification is illegal, and both charges carry hefty prison terms? As a former detective, I would think that you would know that."

"I do. Should I have an attorney present? Cuz my lawyer is in New Hampshire. I can have him here in a couple of hours if needed."

"As of right now, I don't think that will be necessary. Have you, or anyone else on the jury, to your knowledge, made up their mind as to the guilt or innocence of the defendant in this case?"

"Me? No. As for the rest of the jurors, like I said—"

"—'Nobody really talks to you'," the judge finished. "Very well. I advise you not to speak to anyone about the questions that we've posed to you today, and continue not to speak to anyone in the press. Additionally, I want you to assure me that you will refrain from any news organization or news source while on this jury. Am I clear?"

"Very."

"So assure me," Judge Wallace said.

"I assure you that I won't talk to a reporter, even if she has a nice rack."

Wallace didn't even smile.

"You may go back to the deliberation room then."

Deni was then walked back to where he'd been waiting, his escort then called "number eight" as he took his seat.

"Mister Jamar Dubone, yes?"

"Yes, Judge."

"Do you know why we've called you in here?"

"Um. No?"

"Is that a question, Mister Dubone?"

"Um. No."

"None of the previous jurors have told you why we've been calling each of you into chambers?"

"Um. No."

"I have to be honest with you, I'm having difficult time believing that. You seem to be sweating rather profusely, and your knee is vibrating as if you're trying to jackhammer through the floor. So I'll ask you one more time, do you know why you have been called into my chambers?"

Twenty-four year old Jamar Dubone looked into his wringing hands as he sat in front of Judge Wallace, with attorneys in virtually every corner of the office, and shook his head while his shoulders hung in defeat.

"Yes."

"Care to elaborate?"

"The thing on the news."

"I need for you to tell me everything, Sir. Not only for my edification but also for the court record. You do understand that what you've done is serious and is punishable with a lengthy prison sentence?"

"Jamar's head popped up. No. Prison?"

"Yes. Ten year maximum for each offense. You've tampered with a jury, obstructed justice, you spoke to a reporter on behalf of the entire jury, against my instructions, which is contempt of court ..... You've violated the rights of the defendant to get a fair trial. Why, Mister Dubone? Why on earth would you do such a thing?"

"Money. I ..... *My family* needs the coin, man. I been outta work. That lady promised money for tellin' what was happenin' in the jury room," Dubone said. "I think that lady was gonna write a book or suttin'."

"Katrina Brown approached you about this case?"

"Yup."

"And she gave you money?"

"No. Not yet. But she said she would if I told her what was happenin' and said it only to her. She'd grease me some during the trial and some later. After. She said it was a chance to do suttin' good for my fam. Maybe get us outta the projects."

"Did you speak to any of the other jurors about the defendant's guilt or innocence?"

"No."

"Then why did you make the claim that the entire jury had already voted and declared him guilty before all testimony was heard?"

"Cuz a few people was sayin' that in the room. That they think he's guilty."

"So you think that this jury, this *entire* jury, has already come to the determination that the defendant is guilty and cannot receive a fair and impartial trial?"

"I dunno. It's just what I heard a couple a people say. Maybe they can change their mind, I dunno. I told the lady what she wanted to hear. For tha money, Man."

"Very well, Mister Dubone. The officer here is going to read you your rights and take you to a holding cell. I suggest you retain the services of an attorney, if you cannot afford an attorney, we can have one appointed to you from legal aid. You had best hope that if you get in front of a jury on these charges that they have a much more open mind that what you have."

Jamar Dubone was handcuffed and taken into custody, escorted out of the Judge's chambers in a matter of seconds.

"Bring in the first alternate." Judge Wallace looked at a jury list on his large desk. "Marissa Gantse."

15

JUDGE EMILE WALLACE RAISED HIS EYEBROWS AT THE LEAD defense Attorney, Alex Pratt, from behind his desk. It had been a long day in the judge's chambers, made longer by His Honor's decision to work through lunch in order to get through each and every juror and the alternates. None of the attorneys from either side were allowed to ask any of the questions they wanted to pose, having to sit and watch the witch-hunt in silence, some of them with stomachs growling.

They'd made it through the entire jury by the end of business on Wednesday, and Wallace had still not declared a mistrial.

Alexandria was at the end of her rope, stating so to the room. Judge Wallace took exception.

"I beg your pardon, Counselor?"

"Judge, with all due respect, I don't see how you could possibly move this trial forward. You've done due diligence, and even weeding out the leak, this jury is compromised," Pratt said.

"I don't agree."

"The Commonwealth is ready to move forward," Albright added.

"Of course you are," Pratt said. "The tampering only improved your case. According to this Dubone character, who probably should have been disqualified for being mentally incapable in the first place, the jury has already made a decision after only two days of testimony. Both of which were witnesses for the Commonwealth, by the way. My client is just another notch on you belt, eh Justin?"

"Neither of us saw this coming with juror number ten, and you heard him say that he spoke out of turn. I'd chalk this up to tough luck, Alex. The fact that your client is guilty is just an added benefit."

"That's enough, both of you," Wallace said. "The jurors have all gone on the record to say that they haven't made up their minds yet—"

"—Excuse me, your Honor, but what were they supposed to say?"

"I expect them to be honest, which is what we were asking them to do from the start. We want them to listen to all of the testimony and make an honest judgement about the guilt or innocence of your client. We've spent all day polling the jury, on the record, and other than number ten, I see no reason to declare a mistrial."

"This is grounds for an appeal. I can't believe that you think, even for a second, that this is a fair trial at this point. I think anyone who thinks that this jury will come back with a not-guilty verdict, no matter what evidence or testimony I present, should have a seven-thirty exam."

"Watch it, Counselor."

"My apologies, your Honor. I just get a bit irritated when a defendant's rights are thrown to the wind, and regardless of the zealousness of our defense, he gets railroaded into a prison jumpsuit for the rest of his natural life. At this rate, the details of this case will be clues in the Globe Sunday Crossword, and you think we can continue with business as usual?"

"Save the histrionics. Your objection to my ruling is noted, Alex, but if you continue on this soapbox of yours, you'd better get your checkbook ready. You are one more gesture, one more roll of the eyes, or one more comment away from a contempt citation."

Alex Pratt decided not to comment further or even add another apology. The silence that filled the now dimly lit office was as deafening as it was awkward.

"That's what I thought," Wallace said. He looked around the room as he continued. "As far as reversible error on appeal, I can defend my decision to continue this trial. First, I've polled the jury and find no reason to believe that any of the remaining jurors have been affected by the actions of one Jamar Dubone. Second, we haven't exhausted the juror pool alternates. We will bring in the one alternate, Gantse, and have one to spare. Lastly, it is my firm belief that in this day and age, the media is impossible to avoid. Whether we are speaking about television news, radio, newspapers, gossip magazines, Huffington Post, TMZ, or even social media ..... Unless you lock yourself into your house, turn off the electricity and live like a monk, the best you can do is ask for them to ignore what they read, see, hear, and do the best they can. And that is what we are going to ask them to do for the remainder of this case."

The judge paused again, while collecting his thoughts and various documents from his large desk. He then looked at his clerk who nodded in the affirmative, followed by the faces of the attentive attorneys, each visibly showing mixed emotions.

"However, in order to preserve what's left of this jury, I am ordering that they be sequestered. With the media no longer allowed into the courtroom and the jury off limits to both reporters and the news, I believe we can finish this trial, reaching justice in the process."

It was Justin Albright's turn to be unhappy with Wallace.

"Your Honor, sequestering? Not even jurors on the Hernandez trial are sequestered. This in an undue burden on both the jury and a rather large expense for the Common—"

"—Save it, Justin. Declaring a mistrial and starting fresh is much more expensive than sequestering. Seth has taken care of the arrangements, Boston PD will escort each of the jurors to their homes where they will be allowed fifteen minutes to pack a bag. They will then be taken to the undisclosed place of lodging for tonight, and every night until a verdict is in. They will hand over their cell phones and no phone calls will be allowed in or out of their rooms. The televisions will be removed from their rooms as well. Is everyone unhappy?"

Nobody spoke.

She dug into her Michael Kors tote, retrieving her smart phone.

The cell indicated no phone call, and no text message though she knew better than to expect one. Her boyfriend didn't send texts and barely read the ones she sent him.

While the dog continued to whine in an effort to make the attachment of his leash happen with more urgency, Ani had found a note left on the end of the bar next to the dog's leash.

HEY BABE
I'M STILL ON THE FUCKING JURY.
THEY DIDN'T DECLARE A MISTRIAL
AND WE GOT SECKWESTERED - SO I'M
GONNA BE OUT OF POCKET TIL THIS

127

THING IS DONE.   SORRY ABOUT HOBEY — THEY GAVE ME LIKE 2 MINUTES TO THROW A BAG TOGETHER.   HOPE HE DIDN'T LEAVE TOO BIG A MESS.
SEE YA IN A COUPLE WEEKS.
LOVE YA

—D—

"Well, I guess that means no chicken and waffles at Shōjō on Sunday," she said to the dog.   Going to the trendy restaurant in Chinatown was their Sunday routine.   "That poor guy. He went from getting out of it, to complete lock-down."

Ani looked down at Hobey who was still anxiously waiting to relieve himself. She squatted down and pet him, attaching the leash he so craved from the table by the note while doing so.

"Looks like it's just you and me for a while, pal," she said as she closed the door behind her.

16

THERE WASN'T A SINGLE PERSON EMPANELED ON THE JURY
that Thursday, May 15, in good spirits. Not one smile to be seen. In
fact, scowls and looks of complete displeasure adorned each juror,
with various degrees of harsh body language for the garnish.

Prior to being led into the courtroom, each person
complained about the accommodations during their sequestration.
"There's no water pressure." "Does your room smell as musty as
mine?" "Mine smells like moth-balls." "My mattress is so sunken, it
feels like I'm going to fall through to the floor." "There isn't even a
TV. You can see where they unbolted it from the wall."

Marissa Gantse, the newly appointed juror number ten,
asked Deni, "Why don't you have anything to say? Did you get a
better room than us?"

"No point in complaining. Not like it's gonna do me any
good. At least I won't get 'bae' texts every hour," Deni said.

"'Before Anyone Else' texts from your daughter? That's
weird."

"No. Girlfriend."

"What? Gross. Are you dating a teenager?"

Deni gave Marissa a look that told her that the line of
questioning had reached a conclusion, but not before he put his
exclamation point on it.

"The english language isn't bastardized enough, we have to
invent words to misuse."

"What are you, an english professor? You sound like you
barely speak english yourself," Gantse said.

"No, I barely graduated high school, but that's not the point.
You don't like my accent, go talk to someone else."

Regan Avery had been eavesdropping and inserted herself into the conversation.

"My two daughters are always saying stuff like that. Everything is 'obsessed' or 'literally' so 'surreal' or 'blessed'. That's *if* they actually speak. They're always on those damn phones taking pictures or sending emoticons because they're too busy to spell what they're trying to communicate. I know we were all that age once, but now? Every meal, every moment in their lives are tweeted or snapchatted or instagrammed. I swear, never before have lives less lived been so chronicled."

Just then the court officer entered the deliberation room, cutting off any response from either Deni or Marissa.

It was time to go into the courtroom.

Willow Bauer, the lab technician from the Massachusetts Crime Laboratory in Maynard, was the first witness to take the stand Thursday morning. She underwent the same ritual prior to being asked her first question, stating her full name and occupation after swearing on the Bible.

Deni had known Willow for years. They'd had a flirtatious relationship without any payoff when he was a state police detective, when he used to send her evidence to be tested while investigating his various cases. The tech was born and raised in Vermont, attended university there, and always donned the tree-hugger appearance that was stereotypical of someone going to a Phish concert.

Deni watched the witness as she sat on the bench, with virtually the same appearance. Like time hadn't passed. Whatever natural products she used in her daily regimen, it was working. Her long, tightly waved hair, was self-wrapped in such a way as to pull her unruly locks away from her face. Her vegan diet maintained her small frame with virtually no body fat. Willow Bauer seemed to have a natural radiance without the need for makeup. She wore a women's suit made of linen instead of her usual variations of Boho Gypsy dress under a lab coat, which to Deni's eye was the only difference in her appearance since last he'd seen her.

Albright, dressed in black and white like a Blues Brother without a hat, started the questioning with the innocuous at first, then went into such detail that Deni and the other jurors had to write the testimony down on their notepads.

"..... Miss Bauer, as the lab supervisor for the Massachusetts State Crime Lab, you oversee forensic testing for DNA, ballistics, and the like, correct?"

"Correct.   Our facility also does automotive forensics and forensic accounting as well; however, I don't delve into the financial realm. I collaborate and compile reports to be sent to whomever is handling the investigation," Willow said.

"So am I to understand that you don't run any tests yourself?"

"No, that's incorrect. I personally administer bodily fluid, hair, and skin testing that is sent to us from the Crime Scene Unit. I often conduct testing on various objects that are found at the crime scene as well. There are three others in the lab, but as the supervisor, they report to me."

"Did you handle any of the tests in this case?"

"Yes. Because it's a high-profile case, I received instruction from my boss that the forensic testing for the Nichols murder was to be handled personally."

"Because of the attention the case was getting."

"Presumably."

"And what, if any, tests were run?"

Willow Bauer took a deep breath. "Quite a lot of tests were conducted, actually. The knife, the bat, a tube sock, hair fibers, the body of the victim, semen, saliva swabs from the accused .... " The lab supervisor trailed off which left a beat of silence in the room.

"Should we start with the knife?" Assistant District Attorney Justin Albright had already been back to the prosecutor's table to retrieve a fourteen inch Wüsthof chef's knife which had been tagged into evidence. He then announced that he would like to mark the exhibit, which was not met with an objection.

"Is this the knife that was sent to your lab for testing?"

"It is."

"How can you be sure?"

"First, while it is a common, high-end kitchen knife, this particular model is made of carbon steel and retails for about eight hundred bucks. It was part of a kitchen set that goes for five grand. Additionally, once it was tested, it was tagged with the barcode that's attached to it now to preserve the chain of custody."

"What, if anything, did you find on the knife?"

"We matched the victim's skin, blood, tissue and bone to residue found on the knife from tip to handle. Though it is a very sturdy and well-crafted knife, when any knife is presented against a hard surface, such as bone, it leaves microscopic etches in the blade. Over time, that etching is what causes the blade to become dull. Even surgical steel, when used on such surfaces will etch. That line on the adverts that claim that the 'knife will never get dull' is just plain crap."

Several people on the jury began to chuckle.

Willow waited for the mild interruption to pass before continuing.

"The blade on this knife had etching that matched the cuts into the victim's vertebra after going through her jugular. I also found microscopic bone dust between the handle and blade. As you can see," Willow said as she pointed and held the knife for the prosecutor and jury, "high-end knives like these are cast into one piece, so the knife is sturdy. Cheaper knives have a handle that is bonded onto the blade, which is why they tend to break where the handle meets that blade. Wüsthof, the company that manufactures this knife, rivets an ergonomic handle onto the blade, so it's still one piece. I found the evidence I was looking for when I removed the rivets."

"You found Sloane Nichols' bone under the handle?"

"Yes. And blood and tissue from the victim's neck also matched. That is the knife that ultimately killed Sloane Nichols."

Albright then returned the knife to the prosecutor's desk and retrieved the Easton bat.

"Is this the bat that was used to violate the victim?"

"Yes. Again we ran tests on the bat from barrel to handle, those tests confirmed that the blood, tissue and fecal matter emanated from Sloane Nichols' vaginal and anal canals. There was also a trace amount of seminal fluid found on the barrel, which was later matched to Chase Bromley's DNA from a saliva swab."

The bat was returned to the table. A sealed bag with a formerly white tube sock inside it, which had already been entered into evidence was removed from the same table.

"Is this the tube sock you conducted tests on?"

"Yes it is."

"What, if anything, did you conclude after running tests on this sock?"

"The sock was a virtual stew of forensic evidence. We found sweat from the defendant, along with his dead skin cells, trace amounts of the same laundry detergent that the defendant uses, the victim's saliva, blood, part of a chipped tooth …. It was the sock that was shoved into Sloane Nichols' mouth during her torture, and the sock belonged to the defendant, Chase Bromley."

The bag was replaced on the table and Albright repositioned himself so to be directly in front of both the witness and the jury.

"Hair fibers?"

"Many," Willow said. "Many belonging to both the victim and the accused."

"I see. Semen samples? Bloodwork? DNA?"

"Yes. I tested the samples sent in from the CSU, many belonged to either the victim or the defendant."

"Which brought you to the conclusion that the defendant, scientifically speaking, is guilty of the brutal rape and murder of Sloane Nichols?"

"Objection!" Alex Pratt was on her feet. "Leading and argumentative."

"Withdrawn," Albright said before Judge Wallace could make a ruling. As he returned to his seat he said to his counterpart, "Your witness."

Alex straightened her attire as she made way to where Albright had been standing. Today it was a cream colored skirt suit from Ted Baker, London.

"Miss Bauer, is the evidence that is sent to you, at the lab, sent directly from the Crime Scene Unit?"

"In most cases. It can come from the detectives assigned to the case as well."

"Which are sealed in an evidence bag until you open it at the lab?"

"Correct."

"So, hypothetically, if there was any contamination, on purpose or otherwise, at the crime scene or from wherever the detectives might have procured it, that contamination would follow it to your lab?"

"I suppose."

"What do you mean, 'you suppose'? It stands to reason that if someone on the CSU or one of the detectives wanted to steer the evidence in a certain direction, they could taint the evidence in the bag and seal it, which would then be unsealed for you run tests on at the lab. Correct?"

"Objection."

"Sustained."

"How about evidence from the scene that isn't sent to you?"

"I don't understand the question. If it's not collected at the scene and not sent to me, then I couldn't conduct tests on it. I can't conduct tests on what I don't have."

"Exactly my point." Alex looked at the jury, then back at Max Courtland, her jury consultant. He nodded his head in the affirmative. She'd just scored a mild point with the jury. She let the point marinate for a beat, then went back to questioning the witness.

"This lab in Maynard, where you work, how secure is it?"

"Very."

"So no unauthorized personnel could go into the lab and manufacture false-positive results?"

"No. Absolutely not."

"Really? Weren't you working there in 2004 when the facility was infiltrated?"

"Objection. Facts not in evidence."

"Sustained. Watch it, Counselor."

"Fine. Let's assume, which is a big assumption, that all of the evidence that you conducted the various tests upon, was, in fact, unadulterated. Was there any fingerprint analysis conducted on the 'very expensive chef knife' that you were so impressed with?"

"Yes, but the handle had been wiped clean. I couldn't positively identify any prints on the knife."

"So you can't put the knife in my client's hand?"

"No, but—"

"—Just yes or no will do, thank you. How about hair fibers?"

"What about them?"

"You said, 'many' of the hair fibers sent to the lab matched either the victim or my client. What about the rest of them?"

"There were some that didn't match," Willow said with a slight shrug.

"Were there 'many'?"

"Yes. There were many."

"Would you say that just as many matched the victim and my client as didn't match?"

"I would have to say more."

"There were MORE fibers that didn't match samples from my client?"

"Yes."

"Interesting. Did you conclude anything about any of the other hairs sent to you?"

"Yes. Some were from male, some female, but none matched any DNA in our database."

"What kind of hair? Pubic?"

"Yes. Some were pubic."

"So, with the 'MANY' hair samples that were sent you—some from men, some from women, some pubic, some not—what did you conclude?"

"There is only one conclusion that one could make, and that is that at some point several people, male and female, had deposited hair samples in the victim's apartment."

"Pubic hair."

"Yes, pubic hair."

"How does one 'deposit' pubic hair at someone else's house?"

"Objection."

"Overruled. The witness has been deemed a forensic expert and will answer."

"While going to the bathroom, sexually, changing clothes ...."

"So if the victim, Sloane Nichols, was sexually promiscuous, with both males and females, that could explain the bevy of other hair samples that you dismissed?"

"I didn't dismiss anything," Willow exclaimed indignantly. The large, high ceiling made her voice carry and echo loudly. "I test the evidence that is sent to me and pass the report on to the investigating detectives. If they would have sent me swabs to match with any of the other hair strands that were found, I would have done so. I can't match DNA to another exemplar if I don't have another exemplar."

"Thank you. You've just made my other point. But let's look at that report that you alluded to, shall we?"

Alex retrieved the forensics report that had been previously marked as an Exhibit for the prosecution from her table, crossed the room, and handed it to Willow Bauer.

"On this report, you concluded, and you've just testified, that forensic evidence from the semen sample and the sock used in the rape and murder of Sloane Nichols belonged to my client, yes?"

"Yes, I did."

"And you testified that you are an employee of the Commonwealth, correct?"

"Yes."

"And this report is crucial in bringing suspects to justice, correct?"

"Yes, and I see where you're going with this, but my findings are true and accurate. As I said earlier, I have a premed degree from the University of Vermont, a Master's degree in forensic science from Tuft's University, and a Doct—"

"—Nobody is questioning your credentials, Miss Bauer. I am questioning that you conduct forensic tests on evidence for the state, for a state trial, which is prosecuted by the state."

"Objection your Honor. She's badgering the witness," Albright said.

Wallace said, "Do you have a question, Miss Pratt?"

"I do, your Honor." She turned to the witness. "Are you often pressured when conducting your tests by the prosecution?"

"No. Our lab is located in another part of the state and is independent for that reason."

"So you've never bumped up the schedule for a set of tests that either the local police, a sheriff's department, the state police or the DA needs right away?"

"Of course I have. Sometimes—"

"—So they DO have influence over your tests. You said that your lab is independent, but that isn't entirely true is it? You receive calls all of the time from the people that you're submitting the findings to, correct?"

"Yes."

"How very independent of you."

"Objection."

"Withdrawn."

"What type of DNA testing do you run in your lab?"

"PCR. Polymerase Chain Reaction DNA analysis."

"Is PCR the most accurate form of DNA analysis?"

"Yes."

"Isn't there another widely accepted analysis used in DNA testing, Miss Bauer?"

"Well, yes. RFLP is another technique. Restriction Fragment Length Polymorphism, but that technology is now obsolete."

"Because it's inaccurate?"

"No, because it's much more expensive."

"So which technique is more accurate?"

"That is an impossible question to answer," Willow said looking at both the judge and the prosecutors for help.

Alex said to the judge. "Non-responsive, your Honor. I'd like that stricken from the record. Please direct the witness to answer."

Wallace turned to the witness.

"You need to answer the question, Miss Bauer."

"But it's mathematically impossible to say which type is more accurate. They are both more than 99.99% accurate. If I *HAD* to say which, I'd say rif-lip. RFLP. But that is really misleading. Nobody uses it anymore."

Alex turned to the jury. "RFLP is more accurate but nobody uses it anymore? That's what you're telling this court?"

"That's not exactly what I said."

"That's what I heard. I think that's what the jury heard."

"Objection."

"Withdrawn."

"Miss Bauer, is your lab the only lab the Commonwealth uses to analyze forensics?"

"No. Samples are also sometimes sent to an outside facility. A private firm."

"Because your lab gets pressured and makes mistakes?"

"No, we do it to confirm our results."

"That company is Praesen Technologies, correct?"

"Yes."

"Are you aware that they use RFLP analysis?"

"Yes."

"I understood you to say that 'nobody uses it anymore'."

"I misspoke. Because RFLP testing is substantially more expensive to conduct, it is used far less often. Rarely in fact."

"I see. Would you be surprised to learn that Praesen's conclusions were different from yours?"

"Yes. I would."

"Really?"

"Yes, because scientifically it would be impossible. There were two samples, two data markers, two separate DNA strands for comparison …. They both belonged to the same person. *ONE* sample is definitive to one in over fourteen *BILLION*. More than double the number of people currently on the planet. *TWO* samples matching to a false-positive? Mathematically unfathomable."

"I didn't say the findings weren't the same. I said the *conclusions* weren't the same."

"I don't see the distinction," Willow said.

"Can you testify with the same certainty that the semen and the sock that your lab reported both belonged to my client were deposited into the victim at the time of her rape and murder?"

"It stands to reason."

"That's not what I asked you. Can you say with the same 'one in fourteen billion' certainty that the semen and the sock were deposited into the victim at the time of the crimes? Or even on the same day?"

"With *THAT* degree of certainty? No. Not with all of the extraneous hair samples. No."

"Exactly. Which is what Praesen concluded."

Alex entered into evidence a report crafted by Praesen Technologies.

"While the data markers indicate, from using RFLP analysis, that the samples were a match, as you testified, Praesen concluded that *when* each of those separate DNA samples were posited was impossible to pinpoint."

Willow Bauer shrugged her shoulders.

"What was the question?"

"The question is, how can you conclude that semen and sock DNA, which you tie to my client, were inserted into the victim at or about the same time?"

"As I said, it just stands to reason. The victim was raped. The semen and the gag that was used in the commission of that crime matched the DNA of the defendant."

"Stands to reason? Really? My client could have had consensual sex with Sloane Nichols earlier on the day of the murder, for instance, and could also have left his sock in the apartment for whomever later committed the rape and murder to use. Or left the sock on another occasion for another reason altogether. Or, since they used to live together, been a sock that was a straggler which she packed when she moved out. Aren't any of those explanations possible?"

There was a long pause. The silence was deafening. Alex Pratt had come a long way, asked a lot of questions to get to the payoff. The entire day of testimony hung in the balance.

"I'm sorry I didn't hear you, Miss Bauer. Is it possible?"

"Yes, it's possible."
"Which?"
"I'm sorry?"
"Which of those possibilities I just mentioned are possible?"
Another long pause. Willow looked at her lap. Another shrug.

"Any of them."

17

A LONG DAY OF LISTENING TO TESTIMONY WAS MADE MORE so by the fact that Deni couldn't go home. He wasn't going to be able to have a glass or two of Redbreast. He wasn't going to be able to watch the news or NESN. No Sportscenter. He wasn't going to be able to pet the dog he'd been so reluctant to get in the first place, nor was he going to be able to roll around in his own bed with the woman he'd become so attached to. No creature comforts of any sort. Instead, he was stuck in a cheap no-tell motel in Braintree, thirty minutes south of the city, for the second night in a row.

After food was delivered to his room, he paced about the small space for lack of anything else to do. He hadn't brought a book, though he wasn't much of a reader in the first place. Deni's lack of technological know-how ensured a lack of an iPod, which he wasn't sure he'd be allowed to use anyway.

The man was going stir-crazy. Thoughts of missing Ani and Hobey ran through his mind. He wanted to call home. He wanted to be home. Dwelling on the situation about his new accommodations wasn't going to help matters, he finally concluded. But he also knew that sleep wasn't going to come either.

The vending machine with Coca-cola products in it was just three doors down to the left outside of his motel room. As he left his room with the hope that the only two wrinkled dollar bills he had on him would work in the machine, he was stopped by one of the officers on watch.

"Can I help you, Sir?"

"No thanks, Officer. I just need to grab a Coke."

"Make it quick, you're not supposed to leave your rooms after nine."

"Am I the prisoner now? No TV or radio in that tiny shit-hole of a room and I can't get some fresh air?"

"Open a window."

The officer's comment gave Deni and idea.

"Yeah. Yeah. Maybe I will. What time is breakfast?"

"Coffee and pastries at eight, I think."

"Great. Thanks."

Deni went back into his room without a soda, but felt a surge as if he'd had the caffeine. The rear wall of the motel room was lined with a long, narrow window high up near to the ceiling. The window opened in two side-by-side segments with latches on the bottom of the sill. The latches had built-in spacers which opened the windows only eight inches out, holding the bottom of the window away from the back of the motel.

The same type of set-up was in the bathroom, also on the back wall, in the back-left corner of his room. The single bathroom window was much smaller, afforded only to eliminate steam when showering, presumably.

Deni turned on the fan in the bathroom. The poorly serviced fan made a loud noise and caused a slight vibration. Deni knew this from turning on the switch that morning before court, when using the thrown. The fan exhausted nothing, it simply made a loud noise and moved the smell of his bowel movement around.

The noise from the fan cancelled out the noise he was making in trying to disable the latch from the leftmost of the two segments from the larger windows in the main part of the room. He moved the only chair in the room over to the window and opened the section of it to the left. Upon initial inspection, he thought it might be easier to unscrew the hinges from the top of the window, made accessible only when the window was open, but he wouldn't be able to hold the window from falling off the back of the building and making a huge noise. Even if he had a screwdriver, the window falling three stories would certainly attract attention after the weight of the window snapped the latch anyway. Either way, the latch was going to be toast. So that is what he did.

The plastic latch broke relatively easily. The noise it created was masked by the loud fan. Deni eased the window open as wide as the hinge would allow. It was a tight squeeze, even for Deni who was slender and fit. He maneuvered out the window, one leg at a time like he was going over a fence.

Once out the back of the motel room, he looked around to see if it was being watched. He hung from the sill waiting for someone to yell or notice him, but nobody did. There was just a thin line of trees on the back side of the motel, lights from an enormous mall dimly peeked through the branches from the other side of them.

The ledge of the top of the window in the room below him afforded little footing, but enough to shimmy to his left where there was an exposed pipe which ran vertically from the ground to the roof. Deni scaled down the wall using the pipe and was on the ground in short order. He went through the trees to find a chain link fence, which he hopped over and was in the parking lot of the South Shore Plaza Mall within minutes of leaving his motel room.

One of the benefits of not depending upon technology was that he remembered pertinent phone numbers. His first call on the payphone inside the mall was to Ani.

"…..You're going to get into so much trouble," she said after the initial excitement in hearing from him dissipated into pragmatism.

"If I get caught, which I ain't plannin' to do."

"Are you coming here? I miss you, the bed is so lonely."

"No, I can't. As much as I'd love to. I gotta get ahold of She."

"Lisa? Why do you need to see her so bad that you'd risk going to jail?"

"I've got to get her on this case. I need to see where she's at."

"Which case? The trial? Aren't they supposed to provide you with all of the facts during the trial, Bae?"

"Yeah but somethin's not right and I can't wait that long. We're a week in and all I've heard is how much evidence they have that points to him doin' it. Why would he be so careful to wipe evidence clean and be so stupid to leave his sock in her mouth and cum inside her? Why would he risk going to her apartment with a restraining order? And when he was seen in the building, why did he go through with the rape and murder? He must have known he'd be a suspect. With all of the evidence they have, why isn't his legal dream team lookin' to cut a deal? Somethin' ain't stirrin' the Kool-aid and I wanna know what."

"Okay. Be careful. No Chinatown this week, or next at this rate. Guess Hobey will have to keep me company."

"Hun, it's okay to love your pet, just don't *LOVE* your pet."

Deni heard Ani laugh through the phone. He missed her laugh.

"You're a sicko."

"Don't I know it. How ya holdin' up?"

"Another day in the salt mines, picking up the mess that men like Chase Bromley leave behind. I love my job, but I hate my job. Does that make sense?"

"I hear ya. We all just do the best we can and hope it makes a difference," Deni said with a sigh as he looked around the busy mall. Nobody seemed to care about him or pay him any attention.

"I know you think you're doing the right thing by having Lisa investigate your trial, but maybe you should just help convict the sonofabitch. Whether he did it or not, and it sure seems like he did, he's not a nice guy. They showed his criminal record and the times that police have shown up at his door on the news. Nothing has ever happened to this guy for using that poor women as a punching bag because of who his father is. Maybe he should go to prison. On behalf of the battered women of Boston, I know I'd feel better if he was off the streets."

"You've made your opinion abundantly clear, hun. I just gotta know. Ya know?"

"I know."

"Gotta run. I gotta call She."

"I love you," Ani said after a few seconds.

"I know."

"Be careful."

But Deni didn't hear her. He had already disconnected and began dialing his partner, Lisa Sheed.

Lisa wasn't about to have a discussion with her boss over the phone. She left her bed and Reggie, who didn't want her to leave, attained some of the cursory information he requested when he'd called, and met Deni in the Faneuil Hall Marketplace. The spot was her choice to rendezvous. Certainly not his, as it was a rather large pain in his ass to get to the meeting spot on the **T**. Deni had to get on the red line, go through nine stops, switch over to the orange line, to get to the State Street stop. Once he emerged above ground, he had to hoof-it three blocks to the top of Quincy Market, where the cobblestone, pedestrian street for the marketplace begins.

Three hours after making the phone call, he was walking down the street—along North Market opposite the canopy—looking for his partner.

There, on one of the benches lining the pedestrian thoroughfare, sitting next to a statue of a suited man holding a cigar, was Lisa Sheed.

"You have got one gigantic pair of balls on you, my friend."

"Jealous?"

"Hardly. Do you have any idea of much trouble you'll get into when you get caught?"

"So I won't get caught."

"That easy? You just won't get caught?"

"As long as you don't rat me out. By the way, I'm gonna need you to give me a ride back to the mall. It's almost two and I'm gonna miss the last train back to Braintree."

Lisa shook her head in disgust. "I should have just driven out there in the first place."

"So what have you got?"

Sheed handed him a file folder from the shoulder bag that was sitting between them on the bench, followed by an untraceable burner phone.

"Use this if you have to call me again, and I'll keep you updated with what's going on at the office. If you get caught with it, I don't know you."

The fifty or so bars and restaurants in the immediate area were letting out for Thirsty Thursday—which was now very early Friday morning—a weekly institution. No matter the time of year; when the colleges are in session, the dead of winter, mid-summer tourism in full-swing, or blowing off steam during May finals week, students and young professionals take part in the weekly pseudo-holiday.

It was after two in the morning, well after last call, and crowds of young people were stumbling about, making a last attempt at a hookup. Scantily clad females were either searching for their next conquest, or avoiding one, while trying to find purchase on the uneven cobblestone in heels. One such female was laughing hysterically as she fell, managing to keep the scorpion bowl she'd managed to sneak out of Hong Kong from spilling.

Sheed shook her head again. "Fuckin' fools. Then they wonder why men prey on them."

"How about we focus, huh?" Deni wasn't paying attention to the drunks, nor was he interested in the police on horseback that were approaching to control the nightly mess. He was reading through the short file Lisa had assembled in just a few short hours.

"I'll sum it up by saying that although this Chase Bromley is a bad guy, his former girlfriend was no saint. You know me and my past, I have no sympathy for guys who beat women—"

"—I know. And I know that you went through hell before you got out. Probably the reason you switched to women. Less chance of gettin' your ass kicked," Deni said.

"I've always been attracted to women, it just took me a long time to be okay about it. Your vic was into both. Men, women .... Whatever was handy." Sheed pointed to printouts of several profiles Sloane Nichols had posted online.

"What's all this?"

"Oh, I forgot. It's on the internet so you don't have a clue."

"Go fuck ya-self, She. Just tell me what it is. I mean I can read it, but she just posted this for anyone to see?"

"This one is from a website called Booble. But she posted almost the same exact write-up in Kink, Fling, Adult Friend Finder, even old-school Craigslist. She was into orgies. And rough stuff. Like really rough. Some people are into a little B&D or S&M, but this is different. There is this whole niche subculture who are into this kind of stuff. Read it."

Deni read the first ad, shaking his head all the while.

Fun Girl with green blue eyes seeking males and females for one-on-one or group fun (the more the merrier). I'm 27, single, 36-25-36 and like to be dominated. Boys - make me airtight, run train, shower me with that cum. Women - eating box is my best skill, love toys. Message me if you want to come to me, then cum with me.

"Jesus Christ, she might as well have painted a target on herself. What was this girl thinkin'?"

"That was one of the more tame ones. Depending on the site, they get more graphic but say essentially the same thing," Lisa explained. "When she was with Bromley, they were more selective about who they let into his brownstone. When she left him, she got a lot less choosy, as you can see."

"Maybe that's why she left him? Cuz she wanted to be more free to fuck whoever she wanted?"

"Look here," Lisa said, pointing to a police report in the file. "This was buried but I still have Rick Hobbs' PNC password. Same username, same password. Kind of ironic that the people who are entrusted to stop crime can't protect themselves from theft," she said with a proud grin before continuing. "When that doesn't work, I can reach out to a runner over there that I used to see. If I have to."

A moment of relative silence took place while Deni read. Sheed allowed him the time while taking in the drunken shit-show that was Faneuil Hall.

"He was never officially arrested by BPD, but you can't hide every piece of paper along the trail."

Deni skimmed through the DD-5, a police report written by detectives to validate their time, attention, and progress on various cases to their superiors. Deni didn't recognize the detective's name on the report. Not only had he not been a statie for more than a decade, the five was written by a local cop.

"He's a control freak," he said after giving the document a once-over.

"You can say that again. This five was never filed up the chain, but it was held onto to cover this cop's ass just in case it came back to bite him. Cops generally want to stay off the radar if it can be helped, especially when it comes to Kenneth Bromley. He's a powerful man with a lot of friends," Lisa said. "And watch who you share this with. I don't want you or I to get burnt with this either."

"Who am I gonna tell? I'm not even supposed to have this."

"I'm just letting you know. I can't get mad at you for talking out of school if I never told you that you couldn't."

"So Sloane Nichols is under her boyfriend's thumb. And because he has money—or his dad does—she has to listen. Whether he knocks her around or she gets her cuts and bruises from the fun she has, a disagreement over what he wants and when gets the cops involved. They respond to the Double-D, but either Nichols comes to her senses or someone talks her out of moving forward, the charges are never filed. One day, she has enough and leaves the prick, filing a TRO in the process. She's livin' out on her own, but Bromley can't stay away."

"Sounds about right," Sheed said.

"This don't prove he didn't do it. In fact, it gives a pretty clear motive. I wonder why we haven't seen this in the trial yet? Or even heard that we were gonna see it when Albright gave his opening statement? You came up with this in just a few hours, what the hell are the lawyers doin'?"

Lisa gave the international sign for *I have no idea,* but didn't say a word.

"Keep digging."

"Deni, we have other cases. Other *PAYING* cases. I'm running this thing solo. Reggie has been giving me no end of shit about the hours I'm keeping and it's only been a week. Why do you want to investigate this? Why is it so important to you?"

"Because I can't just sit around licking my balls waiting for someone to yell 'fetch'. I can't just depend on the lawyers to spoon-feed me information, if and when they choose to. I have to know the truth and what that fuck-tard Dubone said was right. He may be an idiot but he hit the nail on the head. Everyone on that jury panel is lookin' to hang Bromley by his ball-sack. Already. Maybe he did it, maybe he didn't, but he should get a fair shake. I was a cop once upon a time. I became a cop to see that justice was done, that we got the right bad-guy. But the Mass State Police ain't in the business of justice, it turns out, and it don't seem like the locals are any better. Maybe I been working with Ryan too long, watchin' him defend the rights of our clients. Some of the people are guilty, some not, but they pay for a lawyer so they can get a fair shake. I don't know. I just know that what's happenin' ain't right. And, unfortunately, this time it's my job to help decide if this guy goes free or goes to hell on a shutter. I'd like to do the right thing."

"I get it. Sort of. I just don't have the same instincts about helping a guy who has gotten away with beating his girlfriend, then raping and killing her after she left him."

"If he did it."

"Aren't you always the one who says, 'where there's smoke'? He can't be innocent of all of it. Every time I see his face or hear about the trial on the news, I relive what I went through. I don't know, Deni. I'm more than okay with sitting this one out."

"Then do it because I'm your boss, and I'm tellin' ya to do it. You're an investigator. Investigate. You want to be made a full-partner? Do this and you're in. Now are you motivated?"

She stared into his eyes for a few seconds. Those were words she longed to hear for nearly a year.

"I'll do my best."

After Sheed dropped him off at the South Shore Mall, Deni moved quickly and quietly back toward his motel room. The lights from the parking area lit the long abandoned lot, making him exposed to the mall security vehicles that moved about the property.

Security around the motel was moving about with regularity as well in the early morning hour. But these weren't the mall rent-a-cops. These were actual police officers who could dole out real consequences if Deni was discovered.

He looked up to his third-floor room to see the window still closed, as he had left it. The latch-spacer that kept the window open was broken, by him, and therefore not able to keep the bottom of the window propped outward. The light was on, however, and Deni couldn't remember if he'd left it that way.

A flashlight moved across the back of motel building and went away. Deni made his move, running to the exposed pipe he'd descended. Climbing up the pipe was a different chore all together. The thin brackets that held the pipe to the exterior had been painted over so many times that they were almost flush to the building, which afforded him no holds for purchase.

Deni began to pull himself up the pipe, hand over hand, feet squeezing the pipe like he was climbing a rope without knots in it. As he moved up between the first and second floors, his hands found a soft spot in the pipe. Years of paint hadn't stopped the erosion and rust, they simply masked it. The pipe began to make a very loud noise as it bent. Deni looked left and right, his fear was realized.

Flashlights were moving toward him from the ground.

Fuck.

There was no way to climb the remainder of the pipe, pry the window open and get back inside his motel room before the flashlights illuminated what the police on the ground probably already knew.

Deni let go of the pipe, falling to the ground. He ran back into the thin trees and moved along the perimeter of the grounds of the motel.

Three police cruisers, along with the bus that would bring them to court in a few hours, lined the parking lot on the front side of the building. Each floor had a long, concrete porch that ran the length of the building, each with a vending machine and exterior lighting for the motel's occupants to find their rooms. Getting inside his room via the front door without being seen was going to be impossible. But it was his only way in.

The officers were speaking to each other from all over the motel property over the radio. Flashlights on the building became spotlights from the cruisers scanning the area.

Fuck.

Plan b. If I can't get in, everyone has to come out.

He went back over the fence, back to the mall, and utilized an outside payphone since the mall was closed and locked for nightly cleaning. After making his phone call, he wiped down the phone with bottom of his t-shirt and headed back to the motel.

Within a few minutes, by the time Deni had returned, every light was on in the hotel and the occupants were leaving their rooms. Some were in bathrobes, some in pajamas, some had gotten dressed before gathering in the parking lot where the officers had designated.

Deni messed his hair up, and put on a disgruntled 'just woken up from a sound sleep' face. He melted into the crowd of people gathering along the perimeter of the motel parking lot, all wondering why they'd been evacuated from their shitty rooms and uncomfortable beds. Several were lighting cigarettes as they divulged their theory.

Deni approached one of the officers who was speaking into his radio.

"What the hell is going on? We have court in a few hours."

The officer looked Deni up and down, and pointed for him to go back to the designated gathering spot before answering.

"Somebody called in a bomb-threat."

18

THE TRIAL WAS TAKING ITS TOLL ON EVERYONE INVOLVED.
The attorneys looked as though they'd spent another sleepless night
strategizing over the day to come, the judge's appearance hadn't
improved from his previous few days of fatigue, and each member of
the jury appeared to have aged a decade overnight.

Judge Wallace was made aware of the bomb threat earlier
that morning, and sent word to the jury that he thanked them and
assured them that their safety was his number one priority. An
increase in security protocols were going to take immediate effect.
He also said in his memo, which a court officer read aloud in the
deliberation room, that it was Friday, meaning that there would be
just one more day of testimony and they would have the weekend to
rest. His words brought no comfort.

"Some rest," someone yelled.

"We get to stay in a motel with no TV or radio all weekend?
How wonderful," someone else said.

"We're all gonna die in that shit-hole. Someone tried to blow
us up and they very well might succeed next time."

"It was Bromley!"

"How did I get stuck in this trial?"

The officer had no response. He simply finished reading the
memo that had been typed by Seth Warner on behalf of Judge
Wallace, and withdrew until it was time to lead the disgruntled jury
back into the courtroom.

Constance Reinhardt—who preferred to be called Connie—
was the first witness on the stand that Friday. She was Sloane's

next door neighbor and the first person to speak to the authorities when the victim's apartment was sealed off and ruled a crime scene.

The first witness of the day took the stand with hair pulled up in a bun, thin turtleneck sweater under a business jacket and matching slacks. She had the appearance of a librarian, but stated that her occupation was an executive assistant for an accountant.

She testified under oath that she'd come home after an intense hot-yoga class, experiencing an ungodly odor the moment the elevator opened on her floor. As she approached her own apartment, she saw the commotion outside her neighbor's apartment, where that odor was emanating. Connie had to walk by Sloane's door on a daily basis, which was always interesting, she said. There were usually sounds which gave her pause or piqued her curiosity, this time it was a gaggle of police and an atrocious smell.

The door had been left open as she was allowed to pass to go into her own apartment. Connie said that she peeked through the yellow police tape into Sloane's residence as she walked past; noticing the immense blood spatter and the almost unrecognizable body of her neighbor on the hardwood floor, inside her apartment, between the living room and dining area. The body had not been covered up at that point, pictures were being taken by the personnel inside. She ran the rest of the way to her apartment to shower and think about what to do.

Connie Reinhardt further testified that she decided to go speak to the police in the hall after she'd cleaned herself up. She said that she had seen the accused in the building the previous day, in the early evening when she was returning home from work.

Albright made the point hit home with the jury that, give or take, the witness saw the defendant in the building within the timeframe of the crimes.

The witness went on to say that she had only peripheral knowledge that Sloane had been through a bad breakup, and no knowledge whatsoever that Chase Bromley wasn't allowed in the building due to a restraining order until the police had told her after the murder. She said the detectives who were assigned to the case had her go to Troop H, where the defendant was one of the men in a six-pack photo array. She positively identified Chase Bromley as the man she saw in the building the previous day, on October six.

The witness again noted that Sloane Nichols seemed to be a party girl—after ADA Albright asked the specific question—and always seemed to have mixed company. Albright wanted to get ahead of the defense's attempt to vilify the victim by further inquiring if the victim deserved what happened to her because of the frequent and varied company she kept.

Connie said, "No. Of course not. Nobody deserves what happened to that poor girl. That apartment ..... What happened ..... Just awful. I'll never get that image out of my mind. Not for as long as I live. Oh, that smell. I have still have nightmares all these months later."

The witness for the prosecution was then turned over to the defense attorney, Alex Pratt.

"Miss Reinhardt ..... Is it miss?"

"Yes, but you can just call me Connie," she said.

"I'd love to, but we need to keep things professional for the time being. Were you on a first-name basis with the victim?"

"Yes. As I said, we were neighbors. I'd see her in the hall, or when we got our mail, or in passing."

"And you spoke?"

"Excuse me?"

"When you would see each other 'in the hall, or when you got your mail, or in passing' ..... You would speak to one another or just nod or what?"

"We spoke. Sure."

"Small talk or important stuff?"

"A little of both I guess," Connie said with obvious apprehension.

"I see. Do you live alone, Miss Reinhardt?"

"Yes."

"Boyfriend? Girlfriend? Significant other?"

"Yes."

"Does he or she sleep over?"

"He. I really don't see ....," she said looking for the judge or someone to rescue her. But no help came.

"I'd simply like to know if anyone else might have seen what you testified to seeing, on that day or any other."

"Well, no. It's still early in the relationship."

"Saving yourself for marriage?"

"Objection."

"Sustained."

"You are also in your late twenties, is that right, Miss Reinhardt?"

"Yes."

"About the same age as the victim?"

"Yes. About. It's a young building."

"But not much in common, correct?"

"I don't know," Connie said.

"You don't? I thought you spoke. 'In the hall and in passing' ..... Did you talk about things that you have in common?"

"Well—"

"—Because you didn't really have anything in common, correct? You either made small talk or you complained about the noises and the partying and the random people that she buzzed into the building on a regular basis. Isn't that right?"

"It got loud sometimes, yes. Our building is supposed to be for young professionals. It's priced to be a bit higher than market value in order to keep undesirables out. The landlord promised me when I signed the lease that it was going to be a quiet building with mature, young, working people and it is except for the ..... Well, Sloane. I wanted to let her know that her partying kept me up some nights. I wasn't the only one. She apologized. It wasn't that big of a deal."

"But you formed an opinion about the victim, did you not?"

"No, not at all. I'm a devout Christian. I try not to judge anybody," the uncomfortable witness said. Beads of sweat were forming by her hairline and on her upper lip.

"The parties and the noises that were coming from your neighbor's apartment, they were often sexual in nature, correct?"

"I'm not entirely sure."

"No? You never asked her?"

"Not specifically, no."

"What did the 'loud partying' noises sound like? Didn't they sound like sex parties?   You know, moaning and groaning ..... Domination and submission ..... Vulgar language ..... Isn't that correct?"

"Objection. The witness has already said she didn't know."

"Sustained."

"Okay. Let's try it from another angle. Miss Reinhardt, did you ever see what Sloane's frequent and varying visitors were wearing?"

"Once or twice, yes."

"Can you describe the attire that you saw?"

"It varied. Sometimes it was like leather. Sometimes not."

"Garments one might wear to court?"

"No, I wouldn't think so."

"Because what the many visitors wore was provocative, and revealing, and what one might wear to say ..... A sex party?"

"Objection."

"Overruled.   The witness will answer," Judge Wallace bellowed.

"Maybe, yes."

"And you never spoke to Sloane Nichols about this?"

"Well, it wasn't exactly safe. I mean for the rest of us in the building," she said.

"So you did form an opinion? It's okay. Nobody is saying that it's bad to have an opinion. All I'm asking is if you formed any opinion about the kind of lifestyle that the victim led?"

"I was concerned. Yes."

"And of the many visitors that you saw come in and out of the apartment building, in and out of the victim's apartment, you picked my client out of a line-up?"

"Yes."

"Interesting. Is that because the police told you about him?"

"What? No."

"You said that the police told you about the restraining order. They probably showed you a picture of my client and asked if he'd been in the building, correct?"

"I don't really remember. Maybe. I don't remember when they showed me. Or told me."

"So it could have been when the detectives originally spoke to you after you returned to the apartment to speak with them? Not when you were asked to go to the police station, but when you were still in the building?"

"Maybe. I'm not sure."

"Which is why you picked him out in the line-up, correct? The police had shown you the picture, and you recognized him from the picture."

"No. I saw him. I know that I saw him. We were entering the building about the same time. I was coming home from work and I held the elevator for him. I rode with him up to our floor. He was in the building. I'm certain of it."

"But that was the day before the murder, correct? Did you see him leave?"

"I didn't see him leave, no, but it was about the time that the police said the torturing began."

"Move to strike," your Honor. "The witness is testifying that she saw my client enter the building eighteen to twenty hours before the atrocities against the victim occurred. She is aware of when and how long the victim suffered only because of what she claims the police told her. It's hearsay."

Albright stood but was waved down before he could speak.

"The witnesses' last comment will be stricken from the record and the jury will disregard."

"Miss Reinhardt, isn't it true that my client could have left Sloane Nichols' apartment and the building without you seeing him?"

"Yes."

"Because you weren't spying on your neighbor? Looking out the peephole? Surveilling her?"

"Of course not."

"Did it look like he was sneaking into the building? You testified that you rode with him up to your floor in the elevator. Couldn't he have decided to take the stairs instead?"

"Yes, he could have."

"If he was trying to enter the building unseen, it would make sense for him not to take the elevator with a person on the same floor, correct?"

"Objection."

"Withdrawn."

"Did you hear Sloane Nichols and my client having sex?"

"Not specifically, no."

"But you assumed that's why he was there, just like the others?"

"Objection."

"Withdrawn."

"You liked to listen to Sloane have sex, didn't you?"

"OBJECTION! Your Honor—"

"—I'm way ahead of you, Mister Albright. Counselor, I suggest you watch yourself or you will receive sanctions."

"Yes, your Honor. I apologize," Alex Pratt said.

"Miss Reinhardt, in your opinion—which you reluctantly said that you'd formed—why would someone brazenly walk into a building they weren't legally allowed to be in, in broad daylight, then brutally rape, torture, and murder the occupant of the apartment that someone witnessed them go into?"

"Objection."

"Hypothetically?"

"Sustained. This is your final warning, Miss Pratt. And when there in an objection, you are required to wait until I've ruled on that objection before you ask another question. This isn't your first trial."

"I'm very sorry. One more question, your Honor, if I may."

"At your own peril," Judge Wallace replied with a sigh.

"Isn't it possible, that IF my client was the person that you saw entering the apartment of Sloane Nichols, that he could have been there to have sex, like so many before him, and left with plenty of time for another visitor to enter the same apartment and commit the crimes against her, including her murder?"

The witness looked around to see if another objection was going to be made. After enough time had passed when she was confident that no objection was forthcoming, Connie Reinhardt answered.

"I don't know. I don't think so."

"Because the police said her abuse took twelve to fifteen hours?"

"Correct. Yes. It all happened about the same time."

"Eighteen to twenty hours is the same as twelve to fifteen? Don't you work for an accountant? Those numbers don't match up, do they?"

"I just know that I saw him."

"Three hours ahead of the earliest possible time the murderer entered her apartment."

"I guess. If you say so."

"I didn't say so. The police, the Medical Examiner ..... Everyone says so. Care to clarify your previous answer? Isn't it possible that my client visited and left the victim's apartment hours before the real killer entered the building?"

"Yes. It's possible."

19

THE NEXT WITNESS ON FRIDAY, MAY 16, WAS THE ANTITHESIS of the previous witness. The break had come and gone, and when the jury was led back into the courtroom, the person that replaced the prim and proper Constance Reinhardt on the stand—after everyone came to order—was similar only in gender.

Gena Rivers had been alive for only thirty years, but it was evident that those years had been hard, taking a toll on her body and appearance. Her hair was bleached to the point of lacking color, was teased to make it look as big as possible, and the amount of hairspray that had been applied would have disallowed a hair out of place in a category five hurricane. The garments she'd chosen for court were more suited for a street corner, and even then the female working the corner might rethink the outfit for being too obvious. There wasn't much fabric to begin with, and yet some had been deliberately cut to expose tattoos in places that might have made the artist blush when applying them.

It was obvious to everyone in the courtroom that she didn't belong on the witness stand. As a defendant in her own trial, maybe, but certainly not as a credible witness in someone else's.

The prosecutor must have been desperate for her testimony, was the predominant thought in everyone's mind. The secondary thought was that the woman before them was a train wreck, which brought about the fear of what was she was going to say. This was a flyer that was more than likely going to backfire in the face of Albright and Walsh.

Gena's voice was low and raspy, clearly a smoker. What she smoked was anyone's guess, but all answers were likely correct.

Albright sent his backup, Amy Walsh, to question the witness after going through the usual routine of swearing in. She wore her best suit for the occasion, a stylish indigo sheath dress and two-button jacket. It was her time to shine, and she wanted to dress the part.

"Miss Rivers. How do you know the victim in this case, Sloane Nichols?"

"We used to fu—," Gena began to say as she looked at the prosecution table, where Justin Albright was shaking his head. His witness was about to screw up already.

"—We used to be lovers," she finished.

"Exclusively?"

"No. Sometimes it was just me and her, sometimes she liked to have other people too."

"And this was consensual?"

"Oh very. It was hot."

Everyone in the room tried to hold back laughter as well as their rolling eyes and head shakes.

"I'm sorry, Miss Rivers, I didn't mean sensual, I meant consensual. Did you both agree to it?"

"Yeah. I responded to a profile she placed, then after that she had my number if she wanted some action."

"And she did call you from time to time?"

"Yeah. Like I said."

"Not for pay?"

"No. I wouldn't a charged her anyways. She was a good lay."

"*MISS RIVERS*, you will conduct yourself with decorum or you will be found in contempt and spend some time in jail. Am I clear?"

The judge had had enough of Gena Rivers already. He looked at Albright sitting behind the table, blushing. The look on Wallace's face told anyone with eyes that he questioned the sanity of putting this particular witness on the stand. Her credibility would be zero with this or any jury.

"What? She asked me," Rivers said to the room while the judge made his visual cues.

"My point is the following," Amy ventured on, "You spent time with the victim and she confided in you, correct?"

"When her mouth wasn't occupied, yeah, she told me stuff."

"About the defendant, Chase Bromley?"

"Yeah. She said he was like a control freak and she wanted to be free to fu ..... To have relations with who she wanted to. He wouldn't let her go. He got like super aggro, so she had to cut him loose."

"Objection," Alex said from her seat. "Hearsay."

"Your Honor, direct statements from the victim," ADA Walsh said.

Alex stood. "Which cannot be corroborated." She cocked her head and waved her hand at the witness. "Need I say more, Judge? Really?"

"The testimony is corroborated by the TRO. Sloane Nichols confided in her lover that she wished to stay away from the defendant which is confirmed by the filing of a restraining order. Goes directly to facts in evidence."

"If you allowed the statements of ever lover the victim had, we'd—"

"—The objection is overruled," Wallace interrupted.

"Your Honor—"

"—But your objection is noted. Miss Walsh, please move on."

"I have nothing more for this witness."

Alex Pratt remained standing and waited for Amy to take her seat beside Justin Albright.

As Amy walked past, Alex looked her up and down. She had to admit, she had a slight admiration for the young prosecutor and mildly envied her attire. On this day, however, Alex would win both the daily fashion contest as well as trial acumen. Pratt's sleeveless safari vest and tapered trousers were on the verge of being too risqué for court, though not remotely close to what the witness was wearing.

Alex approached the witness and the jury, shaking her head and gave an exaggerated grin for her audience. It was her way of embellishing amusement.

"You do have sex for money, do you not?"

"I don't do that no more."

"Oh. I apologize. When did you give that up?"

"Objection."

"Credibility, Judge."

"Overruled."

"A couple a months ago."

"Is that because one or both of the ADAs told you to?"

"Yeah. They said it'd be bad if I got up here and said stuff while I was doin' stuff that ain't exactly legal."

Alex laughed outright.

"Prostitution isn't legal, not even a little bit."

"It shouldn't be a crime. I can give it away, but I can't sell it?"

"Be that as it may, it isn't currently legal and you used to do that for a living up until 'a couple of months ago'. Did I hear that correctly?"

"Yeah."

"Did you ever get arrested for solicitation? I'm sorry, being a prostitute?"

"Yeah. Couple a times."

"Do you call seventeen times a 'couple'?"

"I don't think—"

"—I have your arrest history, if you'd like to go through it."

"No, I'm good."

"You might very well be, but not in getting away with it."

"Objection."

"Apologies, your Honor," Alex said. She tried to move along before Wallace ruled, but Gena Rivers cut everyone off with her first outburst.

"You think you're better than me? We all sellin' somethin', lady."

"You're Honor, permission to treat as hostile?"

"Granted." He then turned to the witness.

"Miss Rivers, you've now been qualified a hostile witness; however, there is no onus on you to prove that you're hostile."

"You think that was hostile?"

"Excuse me?"

"Nothin'."

"Very well, Miss Pratt, you may continue."

"Thank you, Judge. Miss Rivers, did you ever bring any of your sexual partners or clients to see Sloane Nichols?"

"Not clients. She wasn't into that kinda thing. It wasn't about money."

"But you did bring non-paying males and females to meet the victim?"

"Yeah, sometimes. If she didn't have any plans or hookups that night, she'd call me and see if I wanted to come over. Sometimes with friends."

"And how long have you been her sexual 'ace in the hole' so to speak?"

"Objection."

"I'll rephrase. How long were you her lover of last resort?"

Albright stood. "Your Honor?"

"Overruled. The witness will answer."

"A few years."

"So while she was living with and in a relationship with my client?"

"Yeah."

"Can you please elaborate?"

"Whattaya mean?"

"I mean, did you and Sloane Nichols and Chase Bromley and whomever else have sex together?"

"No. He didn't know about it. She had people over to his place when he wasn't around. People who responded to her profiles and stuff. Or who I brought over. When he found out about it, he put a stop to it, and right quick."

"And did Miss Nichols get angry about that?"

"Objection. Hearsay."

"Admissions, your Honor," Alex said. "You've already ruled in their favor for the same objection. What's good for the goose is—"

"—Then you will need to specify that to the witness. Sustained."

"Very well. Did Sloane Nichols ever say to you that she was upset or angry about 'putting a stop to it', as you say?"

"Yeah. She was pissed. Said he 'used to be more adventurous'. She was gettin' bored."

"Could you blame him for not wanting any Tom, Dick, or Harriet waltzing into his multimillion dollar brownstone?"

"Objection."

"Withdrawn."

"Do you know if Miss Nichols left my client, or did my client ask her to leave?"

"After a couple a times of him finding out about parties, I think he might'a asked her to leave. But it might'a been a threat to get her to stop. I really can't say."

"I think you just did say."

Albright stood. "Who is testifying here? The counselor or the witness?"

"Please sit down Mister Albright. You're beginning to annoy me. Miss Pratt, do you have anything further for the witness? We seem to be roaming away from what the witness knows and entering into pure speculation."

"I'm almost finished, Judge. Miss Rivers, in that capacity, as a prostitute, did you ever say anything or do anything for the person that hired you that wasn't exactly true or honest?"

"Whattaya mean?"

"Fantasies. People sometimes want you to say or do things that aren't real, correct?"

"Goes with the territory. Ya tell them they got a big ..... Uh ..... They're, like, endowed and stuff. Make like you're having the time of your life, so they can get their kicks."

"So you pretend?"

"Yeah."

"Are you pretending now?"

"No."

"Really? Because I think that your still a prostitute, only now your client is the District Attorney's office."

"*OBJECTION!*" Albright was on his feet, annoyance or not.

"Withdrawn. No further questions."

"Get out your checkbook, Counselor," Emile Wallace bellowed. "Two Thousand dollars. You're in contempt."

In Alex Pratt's estimation, the $2000 fine was money well-spent. She'd pass the cost onto her client, which Kenneth Bromley would happily pay, since it was a result he was ultimately buying.

Alex may have suffered a contempt citation, but she just drove a truck through her client's alleged motive. The prosecution claimed that Chase Bromley wanted Sloane Nichols dead because she'd left him.

She was confident that at least one member of the jury believed that Bromley threw Nichols out of his home, or at the very minimum, believed that it was *possible*.

20

LATER THAT NIGHT, AFTER DENI AND THE REST OF THE JURY had been shuttled back to the motel in Braintree from the courthouse in Downtown Boston, everyone began to reluctantly settle in for a long weekend of sequestration. Some read books. Some chain-smoked cigarettes. Some picked at their cold, leftover takeout from earlier in the evening. Some wrote letters which unbeknownst to them wouldn't be sent until after the trial.

Deni retrieved the disposable cell phone from the hiding spot in the tiny closet behind the footboard within his motel room and began making calls.

The first call was to Ani, of course. She was happy to hear from him and glad he called, though she didn't want him to get into any trouble for it. She talked about her day and asked about his. Deni didn't elaborate other than to say that the days were getting longer and shittier. He was happy to hear her voice. She was happy to hear his. Even Hobey seemed to perk up when Ani placed her cell phone near him and Deni gave a macho 'Hey Pal' into his burner. The call was nice while it lasted but accentuated the separation as the time passed.

His second call was to Ryan Wells, his lawyer-friend in New Hampshire. Deni worked for him conducting various investigations on behalf of Ryan's clients and/or prospective cases. The two men had a long history and considered each other family.

"Hello?"
"Ryan, it's me."
"Deni? Did you get a new number?"
"No, burner phone."

"Uh-oh. Hey, wait. Lisa said that you're mixed up in the Chase Bromley case. I thought that jury got sequest ..... Oh shit. Deni I can't be a party to an illegal communication. I could get disbarred in both Mass and here."

"Relax. This phone is untraceable. You're already on the phone—in for a dime, in for a dollar at this point."

"Great. Thanks for that," Ryan said with a sigh.

"How's Ang?"

"She's great. Getting big."

"Is she still thinking about doing the hippie, mid-wife, water-birth thing?"

"She's not thinking about it, she's going to do it. Hospitals are germ factories. We want to bring our first child into the world in a beautiful, natural way. Not in some sterile environment with a bunch of machines. There isn't any love in a hospital, it's all about the money and beds. Crank'em out and get the next woman with contractions in the stirrups."

"Take it easy, don't get all worked up. I just thought you might want to consider a place that has the equipment to step in if it doesn't go as naturally as you tree-huggers are hoping."

"We will have both a mid-wife and a doctor at the ready. We're not Amish, we just want the experience to be as beautiful as possible."

"Yeah, okay. You go with that. Anyway, I got a couple questions for ya."

"Shoot."

"This case is all about circumstantial evidence and—"

"—Hold up, hold up, hold the eff up. I can't talk to you about the Bromley case, Deni. Let's count the ways this conversation is illegal."

"Fine. Hypothetically. *Hypothetically*, if there was a rape-murder where there was a ton of circumstantial evidence but nothing that directly ties the accused to the crime, can a jury convict?"

"*Hypothetically*, a jury can always convict. We have the worst system of justice in this country, except for all of the others. While the prosecution has the burden of proving their case beyond a reasonable doubt, most people believe that anyone brought to trial is presumed guilty, or they wouldn't be a defendant in the first place.

The prosecutors sit closest to the jury, they speak first and have the last word. They have a jurist presiding over the trial that is supposed to be unbiased but he or she obviously doesn't want criminals roaming the streets ..... The system is stacked against the accused. While the defendant has rights that cannot be infringed upon, the juries are the wild card. Juries can ignore instruction and the law and do whatever the hell they want. Twelve well-meaning people can ruin someone's life or give someone that doesn't deserved to be free the opportunity to have one."

"That's not very helpful, Ry."

"I'm not sure what you want me to say."

"Have you been following this case?"

"Of course. Who hasn't? Three big trials going on in New England right now, and I'm following all of them just like everyone else."

"So you know why we got sequestered?"

"Some idiot spoke to the press. I heard Judge Wallace is going to throw the book at him. What a dumb-ass."

"But it's true. Everyone on that jury is ready to convict him already."

"Well, Deni, as a defense attorney, it's not very cool of me to say that he probably deserves it, but in this case I think your jury might be on to something."

"But there are a lot of questions. Like why would he be so careful to clean fingerprints off the knife and the bat, pour bleach all over the body to destroy evidence, but stupid enough to leave his jiz in her and his dirty sock in her mouth? And why would he be stupid enough to be seen in her building when he had a TRO on him?"

"And the answer is ..... I don't know. Criminals do stupid things sometimes, believe me. You've seen it, you know. And Bromley has the best lawyer that money can buy in Alex Pratt. It's her job to make you have these questions in your mind. I will say this, though. There was enough evidence of abuse to support a restraining order. She moved away from him for a reason. If the allegations are correct, which I admit is a big if, he did get physical with her on more than one occasion."

"Yeah. Seven times according to Albright. But that highly paid lawyer you're so gah-gah over just spent the better part of the day convincing us that Nichols didn't leave him, he tossed her."

"That's what she gets paid to do, Deni. You know this. What's gotten into you? Have you gone soft? He beat her up, seven times you just said, and you think he broke it off with her?"

"The vic didn't press charges for all that rough stuff, because they say it was sex gone too far."

"Or Kenneth Bromley. He has a way of making things go away."

"Maybe. Only none of the cops in those beatings actually filed a fuckin' report, Ry. If he did beat the snot out of her, if it wasn't rough sex like they claim, the Nichol's family should sue the Boston PD. Those guys let him walk every time."

"Thus another flaw in our legal system. Rich defendants don't go to prison at the same rate as the poor ones. I do what I can with pro bono work, but I have to eat too. Everybody deserves a fair shake."

"My point exactly. That's what I've been sayin'. This guy is goin' down no matter what."

"And you want my help so you can live with it. Hypothetically."

"So?"

"So I can't help you with that. It's your conscience, my friend. You've got great instincts, that's why you're good at your job. That's why I hire you."

"I've been wrong before. And recently."

"That's why you have eleven more people on the jury. And that's really all the help I can give you. I'm not on the jury, Deni. You are."

"You don't need to remind me. On another topic, how is Lisa doin' for ya? She said she's been towin' the line. You agree?"

"No complaints here. I don't have her on anything major, but yes. Is she still hounding you to make her a partner?"

"Daily."

"Well, here is where I can give you some advice. Do it. She's a worker and a damn good investigator. Most of what you do is on the computer these days, and that is certainly not your forte. I know you carry the nut on that business, but I seem to remember Jacob forking over the whole ball of wax to start this firm. I don't know where I'd be if my hard work hadn't payed off. He brought me into the fold and look where I am today."

"Fair enough. You heard from him lately?"

"Jake? No. I haven't spoken to him a long while. Jacob Grantes is a funny guy, you know that. He goes in streaks. I hear from him all the time, then nothing for just as long. Honestly, I think he's put this place and the people here behind him. Once in a blue moon he'll get nostalgic, and then he calls every few days for a couple of weeks straight and we make plans to meet, but then it goes back to the way it was. That's life I guess. I take it you haven't spoken to him?"

"Nah. Last time I talked to him he wanted to know if it was okay if Brady came to visit. Ya know, take him to the aquarium, the museum, duck boats, that kinda shit. Ani thought it'd be a hoot, but then it didn't happen. Whattaya gonna do?"

"Practice for when you two have a kid?"

"Bite ya fuckin' tongue. I got a tough enough time rememberin' to feed the dog."

"Okay, Deni. Fight it off all you want, but she's got you on the hook."

"Hey, while I'm thinkin' of it," he said to change the subject, "will you check on my place for me? I haven't been to Barstone for a couple of weeks, I hope my house is still standing."

"I'm sure it's fine, but I'll check on it."

"Thanks."

"Hey Deni?"

"Yeah. Don't overthink this one, okay? Just follow the trial and the judge's instructions."

"She told you didn't she?"

"What, that you have her investigating the case while you're empaneled on the jury? What would give you that idea?"

"She's got a big mouth."

"She's concerned about you, Deni. And so am I. Getting caught doing this, especially on a high-profile case, will really mess up your future plans for the foreseeable future. Please be careful."

"Will-do, Chief."

Deni made his third illegal call on Saturday morning, again from the confines of the motel after a sleepless night. He dared not venture out as he had on Thursday night for several reasons. First, the pipe that he tried to climb had been bent when he tried to climb back into his room and would make a ton of noise again on the way down. He was certain that the fresh bend was noticed when the bomb squad scoured the building looking for the non-existent device. That pipe with a fresh bend in it was just outside his motel window, a window which had been just as recently broken.

Additionally, security had been increased due to that phony bomb threat. While that phone call may have been ingenious at the time, it certainly created another layer of tension.

Lastly, the security detail was knocking on doors and checking in with the jurors infrequently throughout the day. Who knows when they would do so again, and if Deni was out galavanting it would mean certain incarceration.

So he called Lisa Sheed and spoke quietly into his burner phone while sitting on the john, as he did the previous night on his other phone calls.

"How are you holding up, Boss?"

"I'm going out of my fuckin' mind. There's only so many pushups, and squats I can do in this tiny motel room. What are you up to?"

"Oh, working on a Saturday. I think Reggie is going to divorce me at this rate, and we aren't even married yet. I want some time off when this is all behind us, okay? Either way. Partner or no partner, I need to make this up to her. She's my real partner. My world."

"I know. I didn't want this to happen either."

"How is Ani handling this?"

"Bummed out. We go into Chinatown every Sunday, it's like our thing. We don't miss many, but tomorrow is gonna be one of 'em. She'll get over it."

"How are you handling it?"

"I just told you, I'm losing my mind."

"I mean without her."

"I miss her. Ya know. And the dog."

"You're such a typical guy. You never talk about this stuff and just expect that the people in your life are supposed to just know how you're feeling. She needs to hear that you miss her and don't compare it to the dog. I'm sure she knows what makes you tick, but she wants you to say it. She wants you to tell her how much you miss her."

"What? I'm supposed to be some kinda fuckin' sap? I thought women like that strong, silent type?"

"Deni, she wants to marry your sorry ass. If you don't wise-up, you're going to 'strong and silent' yourself into loneliness. Get used to the misery of that motel room, because it's going to be your life if you don't get your shit together."

"With what I do for work, maybe that's the way it should be."

"I don't know how you can be so messed up in noodle from some southern babe that you knew for like two days, but you need to get over that shit. She died. She was a cop and she died. You didn't. You're alive and you need to live your life. If you love Ani, then you need to make a move or you're going to lose her too, only she's still going to be alive to rub your nose it. There, I'm off my soapbox, I said my piece."

"So I guess you got an opinion on it."

"Funny."

"Don't work too late, huh?"

"You don't want to hear what I found out for you? Isn't that the reason you called me?"

"Jesus, She. What the hell we been doing yackin' about our vaginas when we coulda been talkin' about real shit?"

"You're going to love me."

"Tell me."

"It's good."

"I swear to all that is holy, if you don't start talkin' ....."

"This guy has been relatively tame lately. Chase Bromley is a real bag of shit and he started at a young age. Only he never takes the wrap. He never stands up to what he's done, and either pays or bribes other people into falling on their swords for him. Did you know he went to college at Cornell?"

"No. That hasn't come up yet."

"Well, I don't know that it will. Ithaca PD responded to a rape allegation his freshman year. *FRESHMAN*, Deni. Freshman don't normally get that brazen. They try to fit in and not stand out as this timid little kid in a sea of adults who are learning how to think for themselves. You know what I'm saying?"

"No. I never went."

"How did you make detective if you didn't get a degree?"

"Didn't need one back then, you just had to pass the detective exam. Aren't we gettin' off track?"

"Right. Okay. Anyway ..... So this seventeen year old kid is a punk. He's rich and he's privileged and he thinks his shit doesn't stink, and this Stacy Jones apparently set him straight. So he shows her a thing or two and beats the hell out of her, but not before taking her virginity. Campus security shows up but local PD takes charge. She points the finger at Bromley but this kid David Katz gives him an alibi, and another kid, Shane Needer, steps up and says that he was the one that took her out that night. Cops are all kinds of confused and think this chick Stacy is 51-50 and are getting ready to fit her for a straight jacket."

"So look up this Stacy Jones chick. I know it's been a long time, but maybe she can come forward and along with the rest of what is happening now, she might get some sense of closure on it."

"Gee, Deni, I didn't think of that. I did look her up. Ithaca PD wasn't far off, only it was Bromley that made her crazy. Four-point-oh student spiraled into the toilet. She committed suicide six weeks later. Parents say there was a note, but that note disappeared. And that wasn't the only miracle that took place. Huge deposits were made into the financial aid office at Cornell for both David Katz and Shane Needer. Their student loans were paid off before they even finished school. Untraceable, of course, but two and two is still four, even at Cornell."

"So daddy Bromley pays the kids to keep their mouths shut and to keep the cops from figuring out what really went down."

"And it didn't end there. That was just freshman year. This kid razed the place like a goddamned viking and Kenneth Bromley funded the whole thing. Guess who got great jobs working for daddy's urban development empire straight out of college?"

"Let me guess. Katz and Needer."

"Give the man a prize. They're both still working for Daddy right here in Beantown. Chase Bromley does what he wants and to whomever he wants and nothing ever happens to him. He's fucking Teflon. Only this time he can't make it go away."

"I don't know about that, his lawyer is doing a pretty good job. All they got is circumstantial evidence at this point. A very strong circumstantial case, don't get me wrong, but no smoking gun. I was hung up on why he'd be so stupid as to leave unassailable evidence at the scene, still am if I'm bein' honest. But it fits a pattern now that I know all the shit from the past. He just doesn't care because he thinks he can get away with it."

"Well, I'm glad I could help. Now you can sit back and let the rest of the jury do the right thing," Lisa said.

"You did good, She, but keep digging. Go talk to these assholes, Katz and Needer, on Monday. See what they have to say for themselves. Stay below the radar and I'll call you to see where you're at."

"Really? Keep at it?"

"No stone unturned. And Pratt said that there was a ton of other fingerprints and DNA found on the scene, probably from all of the orgies Sloane Nichols had. See if you can't get some names to match all of that evidence. The cops had a hard-on for Bromley and never looked into any of them."

"Okay, if you say so. That is a ton of work and I'm swamped."

"See if Reggie will help you. Maybe she'll ease up on you if you are working together. Make it a family project."

"Maybe. What's the pay?"

"I don't know, you wanna be a partner? Figure it out."

"Gotcha. Maybe she'll do it for free?"

"Now you're thinkin' like a partner."

21

THE MONDAY MORNING BUS RIDE INTO DOWNTOWN WAS fueled with more bickering than on previous trips, as if it was even possible. The weekend was torturous for the jurors and none among them could hold back their resentment any longer. The bad takeout, the pseudo incarceration, the threat of being killed within that would-be prison by the still at-large bomber working for Bromley, and being kept away from their loved ones and their normal lives were all too much to bear. Witness after witness was being paraded into the courtroom to tell the same story, that Chase Bromley raped and murdered the woman who had tried to get away from him. The jury didn't need the testimony of a prostitute, current or former, to convince them of what they already knew. The trial was a colossal waste of time, as far as they were concerned. He was guilty, for the crimes he'd committed and for how they were currently being treated. He was sentenced in the minds of the people on the bus, and the defense hadn't begun to mount a case yet.

Nor would they begin on Monday, May 19. The Assistant District Attorneys, Albright and Walsh, still had another expert that they wanted to belabor their case. The dead horse needed another kick.

Doctor Fred Harris, a psychology professor emeritus and current author and lecturer, would testify as to the defendant's motive for killing Sloane Nichols in such a fashion. Since the Commonwealth didn't have a smoking gun, they felt they needed to bulk up the vast circumstantial evidence with a reestablished motive, which had suffered a few dents with the testimony of Gena Rivers on Friday.

With the shrink's testimony, the prosecution team felt that the crucial elements in their case would be proven. Access, means, and motive. The essential trifecta in sending the defendant to prison for consecutive life terms.

Albright questioned Doctor Harris, since there would be no need for the gentle sensibilities of a female as there had been with the promiscuous witness Amy questioned on Friday. In any event, the strategy was moot. The witness and the testimony rendered from her turned out to be a colossal waste, save for the additional trial experience afforded to Walsh.

"Doctor, you've written numerous publications on the psychoses of gaslighting, psychological manipulation, sexual deviance, and domination, have you not?"

"I have."

"And with respect to Chase Bromley," Albright said as he turned toward the stoic defendant, "have you formed an opinion with regard to his psychological profile?"

"I did. As I illustrated in my report—"

"—This report?" Albright held up what looked to be a bound ream of paper, which he marked for exhibit.

There was no objection from the defense.

"Yes. As I illustrated in that report, because of the defendant's privileged upbringing, his parent's eagerness to display their devotion to their only child by acquiescing to his every whim, the defendant was accustomed to getting whatever he wanted at virtually the moment he wanted it. This entitled sense and expectation of immediate gratification becomes empowering. The thirst for power is further nurtured through witnessing the immense success of his father. That type of success is therefore expected and when it can't be achieved, blame and punishment are necessary to right that wrong. It cannot be his fault, so by default it is the fault of those around him."

"And Sloane Nichols had been around him. The closest to him."

"Yes. She was his former girlfriend. The victim lived with him for several years."

"But she left him. We've heard testimony and entered into evidence the restraining order that she served on the defendant."

"And therefore the biggest of insults. He was constantly reminded of his failures, as he watched his father from the sidelines, and to have his love interest reject him ..... It would be an intolerable circumstance that would be met with retribution. When she said, 'enough', after years of both physical and sexual abuse, his mental make-up insisted that he take action. Nobody would ever reject his father, nor should anybody reject him. And so he retaliated."

"Yet some time had passed between the time she left and the time of the attack. How do you explain that, Doctor?"

"He couldn't very well pile on failure on top of failure, could he? This retaliation had to be calculated. And the manner in which that retribution was executed suggests that he needed to shame her."

"Please expound, Doctor."

"The defendant and the victim had a very sexual relationship. Sexual habits and interests are the most intimate of bonds between two people. Those who share themselves and divulge those interests are willing to offer their most personal vulnerabilities. That is why even married couples sometimes don't share their innermost desires with their spouses, seeking partners outside their marriage to fulfill those desires.

The most damaging way for Mister Bromley to expose and shame the victim was to do so with the most heinous of sexual depravity. He ensured the violation lasted as long as it did because of his need to strip her of all dignity. He wanted her to know and feel the pain that she caused him; and when he felt that he'd achieved that semblance of success, he brought about her death. He controlled her last moments, he controlled every perverse act he performed on her, he even controlled when she died. The defendant was essentially regaining what he felt she took away from him. Control."

"Thank you, Doctor." Albright went back to his seat, offering his witness for cross examination without saying as much.

Alex Pratt rose from her seat, again straightening out her attire. Today it was a silver patterned Calvin Klein Sheath Dress—rivaling Amy's from Friday—with a black BASLER three button pleated blazer covering her shoulders. She then picked up the enormous report that had been crafted by Harris from Albright's desk on the way toward the witness.

"How many times and for how long did you examine my client, Doctor Harris?"

"I didn't."

"I'm sorry, can you say that again?   I don't believe I understood you."

"I've never directly spoken with your client, Chase Bromley."

Alex dramatically dropped the heavy tome in front of the witness. The loud 'thud' echoed through the courtroom.

"This report is almost *seventeen hundred* pages, Doctor. Are you telling me that you generated all of this out of whole cloth?"

"I beg your pardon. I did not make up anything. I studied the events and evidence that was provided to me from this case, and with my vast research—"

"—Oh, I'm sorry.   You wrote this encyclopedia about my client from what the District Attorney gave you?"

"As I said—"

"—What if he gave you misinformation?   That would drastically affect your findings in this report?"

"Well, yes. But—"

"—But you couldn't actually speak to my client because an insanity plea wasn't offered, correct?"

"That's correct. My requests to examine him were denied and in fact forbidden by your office because he wasn't invoking an insanity defense."

"Because nobody is questioning his mental state, you couldn't legally examine him without his consent. Which he didn't give, correct?"

"Also correct. I believe at your insistence."

"Basically this report is merely hours upon hours of guesswork, correct? My client is as sane as anybody."

"I wouldn't go so far as to say—"

"—Your Honor, I would like this witness's testimony stricken from the record and I would ask that you instruct the jury to disregard his entire testimony. He has no direct knowledge of my client, he merely has the self-serving opinion that was spoon-fed to him by the District Attorney's office. Everything he's testified to is academic at best."

Albright stood to argue but was thwarted by Judge Wallace's ruling without hearing from him.

"I agree. Sit down Mister Albright. The witness is excused, the report is taken out of evidence, and the jury will disregard his entire testimony."

"Fantastic. That was an entire morning that we will never get back," Jordan Raines, juror six, blurted out as they entered the deliberation room for their preordered lunch. "We had to hear that gas-bag go on for three hours for nothing."

"Relax. They're probably going to rest their case, so now we move on to the defense witnesses," Deni said as he took his usual seat next to her.

Each of the jury members sat around the table in their assigned seats by juror number. It was easier for food ordering in the morning, and the delivery of that food when it arrived to insist that the jurors sit in the same spot every day at lunchtime.

Evelyn Rocher, juror number eight, leaned across Deni to speak to Jordan. Deni couldn't help but feel encroached, her white hair and elderly woman's perfume invaded his space.

"I can't help but get sick to my stomach when they describe what happened to that poor woman. To be raped is bad enough, but what she went through," Evelyn said with hand to stomach. She pushed her food away from her on the table when she leaned back into her own space.

"I get your point," Jordan said without an attempt at whispering. "But hasn't every woman been a rape victim? When you get right down to it? Not like that, but you know ..... I mean, there isn't a woman alive who hasn't had sex with someone that she really didn't want to. You're laying there knowing what a huge mistake it is, and you want out, but he's already inside you, so what are you going to do? You can't expect to cut a guy off three pumps before he finishes his business and expect that things are going to go smoothly. So you lay there and figure out a way to get rid of him so you never have to do it again."

The elderly woman looked horrified, silently making her judgements about juror six.

Deni looked at Evelyn. "I don't think she was talking about the case anymore." Then back to Jordan. "I'm not sure that's rape."

"What do you know?"

Deni rolled his eyes and looked across the table at Regan Avery, juror four. She moved forward to involve herself in the conversation.

"I think he's right. Everyone smells the morning-breath of a bad decision at some point in their life. Some more than others. Caveat emptor—buyer beware. You can't blame someone else for the decisions you made to get you where you are. If you're in bed with someone and realize at that point that it's a mistake, or when he's on top of you, you can't then call it rape. You can't Monday morning quarterback the Sunday game and blame everybody but yourself. The real question is, can you live with the repercussions of a bad decision versus surrendering to the what-ifs that will always be peering out from behind a dark and murky corner of your brain?"

Jordan looked around the deliberation room, at every face at the conference table. All eyes were on her.

"What are you a shrink? Who asked you?"

"I think this is kind of pertinent to the case, don't you?" Regan also looked around the table. "The victim, Sloane Nichols, got involved with a guy that she probably shouldn't have. He had money and obviously shared some of the same adventurous sexual appetites she had, but she stayed with him longer than she probably wanted to. She waited too long to get out and he went nuts."

"You're not saying what happened to her is her fault, are you?" Renaldo Ramos Gomez, juror number two, was nearly incensed.

"No. Of course not. But that's my point. We all make some decisions in our lives and when we look back at them, can you live with them or not? Did she deserve what she got? Absolutely not. But I'm not so sure she helped herself either."

Deni kept quiet. He knew more information about the lifestyle of Sloane Nichols than the rest of jury. The jury had heard testimony that the victim was promiscuous, that she set up profiles on various sex websites. But they didn't know with as much detail, at least not definitively. Not like Deni did. Not yet.

He knew that Nichols exposed herself to dangers that weren't widely known. Deni had seen and read the ads and profiles and the explicit pictures and language therein. Maybe those truths would be exposed by Chase Bromley's defense team, maybe not. Deni might have to divulge that information to the jury if the defense didn't, and decided to cross that bridge when and if he came to it. But for now, Deni couldn't and didn't say anything about it for fear of having to explain how he came about this knowledge, which was not legal in any sense.

Denai Moshe, Juror twelve, spoke up.

"Now wait just a damn minute, lady. Are you sayin' that if I park my car outside a store 'cuz I'm waiting for a friend to come out —with the windows down and the car runnin'—and I get car jacked, that it's MY fault? I live in Roxbury, and I know not to do that, but if I did? Is that what you sayin'?"

"No. That's not what I'm saying. Not exactly. What I'm saying is that what happened to the victim in this case is NOT her fault and is horrific and criminal. Chase Bromley should go to prison for the rest of his life, and they should throw away the key. However, if Sloane Nichols had made some different choices, she might be alive today to regret ever having called Chase Bromley her ex-boyfriend."

Sherlie Lovett, juror eleven and madam foreperson, stood and spoke at a volume louder than the escalating conversation.

"That's enough everyone. The topic is purely academic anyway, because we aren't ever going to have to make a decision on the what the victim should or shouldn't have done. We're eventually going to have to render a decision on the defendant's guilt or innocence, but not today.   We're not even supposed to be discussing it yet."

Sherlie may have had more to say, but the door to the deliberation room opened. The detritus from lunch was to be picked up by the officer who entered. Paper wrappers and cups and straws and napkins were all being pushed off the table and into a trash can along with the food leftovers, which came as a welcome interruption.

"We should be ready to go back into the courtroom in few minutes, ladies and gentlemen. You have that amount of time to use the bathroom if necessary."

22

AMANDA HUNT TOOK THE STAND IMMEDIATELY AFTER THE
lunch break. The Commonwealth did not rest their case, as Deni
had thought and shared with the rest of the jury. Instead, they chose
to add one witness, one that they had at the ready in case they
needed her. Albright and Walsh determined that they needed to
make Chase Bromley appear worse than the victim. A former
girlfriend would do the trick.

The curvy red-head made way down the aisle of the gallery,
through the gate leading to the witness chair next to Judge Wallace.
She was well-dressed in a baby blue herringbone skirt suit, the color
highlighted her hair, eyes and curves. The neckline plunged and the
nineteen inch skirt was well above the knee, the ensemble teetered
on the line between serious business and flirtatious. This would be
the prosecution's last and final witness, based upon her familiarity
with the defendant, and needed to drive the point home with the jury
that Bromley is a violent person, a monster, and had been for a long
time.

Alex Pratt and her team had known about the probable and
eventual testimony of Amanda Hunt, of course, and had objected to
her being on the witness list months prior, when the list was
compiled by ADA Walsh and sent to the high-rise office of Taylor,
Higgs & Pratt. The argument for Hunt being taken off the list of
potential witnesses was because her testimony was hearsay and
would be prejudicial to the jury. This was another one of the pretrial
motions that was lost by the defense.

But that didn't stop Pratt from standing to object in one last-
ditch effort to preclude her testimony. As Amanda Hunt worked the

runway toward her seat, front and center, Alex raised her objection in front of the jury.

"I renew my objection to this witness, Judge. Her testimony is prejudicial and outweighs any probative value. When we deposed her in preparing for trial, she admitted to having no knowledge of any of the events that took place on the date of murder, nor any knowledge of the relationship between my client and the victim. She can only testify as to events that took place between them, during the course of their relationship. What happened between them may or may not have taken place between the victim and my client. Additionally, her testimony could be completely fabricated as there is a history of animosity between the witness and my client, which I submit is the real motive for testifying here today."

"Prior bad acts, your Honor," Albright said. "The witness will testify to a pattern of behavior consistent with the crimes against the victim. You've already ruled on this."

Judge Wallace nodded.

"Indeed I did. Objection is overruled but noted. The witness will testify, and the defense can inquire as to the veracity of her statements in cross. But don't stray too far, Mister Albright, we've already spent the morning with disregarded testimony and I don't wish to repeat it."

"Thank You."

Alex Hunt was sworn in and took her seat. Albright then began his questioning.

"Miss Hunt. You are familiar with the defendant, Chase Bromley, correct?"

"Yes."

"And how do you know him?"

"He is my ex-boyfriend."

"We've heard testimony that Sloane Nichols was his ex-girlfriend."

"I lived with Chase before her."

"I see," Albright said. "How long did you live with him prior to your separation?"

"About two years."

"And did you move in with him right away, or did you two see each other for a period of time before you decided to move in with him?"

"I saw him for about a year before I moved into his brownstone. But we weren't serious."

"You moved in with him, but you weren't serious? What does that mean, that you both saw other people?"

"*HE* saw other people. I said it was them or me, and he chose me. He wanted me to move in with him to prove that it was over with the other women."

"Which made you happy?"

"For a time."

"When did you realize that moving in with him was a mistake?"

"Objection. Leading. She never said it was a mistake," Pratt stood.

"Sustained."

"I'll rephrase. How long after you moved in with him did you become unhappy?"

"Objection, your Honor. She didn't say she was unhappy."

"I asked if moving in with him made her happy, and she said, 'for a time'." Albright opened his exaggeratedly opened his arms. "Meaning that she became unhappy at some point. It's common sense, Judge."

"Sustained. Rephrase or move on."

Albright had made his point, so he moved on after taking a beat to let his point linger with the jury.

"Were you ever intimate with the defendant?"

"Yes."

"And what, if any, peculiarities did he have in that regard?"

"Objection—"

"—Preferences. If Miss Pratt has an issue with the word, 'peculiarities', I can use 'preferences' if it makes her feel better."

Alex sat down and Albright turned back to his witness.

"Were there any sexual *preferences* that the defendant asked of you?"

187

"Yes. Several."

"As uncomfortable as they may be, can you please tell us about them?"

"He was very aggressive. He always had be in control. Sex was always his way. If he wanted to do something, that's what we did. If I wanted it a certain way, or if I asked him to do a certain thing, he would ignore it and do what he wanted unless it was his idea. Same for if I didn't want to do something. If it wasn't his idea, or if he wasn't into it at that moment, we didn't do it. It wasn't like that before."

"Before?"

"Before I moved in. He was everything I wanted before I moved in, except for his openly dating other women. Rich, Good-looking. Doting ..... But the attentiveness changed after I moved in. I guess he did those other things to the other women."

"Objection. Speculation."

"Sustained."

"What do you mean by 'other things'?"

She looked at Judge Wallace. "Do I have to say?"

"Yes, Miss Hunt. Please answer."

There was a long pause. She looked uncomfortable and yet was milking the spotlight at the same time.

Albright grew tired of waiting for his answer.

"Miss Hunt, What did you mean by other things? What changed about your relationship after you decided to move in with the defendant?"

"Like I said. He was aggressive and controlling. Sex became more rough. Anal. Large toys. Fisting. I had to use a safe word, and even then ....."

"And even then?"

"And even then, if he didn't feel like stopping, he didn't stop."

"Can you tell us what you mean by aggressive? Can you expound on that please? I know it's uncomfortable, but it is very important that we hear what he did in that regard."

"Objection. Asked and answered."

"I'd like the witness to expound upon her testimony. While those sex acts might be abhorrent to some, it might not be to others. I'd like for her to explain how she felt to the jury," Albright defended.

"Get where you're going quickly, Counselor. This is a courtroom not Penthouse Forum."

"Thank you. Miss Hunt?"

"He liked it rough. He said that there was pleasure in pain. He liked to push the envelope to see how far he could go with me. With how much pain I could take. He said that if I let myself go and embraced the pain, when it stopped it would be euphoric. But he didn't like pain. It was always me."

"Explain that please."

Alex Pratt stood to object but was waved off by Wallace before a word was uttered.

"It started with handcuffs and slapping. Then it escalated to whips and paddles. I was getting some pretty severe bruises, but it didn't stop. Chase kept getting more aggressive, more invasive. He brought home these big dildos and he liked to use them on me. These things were enormous. I was getting abdominal and intestinal pains from how deeply they went inside me. We used to watch pornography together and I've never seen a penis even close to the size of the things that he stuck inside me. At first I refused, but he said that he would be gentle. He just wanted to see how they felt. I tried to give one to him in the anus, so he'd know how it felt, but he went insane."

"Objection. The witness isn't qualified to testify as to the defendant's mental state."

"Sustained."

"Can you clarify your last statement?"

"When I said that I would try it, he was gentle at first. So I agreed to try it again when I was handcuffed because it really got him off. But then it got much worse, he would take these things and shove them inside me. He just kept jamming them into me trying to see how far they would go? I don't know. They were really long and wide and painful. He pushed one into my anus, and the other in my vagina while I performed oral sex on him. He said that watching me be 'air-tight' made him really hard. My safe word was 'apple'. Every time I would try to scream 'apple' he would put himself in my mouth so he couldn't hear the word. One time I tried to put the big blue one into his anus, so he would understand that while it might make him really hard, it really really hurt me. He got so mad. Chase ripped it out of my hand and beat me with it."

"He raped you with it?"

"Objection. The witness never said she was raped."

"Sustained.

"Was that the only time he was violent?"

"He did that to me many times. It got more violent each time. I tried to understand it. I tried to go along with it because he enjoyed it. That's what you do for the person you love, right? But then he started choking me. It's difficult to say 'apple' with a penis in your mouth, but it's impossible when you're being choked. Light choking became choking me out. I passed out and would come to with all of these things stuck in me. He left them in me after he was finished. I'd be tied up and he'd be in the living room watching TV or playing a video game."

"Did you ever ask him to stop?"

"*EVERY* time. If I could. It would escalate every time, each time getting worse and more painful than the time before. I'd tell him enough, say the safe word, and he would keep right on. I wanted to go see a counselor. You know, like a sex therapist or something. But he refused. He said that a healthy and experimental sex life was important. I finally realized that I had to leave."

"Thank you," Albright said to Amanda Hunt. On his way back to his seat he said, "Your witness," to Alex Pratt.

"You dated my client for three years, correct? One year before you moved in with him, then two years together in the brownstone?"

"Yes."

"So your sex life was so intolerable, that you stayed with him for three years?"

"It didn't start out like that."

"Oh yeah, right, I forgot. You testified that it got bad after you moved in with him."

"Right."

"And you lived with him for two years?"

"Well, yes, but—"

"—Your sex life was so intolerable, that you stayed with him for two years."

"I didn't have anywhere to go. I moved out of my apartment when I moved in with him," Amanda said. She began shifting in her seat on the witness stand.

"Didn't you leave because he refused to marry you?"

"No. Not only that."

"Are you married now?"

"I'm engaged," Amanda said. She proudly showed her engagement ring to the courtroom. When the jury seemed to have had their fill, she showed the judge. Even those with bad eyesight could see the diamond from a distance. It was big and shiny and, if it was real, it was real expensive.

"Wow. That's a big rock," Alex exaggerated for effect.

"He loves me."

"Does your fiancé do any of those sexual things you described earlier to you?"

"Objection." Albright was on his feet.

"Goes to credibility. He put her sex life in play," Pratt said.

"Overruled. But you're on a short leash also, Counselor. Make your point quickly."

Alex turned back to the blushing red head. Her face and neck were beginning to match her hair.

"How about it, Miss Hunt. Does your fiancé do any of those sexual things you described earlier to you?"

"No. Not like that, no."

"What do you mean, 'not like that'? Does he do some or all of those things, yes or no?"

"Some of them, yes. But not like Chase did."

"Does he like you to do things that you would prefer not to do?"

"No," Amanda said defiantly. "I love him. My preference is to make him happy."

"Like you did for Chase."

"No."

"Then why stick it out for two years?   You saw a golden goose, and if he liked some kinky stuff, well then that was just the price to pay for the good life, right?"

"No. I'm not like that."

"Like what? A whore?"

"*OBJECTION!* That's uncalled for, your Honor."

"Sustained," Wallace said. "Counselor—"

"—I'm sorry, Judge. I got carried away. Miss Hunt, do you currently work?"

"No."

"So your fiancé supports you?"

"He has plenty of money. I don't have to work. I stay at home. When we have kids—"

"—You're basically a homemaker without the kids?"

"He travels all of the time for work. He's not home as often as I'd like. He likes me to stay home and take care of his condo while he's away."

"So you're a maid?"

Amanda looked disgusted and insulted.

"We have a maid."

"A cook?"

"We have a chef."

"*WE* huh? Sounds nice."

"It is. Very."

"And you like that lifestyle? Having 'plenty of money'?"

"Who wouldn't?"

"—And Chase Bromley is from a prominent family with 'plenty of money' also, meaning you wouldn't have had to work if you'd married him, correct?"

"I don't know."

"Did you work in the two years that you lived with him in his brownstone?"

"Well, no."

"A year before that? When you had your apartment?"

"For a while. Then Chase ....."

"Then Chase, what? Paid for your apartment and all of your living expenses?"

Amanda shrugged.

"The court stenographer has to write down what you say, dear. You have to actually say the words 'yes he paid for everything and I haven't had to work in a very long time'."

"Objection."

"Sustained. But the witness will answer."

"He paid my bills, yes. I felt bad, so I moved in to save him money."

"How nice of you," Alex said then immediately raised her hands knowing an objection was imminent. "Withdrawn."

"So you let him do those things to you, Miss Hunt? The things that he allegedly preferred and you supposedly didn't enjoy, for over two years, because you didn't want to have to work?"

"Absolutely not."

"When did you start seeing your current fiancé? Immediately after leaving Chase?"

"Yes, but you're twisting—"

"—I'm not twisting anything. These are the facts. You're angry with my client because he wouldn't marry you. When you finally realized that, you found another golden goose to support your lifestyle. You were perfectly willing to do whatever sexual act my client allegedly preferred as long as you were provided for in the elevated custom that you thought you deserved. But when that was put in jeopardy, because he wouldn't put an enormous ring on your finger like the one you have now, you had to find someone else. My client, the man who scorned you, has been accused of crimes, crimes that he didn't commit, and you now have an opportunity for revenge. Is that why you're testifying here today?"

"No, I'm telling you the truth."

"Did you follow this case in the news?"

"Of course. It was everywhere. Papers, TV ..... Everywhere."

"So you knew about the restraints and the bat the killer used on Sloane Nichols and concocted these allegations of things he 'used to do to you' as a way of getting back at him. Correct?"

"No, he used to do those things to me."

"Did you ever call the police?"

"His father—"

"—I'll take that as a 'NO'. Tell a friend?"

"Well, no, but—"

"—So nobody can corroborate your story that all of these things happened against your will? Did you two have other partners involved in your sexual relations?"

"No, I didn't have somebody come watch us. Sex is private."

"Not for Sloane and Chase it wasn't. They invited other people into their bed all of the time and yet none of them are saying what you've said."

"I'm telling the truth."

Alex Pratt turned to the jury, scanning the faces of each member.

"I think we all see the truth, Miss Hunt."

23

ALEX PRATT'S FIRST ORDER OF BUSINESS ON TUESDAY morning, at the recommencement of trial, was to ask the judge to dismiss the case against her client. The Commonwealth rested its case against her client, Chase Bromley, at the conclusion of Amanda Hunt's testimony, after opting not to redirect. Instead of looking weak, asking more questions on Monday in an effort to control the amount of damage Alexandria Pratt inflicted upon their case, Albright stated to the courtroom that he'd finished presenting the facts against the defendant.

Pratt's contention was that Albright and Walsh, on behalf of the Commonwealth of Massachusetts, didn't meet their burden of proof and requested a dismissal with prejudice. This is done by every defense attorney in virtually every criminal case. It's an unwritten rule. The counsel for the accused invariably claim that the prosecution hasn't proven their prima facie case, and in this case what the Commonwealth claims to have happened has not been proven to the extent of meeting the burden of proof threshold. Should the judge agree and dismiss the case, which happens with the same rarity as winning the lottery, double jeopardy is attached and the defendant cannot be retried for the same set of crimes.

Judge Wallace, of course, just as routinely denied the motion to dismiss the case, as was expected, which brought about Pratt's next order of business. Her opening statement.

The defense attorney waived her opening statement when it was supposed to have been given, after Albright's on the first day of the trial. Through a technicality in the language of the Commonwealth of Massachusetts Criminal Court Procedure guidelines, Alex Pratt won the right to preview the defense's case immediately before she began to present it. That time was a week into the trial, on Tuesday, May 20.

Alex donned yet another business suit from her vast closet, this particular day was an ensemble in shades of royal blue. Her Calvin Klein speckled pencil skirt and matching sleeveless cowl neck blouse by Tahari Arthur S. Levine were both partially covered by an Anne Klein one-button blazer. The five inch Jimmy Choo Anouk suede pointy toe pumps added height, making her taller than her prosecutorial counterpart. It was one of her 'performance' suits. She had a few choices, classified as such for the opening and closing monologues she gave to juries. The suits made a statement. The garments said that she was trustworthy. That she was well put together, honest, and that she knew what she was talking about. That she was good at her job. She stood tall and proud and on the side of righteousness.

Women loved her fashion because they wanted it. Men loved the attire because it was flattering. Alex Pratt had a track record for success, her ability to litigate was only part of it. The way she looked and carried herself was just as important. She spent a great deal of time and money to look the way she did. Her look begat confidence. And confidence wins trials.

"Ladies and gentlemen of the jury, the Assistant District Attorneys, Albright and Walsh, have rested their case. That means that every piece of evidence that they have at their disposal; through medical evidence, forensic evidence, physical evidence, and all of the witnesses that they have presented, the exhibits that you looked at, are the sum total of their case against my client, Chase Bromley.

Let's go back to the beginning of the trial. Mister Albright said that he would prove that my client was guilty of the brutal rape and murder of the victim, Sloane Nichols. As if there are nice ways to rape and murder someone. I intend to look at that right now with you.

I am in no way denying that Sloane Nichols was violated, at length, and tortured for hours upon hours before her killer unmercifully finished the job. How can I? Scientific evidence proves this. The pictures and the bat and the testimony from experts are undeniable. Sloane Nichols is dead for a reason.

The prosecution wants you to believe that my client, Chase Bromley, is that reason. That he is responsible for her death.

Why? Because they didn't investigate any other suspect. This defendant is one of convenience.

Yes, he used to date her.

Yes, they lived together at one time.

Yes, they had fights, just like any couple.

And sometimes those fights escalated to a point that is regrettable. Like some of the fights that either you or I might get into. And just like we would probably say, Chase Bromley and Sloane Nichols had one too many of those fights.

Some people fight about money. I yell at my boyfriend because he's a slob."

The jury was allowed to chuckle for a beat.

"Their fights were about sex. Rough sex, multiple partners, orgies ..... The victim placed profiles on sex websites, basically sexual advertisements, to attract other partners behind my client's back. So they fought. And they fought. And he eventually told her to leave. It was a veiled threat to get her to stop.

But she didn't.

And she left. Sloane Nichols left and filed a temporary restraining order. One that wasn't violated for months after she filed it.

None of these facts are disputed. But that doesn't make my client a murderer. It certainly doesn't make him a rapist."

Alex pointed to the prosecutor's table as she moved around the floor in front of the jury, prosecutor's table and judge. She used the space to command attention. She had it.

"They would have you believe that he is both of those things because they shocked you and horrified you with pictures and stories from a gold-digging, scorned ex-girlfriend. And a softball bat. And a knife. And the circumstantial evidence of my client being in Sloane Nichols' building. And because they had sex at some point before her violation and murder."

She moved back toward the jury.

"Should he have been there?

Legally? ..... No, not by the letter of the law. Spirit of the law is debatable.

His decision to violate the TRO is lamentable, because he was invited there. Chase and Sloane were back on good terms. Such good terms that the victim invited him into her apartment and into her bed. They had sexual chemistry. They shared the same appetites, ones that Miss Nichols couldn't satiate from the numerous conquests she'd sought through all of the adult mating websites.

The only thing that the Commonwealth of Massachusetts has proven beyond a reasonable doubt, is that the victim was victimized. They have proven that she is dead and her last hours on this earth were some of the most horrible that a person can imagine, made so by her tormentor. They will get no argument from me on that front."

She slowly paced back and forth in front of the jurists. Making eye contact at the right times, looking around the courtroom at others.

"But they haven't proven who that tormentor is. Not by a long shot.

Just because he was in the building, because he'd had unprotected sexual relations with his ex-girlfriend, the police stopped investigating. They had their man.

But they didn't.

The timeline is off. Chase was seen entering the building eighteen to twenty hours before her throat was cut, according to the Medical Examiner. So did my client enter into Sloane's apartment, hang out for six to eight hours, *then* start abusing her?

Of course not.

He had sex with the victim, left her apartment, and somebody else came hours later. That person is who the police should have been—and still should be—looking for.

We intend to prove that Sloane Nichols was a victim because of her risky lifestyle. We're not saying that she deserved it, we aren't even insinuating it. What we are saying, what I'm saying on behalf of my client, is that she created profiles—sexual advertisements—to attain partners in potentially dangerous sexual acts.

Further adding to her risk, was her addiction to drugs, specifically valium. You've heard from their witnesses. Their ME, their detectives, the Crime Scene Unit. A multitude of drugs were found in her system yet none were found in her apartment.

The prosecution won't argue these facts. Because they can't.

There was no forced entry into her apartment, which indicates at the very least that she expected her killer, and likely knew him.

Was he there to sell her drugs? For sex?

We don't know because the police stopped investigating.

Her lifestyle is not one that I would choose. It may or may not be one that you would choose," she said, again making eye contact with as many members of the jury as possible. "Because it's risky. It's dangerous. But I'm not blaming her.

As I said, Sloane Nichols had many sexual partners because of the many profiles she posted on various websites. We could show them to you, but what is the point? Why drag the victim's name through the mud. She's dead. But you do need to understand that some of her conquests she engaged with more than once, some in groups, some not. In these conquests, there were restraints and paraphernalia that could be dangerous and put her at significant risk. The victim invited strangers into her apartment to engage in these risky behaviors for her own sexual satisfaction.

Any one of those partners could have raped and murdered her.

Because it wasn't my client. It wasn't Chase Bromley who betrayed her. He loved her. He wanted her back. He never wanted her to leave in the first place. She might have even wanted him back, we will never know what was in her heart.

Yes, he went into her building at her request. And yes, he engaged in the sex acts that the two engaged in for years prior to their separation. Again, at her request. What would you have done? The person you love invites you to reconnect, and so you do. They made love in the familiar way that they used to. Maybe not the way you or I do with our partners. But it's not illegal. It was consensual and took place hours before the real murderer entered the victim's apartment."

Alex took a long look at the jury for one final time. She paused to ensure that she not only said what she wanted to say, but that the jury had listened to it. That they truly heard her, and God willing, bought into it.

"After we present our case, you will have no choice but to demand real justice. You will have no choice but to send the police out to investigate who actually committed these crimes against Sloane Nichols. You will have no choice but to render a verdict in favor of my client, Chase Bromley. A verdict of Not-Guilty.

Because he isn't.

Thank you."

24

IN LIEU OF USING THE TUESDAY LUNCH BREAK FOR A
meal, the defense team gathered in a vacant conference room on
the first floor of the courthouse.

Bromley complained that he was hungry, telling his defense
team that he would just go out and get his own lunch, but was
thwarted in his effort at sustenance.

"You can't go out there and risk being accosted by the media
on your own. I'll buy you the biggest steak you can eat at Abe &
Louie's if you just sit down and shut up," Alex told him.

She was stressed and everyone in the small conference room
knew it.

The hour was used as a strategy session and to discuss how
impactful Alex Pratt's opening statement was, or if it had any impact
at all. If even part of what the idiot and former juror, Jamar Dubone,
had said was true, the majority if not all of the jury was ready to
throw their client into a cage and throw away the key. If she didn't
win over any members of the jury, the only way Chase Bromley
would come out of prison would be in a bag.

She had a rock-solid case for an appeal, but it simply
couldn't get that far. Moving forward with the trial when the jury was
compromised was an error on the judge's part, she was convinced
of it. The likelihood, however, of winning this or any appeal was slim
at best. Judges don't like to second-guess other judges, nor the
unanimous verdict of a jury. In the improbable event that she did win
an appeal, she'd win the right to have to try the case all over again,
only to have to go win over another jury.

Max, Ben, and Jack sat around the table while Alex did laps
around the table in her opening statement attire. She was still

commanding attention, necks hurt as they followed her. The client slumped in a chair in the corner, making his feelings known through body language.

Nobody on the defense team had any illusions about theres' being an uphill battle. What they were meeting to decide was if lead counsel's opening statement—in the middle of the trial—had decreased the size of that hill, and how to flatten it moving forward.

The jury consultant, Max Courtland, thought it about as successful as the team could have hoped. He seemed the most positive about their mini 'state of the union'.

"You definitely made a dent. I mean, you made your mark. Some of the jurors were nodding their heads. Some taking notes. If you've already made up your mind, you aren't listening. You aren't writing things down to discuss or to contemplate later."

"All I need is one," Alex said.

"One just gets you a hung jury. A mistrial," Jack said. "You'd have to try this case all over again."

Alex looked at the youngster like he was an idiot.

"You're right," Kevin said. "But would the DA's office choose to try this case again? Would we get a more beneficial jury? I mean if he can't get a conviction with a jury that was predisposed to find him guilty? Who knows? With one juror, we live to fight another day —if we have to."

"They might feel bad for her, but they probably don't like her," Max said.

"I'm not sure making a villain out of the victim is the wisest choice," Kevin interjected. "I've been saying that from the beginning. They see those photos and hear all of the medical testimony and the jury feels for her. Who wouldn't? You'd have to be one cold bastard not to feel empathy for her. You're right, Max, they might not like her but to have the attorney of the person who is accused of doing all of that damage say, 'it's her own damn fault' doesn't play."

"Kevin, were you not in the room when I said that she didn't deserve half of what she got? That I didn't blame her? I meant it.

No matter what fucked-up decision a person makes, they don't deserve to be violated in every orifice and then nearly decapitated."

"Agreed. Just make sure that while you're saying she opened the door, you're also telling the jury that you want to have whomever did it, to pay for it."

"I think she did that, Kevin," Max said. "She's a partner at the largest law firm in New England, she knows what she's doing. And I saw the jury. I know we have at least one."

This caught Jack Elders, the youngest of the team, by surprise.

"Really? Who?"

"Number seven. The investigator. The ex-cop." He flipped through a file folder. "Dennihan. Warren Dennihan."

"There is no way that you know that," Kevin interjected.

"I have a seven figure salary for a reason. I know how to read a jury. He's not convinced that Chase did it, which is great for us. He hates him, but he's not convinced."

Chase was seated at one end of the conference table, a smile began to form but he remained silent.

"Don't get cocky," Alex said. "We've got a long way to go. I just told twelve people that you loved her and that you were close to reconciling. Putting you on the stand is a big-fat risk, one that I'm not sure we should take. But if we need you, you better be ready. That Albright is going to come at you with a blazing bazooka."

"I'll be ready. I want to testify. I'm telling the truth," Bromley said.

"I won't put you on the stand unless we have to, but we may have to. I can't knowingly suborn perjury or I'll be disbarred at the very least. Whether you did it or not, they can't prove that you did it with the evidence they've presented. So you damn-well better know that he's going to ask you on the stand. Albright will flat-out ask you if you did it, and if you have that shit-eating grin on your face like you have right now, you're toast. He's going to try to trip you up when he cross-examines you and there's only so much I can do to protect you. Don't tell them a provable lie or they will bury you. Take a valium if you have to, but whatever you do—*STAY CALM.*"

Again, Elders was taken by surprise.

"Was that a joke?"

"The valium thing? Yes. Mostly."

"I meant he's not going to testifying today is he?"

Alex rolled her eyes.

"No. I just want to be sure he knows the score going in."

Kevin was seated next to Jack and leaned toward him.

"The first witness is the psych professor from Columbia, remember?"

"Yeah. Right. That's what I thought. That's what we discussed."

"That's what *WE* discussed, Jack. You're hear to listen and learn. Ask a question if you need to, but remember there is such a thing as a stupid question," Alex said.

Kevin leaned in again.

"Don't take it personally, she's stressed out. If you have a question, write it down and ask me later."

The young attorney nodded.

"We start with the shrink, then put Chase on the stand. After that, I'll call up a few of the people that responded to the profiles online and had sex with Nichols. Kevin, be ready with rebuttal witnesses in case Chase tanks his testimony or one of the sex fiends lies on the stand. And we're going to need some high-profile character witnesses."

"Will do."

"And that really should do it. That really should be enough to get our verdict."

"If nothing else, you've got a hanger," Courtland added.

"Let's not bank on a hung jury, Max."

"I'm just saying, Alex, you've got one in the bag right now."

"You really like seven that much?"

"You're going to want to name your babies after me when he hangs this thing. He might even turn the rest of the jury our way. I called him from the jump. He's tough and nobody is going to sway him. You win him, you'll hang at the very least. If we convince him enough, he'll swing it our way."

"I don't know. Who's the foreperson?"

"Eleven," Max said as he flipped through the file again. "Sherlie Lovett. HR Exec. She's a politically correct nightmare, but a prude. She could be persuaded to see all this sexual deviance as just desserts for the vic, but right now she hates Chase." He looked at their client at the end of the table. "Sorry Pal. Just calling it like I see it."

He shrugged it off like he was used to it.

"My money is on seven. When in doubt, focus on convincing him. Trust me."

"Okay," Alex said. She looked at Kevin who nodded in agreement.

"We focus on seven."

25

DOCTOR ELIZABETH BAXTER, A TENURED PSYCHOLOGY professor from the preeminent Columbia University—and experienced trial expert for-hire when a published shrink was needed—took the stand on Wednesday, May 21. She was the first witness for the defense and the only person to take the stand that day.

The good doctor carried herself with an air of superiority, not just in the courtroom but on a daily basis, in any given situation. She was, after all, an expert in the field of the human brain and behavioral science. She knew why people acted the way they did, what neurons and synapses were firing to produce the chemical reactions that manifested into human behavior. She felt God-like in her knowledge of how to identify, explain, and treat all forms of psychological deviance.

Elizabeth Baxter walked down the aisle toward the witness stand after her name was announced to Judge Wallace by lead defense counsel, Alexandria Pratt. The full-figured expert donned a red Julien Macdonald dress with an empire waist to push her form up and out, strutting her stuff with chin high and hips swaying between the empty pews toward her perch.

After undergoing the ritualistic formalities that come with being a witness in a courtroom, Doctor Baxter took her seat and waited for Alex to approach both her and the jury to her left. None of the questions that would be posed to her from the defense attorney would come as a surprise, as all questions had been forwarded to her far in advance by Alex's underling, Jack Elders. Baxter could have both asked the list of questions herself and answered them, if such protocol was allowed in a court of law.

Witnesses are always prepared by the side of the aisle that calls upon them, for the good of both parties in the Q&A. Lawyers want to know with a high degree of certainty what their witness will say before they say it, and testimony that seems shaky comes off as untrue. A prepared witness is the most beneficial one. This particular witness was not only prepared but had also been apprised of how important her testimony would be for the defendant. While her natural confidence was desired, it was essential for Chase Bromley's defense.

Pratt's only concern with Doctor Baxter's upcoming testimony was if she would come off as *too* arrogant for the jury. She decided to take things slowly and watch both her witness and her consultant, Max Courtland, to gauge the jury's buy-in. The first few questions set up a foundation for the remainder of Baxter's assertions, getting her pedigree information out of the way.

" ..... And as a renowned psychologist, you have experience in identifying and treating what would be considered mental disorders, correct?"

"I have taught, lectured, and published about virtually every mental disorder in the DSM."

"DSM?"

"Diagnostic and Statistical Manual for mental disorders. It is considered *the* published authority on the subject. The manual is consulted both in the US and internationally. It is psychiatry's bible and sets the legal standards for dealing with crimes committed by persons with a mental disorder," Baxter explained while the attorney picked up a copy of the thick manual for the jury to see. Alex offered it into evidence before allowing the witness to proceed, as prepared.

"I've been involved with several research projects where the results have been incorporated into the DSM. I've published my own findings from various patients I've treated, some of which have been the basis for manual updates as well as grants that have been issued for other studies. I have written as many books about the human brain as I have years of teaching at Columbia."

"You are so widely respected in your field, Doctor, that you have testified in many trials and been consulted by a litany of police forces for psychological profiling, is that correct?"

"I have testified as an expert witness in more than two dozen criminal trials and have crafted nearly a hundred profiles for investigators all over the country, ranging from local police to the FBI. I was even asked to consult for Scotland Yard but I had an unfortunate scheduling conflict."

She said, "shed-yuling" like a Brit in order to achieve some levity. A few chuckles were all that could be mustered from the room, and may have been more out of pity.

Albright stood.

"Your Honor, we stipulate to the witness's expertise if it would speed up the process and cease the redundant patting herself on the back for her achievements."

"I'm laying a foundation your Honor. I'll connect if I'm afforded some latitude."

"Overruled."

Alex looked to Max Courtland who was seated in the same chair behind the defense table that he'd taken up for the entire trial to date. He slightly nodded his head, indicating to lead counsel that if the jury hadn't bought into the fact that their witness was an expert by her own testimony, the prosecutor's stipulation sealed the deal. The witness may or may not be well-liked by the conclusion of her testimony, but she would be well-respected, which was the ultimate goal when all was said and done.

"Did you have the opportunity to examine my client, Chase Bromley?"

"I did. Over the course of several weeks, I met with him for three-hour increments, once or twice per week. Eight sessions in total."

"And what, if any, conclusions did you have with regard to his mental state?"

Doctor Baxter looked to Bromley and then back at Alex Pratt.

"Since he waived his right to doctor-patient privilege with regard to this case, I can say that he is no more dysfunctional than any of us."

"Can you further explain that statement please, I'm afraid I don't understand."

"Every human being has a complex network of electrical signals, if you will, which fire off at millions of times per second in various parts of the brain. Those firings create chemical reactions within the brain that motivate us to respond in the way that we do. No two people react *exactly* the same way—even with similar brain functioning. Past experiences create neurological pathways or highways which recreate like responses."

Alex could see that the doctor was beginning to lose some of the jury members, confirmed by Max's signaling.

"Maybe you could simplify what you mean. I don't know about the jury, but you lost me with 'neurological pathways'."

"Of course. I apologize," Baxter said like she was used to speaking with intellectual inferiors. "Let me rephrase. It's like the roadways we drive every day. We have back roads and highways and interstates and turnpikes all over this nation of ours. There are a seemingly infinite number of ways to get from point A to point B, but each of us have a preferred way in which we like to travel if we have taken that same journey before. If we haven't, we tend to forge our way through it and remember how we did it for the next time, unless we got lost or learn a better route."

She again achieved a few chuckles from the same individuals who found her previous pun semi-funny. She paused for the lackluster effect.

"But once that preference to drive that route has been forged, we tend to take that route each and every time we need to.

That is what I mean by pathways. As a person gets older and has had a wide variety of experiences, the brain gets used to dealing with that set of problems and solves it with increasing ease by using those preferred pathways. But yours are not like mine. And a third person's might be another way altogether.

The DSM, as I mentioned earlier, sets the standard for a spectrum of what we will call *acceptable pathways*, for the sake of simplicity. Basically, if the brain reacts to a certain set of problems— on a forged highway or one that has to be built because the situation is new to that person—in a way that doesn't cause harm to another person, it is typically considered acceptable behavior. Whether it turns out to be a mistake or if it was the correct decision, either way, as long as it doesn't hurt anyone else, it's generally acceptable. Meaning *NOT* criminal."

Alex took a beat, letting the explanation linger in the air.

"Hmm. Could you give an example?"

"Of Course. There are millions of examples. But since we are discussing your client, let's put in the context of sexual intercourse."

"Go on."

"When we have sex for the first time, the situation is new and we have to sort of fumble through it."

Baxter gained more laughter than she had previously. She soaked it up, milking it for all she could.

"But once we do it a few times, our brains create pathways to attain the goal of achieving an orgasm. We have certain preferences. We have certain movements that our brain tells us will get us the pleasure we desire. That is why couples who have been together for a period of time will sometimes get the feeling of being bored with sex from their partner. Our brains have those pathways and we just go on autopilot to get to the orgasm. We know what works, so we stick with it.

According to the DSM, none of what we do in terms of sex is considered illegal unless; there is an unwilling or an unknowing participant, are under a certain age to give that consent, or—and this can be argued on whether it should or shouldn't be illegal in another discussion—if one of the two people involved is being paid. What might be considered sexually deviant to one person, might be vanilla to the next.

Your client, Chase Bromley, doesn't achieve sexual pleasure the way most people do."

"Does that make him a criminal, Doctor?"

"No. Not unless his behavior is outside the aforementioned guidelines. If he is engaging in behavior that is consensual with his partner or partners, no. It may seem repugnant to some, but it's not criminal per se. It could be argued that it's abnormal, but not criminal.

Sex is not something that is cookie-cutter. Homosexuality, bi-sexuality, dominance, submission ..... All of these things were either taboo or illegal or considered deviant, even in the DSM, until relatively recently. Some people still feel that way. But again, that is a different discussion.

Chase Bromley gets pleasure through dominance, through creating new neurological pathways by creating different experiences."

Alex turned to the jury but continued to question Doctor Baxter.

"Different experiences? You mean different types of sex acts?"

"Yes. And different stimuli, such as pain. It will always come back to dominance at some point with him, he has to be in control of those new experiences. Any partner who chooses to enter into a sexual liaison with Chase Bromley, has to get the same level of pleasure, only through submission."

"How about necrophilia?"

"With Chase? No. He cannot assert his dominance over someone who is dead or comatose. He wouldn't be aroused by someone who couldn't succumb to his puissance or give the semblance of not wanting it. What you described, necrophilia, would be considered illegal, by the way, and is covered in the DSM. Someone who is deceased cannot obviously give consent, which is therefore illegal."

"So he's not a necrophiliac, is he a compulsive rapist?" Pratt was proactively taking the teeth out of any argument Albright would have on cross.

"No. Raping someone would pose a threat to himself. A woman who was actually being raped would presumably fight back, which would endanger himself. Chase Bromley has led a life of privilege. Spoiled and coddled. He wouldn't want to put himself in actual harm, he just wants whatever he wants and expects others to acquiesce. Your client likes to act out fantasies of raping someone, but needs a willing participant in his role play. Any attempt to fight him off would simply be acting or he would instantly lose interest. No real threat."

"Am I to understand that he's also lazy?"

"To a certain degree. He has, in psychological terms, the sexual deviation known as preferential dominance. As I indicated, he has to be in control, be it sex or any other facet of his life. Rape is just a sexual role playing that he prefers as part of his preferential dominance."

"Let me get this straight. My client has to pretend to be raping his partner in order to achieve sexual pleasure?"

The defendant was getting visibly uncomfortable. Stoic was no longer an option for him. Chase remained silent but his sexual preferences and mental state being paraded in front of strangers for the world to see was more than unsettling. He didn't want to die in prison, but he didn't want the world to know his most private thoughts and desires either.

"That is also incorrect. That is his *preference*. From every report I've seen from his primary care physician, he is a healthy male with normal blood-flow, a healthy prostate, and can achieve an erection without the need for any chemical enhancement."

"Like Viagra."

"Or Cialis or any other medicine for males with erectile dysfunction. He finds sex appetizing. Women, men, groups ..... He simply prefers to act out fantasies which cater to his preferential dominance. He can have what some might call regular sex, meaning his sex drive can be reconditioned for a more conventional type of liaison if he couldn't find a willing participant, but he would prefer to be with someone who prefers to be sexually dominated. A submissive. Someone who enjoys the *fantasy* of being raped."

Alex Pratt paused again so she could change tact.

"The medical examiner testified for the Commonwealth several days ago that the victim in this case, Sloane Nichols, was in and out of consciousness while she was being brutally raped over the course of many hours." Alex turned toward the two prosecutors and pointed at them. "They contend that my client penetrated the victim vaginally and anally, ejaculating into her over the course of that abuse while she was in and out of unconsciousness. Does that make any sense to you, Doctor?"

"No, it does not."

"How do you reconcile the evidence of his DNA and fingerprints at the scene with my client's profession of innocence?"

"I don't think that anyone can dispute that he had sex with the victim. *He* doesn't deny it. But, after spending the amount of time that I did with your client and after having thoroughly read the medical report, there are a number of issues that force me to conclude that Chase Bromley didn't rape and murder Sloane Nichols."

Alex turned to the jury. This was the payoff. She needed them to hear her witness. She needed them to believe her witness.

"Please explain, Doctor."

"As I said, he wouldn't put himself in a situation where he might be injured. Second, the medical report that I was provided indicated that the examiner found trace amounts of polyethylene glycol inside Sloane Nichols vagina and anus. Polyethylene glycol is used to lubricate condoms manufactured from latex rubber. Why would your client use one or more condoms only to leave the DNA evidence inside her anyway?"

"Interesting. Are those the only 'issues', as you put it, which add to your conclusion that Chase Bromley is innocent?"

"No. Additionally, and without placing any blame on the victim, her preferences as indicated from the profiles she placed seeking her many sexual partners, leads me to believe that Sloane Nichols had some sexual deviations of her own. From what I can determine, she liked to be dominated, she liked group sex, and enjoyed male and female partners. The word nymphomania is overly used and often misrepresented. The clinical term is hypersexuality, and it is diagnosed to those—male or female—that have an addiction to sexual release. While I've never met the victim, it seems clear to me that she liked sex, she liked it to be rough—or at least role played to be—and she like it often."

"And why would her sexual appetites be pertinent to this case?"

"Her appetites are important because she sought out a number of partners through casual sex websites. While I don't want to impose any blame on the victim for what happened to her, she put herself in high-risk situations by inviting strangers where she lives to dominate her. Previously, she'd engage in these trysts with the defendant, which added some degree of security. After the relationship ended, she was seeking out these random people on her own."

"For starters?"

"Yes. In addition to Sloane's hypersexuality, she was a frequent drug user. I can't comment on her addiction because I've never examined or treated her. But drug use, especially over a long period of time, affects how the brain works, not surprisingly. The brain will over time slow or stop responding to problems and dealing with these 'pathways' I described."

"Fascinating. Go on, Doctor."

"It would be like driving a route well-known to you, and encountering a number of detours along the way. Every time you seem to get your bearings, a new detour pops up and takes you further off course. I said, 'for starters' because Sloane Nichols' appetites alone put her in a great deal of risk, not only in terms of sexual diseases but physical harm as well. Her drug use only exacerbated her risk by continuing to make choices that posed significant risk to her well-being. Inviting strangers into her home for sex is dangerous enough, add a criminal element with the sale of controlled substances ....."

"And it's your opinion that one of those random lovers took dominating her to the extreme. Or a drug dealer? Or both? That this was the type of person who brutally raped and killed Sloane Nichols, not my client?"

"Yes. I prepared a psychological profile of the killer."

Kevin Bishop stood behind the defense table, retrieved a large file folder box from the floor and took the lid off. He began taking out stacks of black slide-n-grip bound reports, each seventy-five pages in length.

Alex began passing out the reports to the jury members, each getting their own copy.

"I'd like to offer this psychological profile as Defense Exhibit —"

"—Objection!" Albright was now also on his feet.

Alex tossed two copies on the table in front of both prosecutors.

"Don't worry, I have copies for you also."

"Your Honor, is this really necessary? One for the jury to examine during deliberation will suffice."

"The report is rather lengthy, Judge. I didn't think you wanted to waste the court's time by having to read it out loud, so I provided a copy for each juror. I thought it both reasonable and expeditious."

Albright was incensed. "May we approach?"

"Very well."

The entire defense team moved from their chairs to join lead counsel, ADA Walsh followed her boss to the bench who was already spitting venom when the stragglers arrived.

"Your Honor, this report is not only prejudicial, but also cannot be proven. The witness is highly paid to concoct some other suspect out of thin air in order to free the client who ultimately paid the bill," Albright whispered loudly so His Honor would sense his outrage without the jury hearing him.

Wallace's hand was over the microphone to ensure it.

Alex Pratt would have no truck with Albright, speaking with the judge directly.

"We have a right to present alternate theories of the crime, and offer alternate suspects. The ADA himself said that she was an expert and now he wants to refute her findings?"

"She has provided hand-outs for the jury to hold and lament over. If you allow this, I want to be able to provide each member of the jury with copies of the crime scene photos, of the—"

"—ENOUGH," Judge Wallace said in a louder whisper. "The defendant has the right to pose a plausible defense. That being said, one copy for the court, one for the jury and one for Mister Albright and Miss Walsh to share will do. Now everybody but Miss Pratt can go back to their seats."

The foreperson took the copy for the jury from Alex, who entered the report into evidence and went back to questioning her witness.

"So that report says what? Briefly."

"It highlights the attributes of a violent misogynist. The killer not only hates women, but wants them to suffer. He wants to watch them suffer. He has issues with his mother. He feels that all of his mental and emotional pain is manifest from a maternal lack of affection. He likely uses narcotics to deaden that pain.

In short—the killer is not Chase Bromley."

26

THE TESTIMONY OF DOCTOR ELIZABETH BAXTER WAS punctuated on Wednesday by another lunch break. When the words "I have nothing further for this witness" fell from Alex Pratt's lips, Judge Emile Wallace decided it was a good time to take a meal. The jury left the courtroom to eat their preordered lunch, and used the time to discuss the case amongst themselves in the deliberation room.

Cherelle Garrison, the twenty-seven year old African-American and juror number five was the first to give her opinion.

"I still think he done did it. He got all that money to pay for that lady to say he din't do it, but he damn sho did."

Denai Moshe, the fifty-six year old MBTA worker and juror twelve, had her back.

"Damn straight. Rich people never have no account for themselves. We gotta make that sum-bitch pay."

"We shouldn't be discussing the case yet," Sherlie Lovett, madam foreperson, said to the room while finishing her bite of ciabatta bread that she picked off her sandwich.

"We in the deliberation room ain't we? Me and my black brotha be deliberatin'."

"You wonder why people are racist? When people like you say stupid stuff like 'black brotha'. You don't see white people say 'brother' and 'sister' because they have the same pale skin, do you? I agree with you, Cherelle, that the man is guilty and should only come out of prison in a pine box, but not because you're black. I agree with you because it's correct."

217

"And we shouldn't be discussing it yet," Sherlie said again.

Deni wasn't eating the ramen that he'd ordered, deciding instead to push it toward the center of the table, where Sherlie was trying to multitask opposite him.

"Just let it happen, Sherl. It'll save time when we have to vote."

"We were instructed not to discuss the trial yet. It's my job to maintain order," she said through another dainty bite of her sandwich that she again pinched off.

"Fuck it or fight it, it's all the same," Deni mumbled.

"What did you say? 'Fuck it or fight it'? Is that some kind of Zen thing?"

"You must be a music lover."

Sherlie looked around the room for help, but initially received none.

Ben Post eventually gave an exaggerated expression of exasperation, leaned across Marissa Gantse and whispered to his foreperson.

"It's actually 'Fuckin' or Fightin', it's all the same', honey. It's a Sublime song."

The forty-three year old Human Resources Exec still looked lost.

"*What I got*? No? Well, you should google it. Do you know what google is, sweetie?"

"Very funny."

Marissa was tired of juror nine invading her personal space. Ben's left ear was against her chest like he was listening to her heart beat while he informed Sherlie about the referenced music lyrics.

"Can you rest your head on someone else's tits please?"

"Oh, Puh-lease, honey. You call those tits?"

"Jealous?"

"Of those? How many rug-rats have sucked the life out of 'em? I don't think so."

"Will you two please knock it off? You should be ashamed of yourselves," Regan Avery, juror four, exclaimed from across the table.

Ben rolled his eyes for the world to see.

"Moms gotta stick together," Reagan said to Marissa.

It was Jordan Raines who brought the conversation back to the trial.

"What I don't get is what makes men fall for women like that?"

Paul Weist, juror three, looked to his right at Jordan as he asked her to elaborate.

"What do you mean?"

"I mean she lived with him for how long before she left him? He let her live in his house for all that time knowing what she was. I know it's not nice to speak ill of the dead, but when you have sex with literally anyone, what made him still attracted to her?"

"He was into the same shit," Deni said. "They both fucked anything with a pulse. Two peas in an orgy."

"That's just gross. I don't see the attraction to someone like that. I'm not that old, but I guess I'm old-fashioned. I prefer the men I date to not have slept with women in the triple digits. I would think it would be worse for men who date women who've slept with that many people. It's just gross. Who could love someone that has had that much ..... Love. Guh."

"I guess you'd have to be there," Deni responded with a shrug.

Sherlie Lovett had given up on trying to derail the topic. She decided to sit back in her chair with the mini bag of potato chips that accompanied her sandwich, crunching loudly on individual chips to avoid hearing the dialogue.

Oscar Brenowitz chimed in.

"Back in my day, we used to call them 'good-time girls'."

"I think they still call them that. Or worse," Jordan said.

"We didn't look too fondly at those kinds of girls back then," Evelyn Rocher said. "But they didn't deserve to be killed, let alone what this poor girl had to endure. Times may have changed, but nobody deserves ..... A baseball bat? It's just so horrific."

The room nodded. Nobody corrected that it was a softball bat, not a baseball bat, as the distinction wasn't necessary.

Renaldo Ramos Gomez spoke after a time.

"I don't know if this is the expression, but you play with fire and it burn you. This woman, Sloane, she ask for it. Sometimes people don't know what they wish for."

"So are you saying, are *any* of you saying, that she asked for this? That she should have seen this coming?" Regan put her hands on the table in front of her and leaned in to see the faces of the entire jury.

"She was a ho," Cherelle said. "I ain't sayin' she deserved what that mu-fucka gave her, but she shoulda' seen some of what came. You can't just do what she do and expect a mu-fuckin' rainbow."

"I have two teenage daughters," Regan said. "I have no illusions that they are saving themselves for marriage, no matter how much I preach. So I tell them that they should wait, at least until college, and hope for the best. I tell them that if it's that important to them, to at the very minimum use a condom, but the best decision is to wait. But if they don't? What if they don't? What if they decide to have intercourse with not just one boy, but date a couple of boys? They're in high school. Word will get around. What if one boy gets jealous? Should they expect to be beaten or raped or worse?

This Sloane Nichols made some poor decisions. For whatever reasons, she decided to get involved with God knows how many people. Maybe she was looking for something. Maybe she had some mental or emotional issues that made her seek out all of these partners like that shrink just said. Who knows? But there is no way that any of you can tell me that she should have seen a brutal rape and murder coming. An STD? Sure. More physical abuse from Chase Bromley or someone else? Maybe. AIDS? A pregnancy? Okay. But not rape, torture, and murder. Please tell me that we're not going to let this guy do this to someone else. I have daughters. We all have women that we know and love. We have to protect them."

Paul put his left hand on her right forearm.

"I don't think any of us are saying that, Jordan." He looked around the table for confirmation before continuing.

"We're just talking. Just hashing things out. We're gonna do the right thing."

It was Assistant District Attorney, Justin Albright's turn to interrogate Doctor Elizabeth Baxter. His cross examination would consume the rest of Wednesday, and he would need it, he thought. And maybe all of Thursday. He needed to roll up his shirt sleeves because he had some work to do.

The psychology professor had done some damage to the Commonwealth's case. She was an expert on the human brain, his own words were used to solidify that with the jury. Doctor Baxter had been consulted on many different cases, many different trials, by many different local, state, and federal investigators.

And she said Chase Bromley couldn't have committed the murder.

Albright had discussed the state of affairs with his second chair, Amy Walsh, during the break. She agreed that they had taken a hit. Their boat wasn't sinking, but damage control had to be conducted. In keeping with the metaphor, Amy suggested that they patch up the holes or else risk taking on significant water.

An acquittal was not an option.

So Justin Albright went in with both guns blazing.

"Doctor Baxter, you've never been in practice, have you? Never put out a shingle and treated patients, correct?"

"'Put out a shingle'? No. However, I have treated patients."

"But you primarily teach."

"Yes. At Columbia University. That's in New York City. It's in the top five universities in the country. You may have heard of it."

Albright looked to Judge Wallace.

"Permission to treat the witness as hostile?"

"Granted."

"I'm not being hostile, Mister Albright. I'm merely trying to illustrate to you that I'm not some five-and-dime shrink who teaches a course at a learning annex. I'm preeminent in my field, teaching at one of the top universities in the country, arguably the world."

"I didn't ask you a question, Doctor Baxter. Your Honor, can you instruct the witness to speak only when asked a question?"

"Doctor Baxter, if you could limit your responses to when you are asked a direct question please?"

She returned her gaze to the ADA in front of her while pretending to preen herself. There were no dents in her armor.

"You teach instead of taking patients, and you have for nearly twenty years. Would you say that you might be out of practice, since you've never accepted patients in that time?"

"As I said to you before, I *have* and *do* treat patients. I take on patients and cases that intrigue me. I involve myself in research studies that interest me, which necessitates me seeing patients. As a tenured professor, I'm afforded time to conduct work outside the university."

"Have you ever heard the expression, 'Those that can't do, teach'?"

"Objection." Alex Pratt was on her feet.

"Withdrawn. I'll rephrase."

"You've never met Sloane Nichols Correct? So any mental diagnosis you gave earlier is purely academic? You have no idea what might have been her motivation behind seeking out lovers on various websites, do you? Maybe she was just a very sexual person. Is that possible?"

Doctor Baxter looked to the judge.

"Your Honor, I counted at least four questions there."

"We have the rest of the day, counselor. And tomorrow if you need it. Please ask one question at a time."

"Sorry, Judge. Did you ever meet Sloane Nichols, yes or no?"

"No. I believe I've already testified to that, if you'd care to go back and read my statements."

"Just 'yes' or 'no' please and thank you. Now, the diagnosis you alluded to earlier ....." Albright consulted his yellow legal pad, "..... 'hypersexuality' ..... Is purely hypothetical."

There was a long pause. Albright finally realized he hadn't asked a question.

"Correct? Yes or no?"

"No."

"No? How can you say 'no' when you've admittedly never met the victim?"

"Because I've published findings on the subject. I've interviewed, conducted MRI brain scans, diagnosed, and prescribed treatment to several people with the same presentations. While I've never met the victim, nor do I assert any blame for what happened to her, her hypersexuality was a contributing factor in her death. Whomever killed her, did so in part, because he felt a passionate abhorrence to that sexuality. As I've testified, that abhorrence does not exist in the defendant."

Albright, deflated, changed course.

"You testified earlier that one of the issues you had with Chase Bromley being convicted of the rape and murder of Sloane Nichols was the existence of ....." Albright consulted his legal pad again, " ..... Polyethylene glycol ..... In both her vagina and anus."

Another long pause.

"Yes or no, Doctor?"

"Yes."

"Have you ever heard of a condom breaking?"

"Yes."

"And that could have occurred in this case, correct? The defendant was raping the victim while using a condom, the condom broke, spilling the semen into the cavities. Is that possible? Yes or no?"

"No."

"That's not possible?"

"Not in this case, no."

Albright feigned righteous indignation.

"Really, Doctor? I have to know how you can possibly come to that conclusion."

"Have *you* ever had a condom break?"

"I'm asking the questions here."

"Fine. Then I'll explain. When men use a condom, they do it for safety—not because it feels better. Rapists use them so they don't leave any epithelial cells or pre-ejaculate inside the victim, not because it feels better. The sensations between using a condom and not, are like night and day. No matter what brand, no matter what the condom is made from—lamb's skin or latex rubber or the numerous other types that try to claim that it maintains the same sensation. Regardless of what anyone will tell you, if you haven't experienced it yourself, male or female, all parties involved immediately know when a condom breaks. The moment it does, the sensation becomes markedly more intense. Or, if you like, better."

"And you claim to know that it didn't occur in this case, how?"

"The rapist would have immediately known that the condom was compromised and would have immediately removed himself from the victim in order to conceal his identity."

"Or maybe when the condom broke, the defendant's DNA spilled into the victim."

"Was that a question?"

"Is that possible, yes or no?"

"Once, yes. Not twice or more."

"Your Honor?" Albright looked to Judge Wallace with obvious frustration.

"Please answer his question with either a yes or no, Doctor."

"No. Now you're going to ask me to explain why, which I was attempting to—"

"—Judge, I move that this witnesses' entire testimony be stricken from the record. She is unresponsive, and shows obvious contempt for an officer of this court. I further demand—"

"—*ENOUGH*, Counselor. She is being the opposite of unresponsive, which is why you have continually asked me to re-instruct the witness. I do sense contempt on both sides here so I'm going to ask that your second chair take over the cross. Miss Walsh, your up."

"Your Honor."

"*SIT DOWN*, Mister Albright."

It took a few moments for ADAs Albright and Walsh to do-si-do. It took a few more moments still for Amy Walsh to collect her thoughts and insert herself into the examination.

"Uhm..... Doctor Baxter. Uh, would you like me to have the court stenographer read you back the last question?"

"No, thank you. I'm very good at remembering things. Your boss asked me if it was possible that the defendant's condom ruptured—I think he used the word 'broke'—while he was raping and before murdering the victim, and my response was 'no'. I tried to explain the sound logic behind that reasoning but he seemed to want to avoid hearing my answer. Would you like me to continue to explain or would you like to move on?"

"Yes. Please explain."

"Thank you. The existence of the defendant's semen inside the victim was from sex prior to the rape and murder. I'm not going to testify that when the defendant had sexual relations with the victim that it was consensual, though there is significant evidence to suggest that it was. What I am saying, is that the male who raped and murdered the victim—subsequent to her relations with Chase Bromley—used a condom or condoms that did not break. I know this because semen was identified in both the victim's vagina *and* anus. The defendant's semen. If he was the murderer, and the condom ruptured as your boss suggested, it would have spilled DNA into one orifice or the other. Not both.

What your boss is suggesting is that the murderer had the misfortune of having his condom break while raping the victim, meaning his DNA spilled into her, only to have the same scenario happen again in a different orifice.   That is beyond bad luck and rounding the corner to ludicrous."

"But it is possible?"

"No. Why use a condom at all? After the first incident, why even bother?   You're already done, so to speak.   Cooked. Investigators are going to run DNA analysis and find you out, why not get all you can out of the experience?   From the rapist's standpoint, why not get every sensation you can from it since it will likely be the last time you have the opportunity to be the rape-*ist* instead of the rape-*ee* for the remainder of your life?"

Amy Walsh turned to her boss for guidance. He gave none.

She looked to the jury, who had the same look of uncertainty as Albright. The expert was arguing salient points that had not been thought of or addressed.

The silence was deafening.

"Nothing further for this witness."

27

"I THINK WE SHOULD AT LEAST EXPLORE THE IDEA OF offering a deal," ADA Walsh said to Albright as they left the courtroom for the day. The two were walking back to the DA's office, located on Bullfinch Place. The walk would take no more than four minutes down Somerset Street.

"No way. No deals. This is a slam-dunk case. A marquee case. The people of Boston are watching and waiting for justice here, Amy. We can't let a little thing like getting absolutely destroyed by their expert witness take our eyes off the prize. Chase Bromley goes to prison until hell freezes over if I have to drive him there myself."

"Is that your career talking or are you that confident that we can bounce back from what just happened today?"

"What are you talking about?"

"A conviction in this 'marquee case' is going to get you elected to District Attorney next year. I'm not an idiot, Justin. Is that what's driving you? Because losing this case—"

"—We're not going to lose this case. How can we? He beat the hell out of this poor woman time and time again. And where were the police? In the hip pocket of Kenneth Bromley, that's where. A TRO didn't keep Bromley junior away, his fingerprints were found in the victim's apartment. His semen was found inside her corpse, Amy. We don't make deals with guys like this. Pedal to the floor."

"Justin, did you see the jury? Were you in that courtroom? Were you paying attention at all? Judge Wallace tossed you from cross examining a witness that *YOU* pronounced an expert."

"Emile Wallace. The man isn't qualified to judge a beauty pageant, let alone a criminal trial."

"You weren't saying that yesterday."

"He didn't bias the jury against me yesterday."

"Justin. He didn't bias the jury against you at all. He just put you out of your misery and gave me my share. You weren't getting anything out of that pompous windbag, and he made sure that I took the hit. The jury felt sorry for me. I'm just the second chair thrown to the wolves. But I saw them. The jurors. That shrink-doctor of theirs put reasonable doubt into their minds. Can we still win? Sure. If we don't take any more hits like that one. We've got a strong circumstantial case that took a big shot to the chin. I think if we put a top count of murder-two on the table, they might go for it. Roll in a few of the lesser-included felonies to run concurrent? What can it hurt to discuss it?"

"Do you know Alexandria Pratt?"

"I've heard of her," Amy said with sufficient sarcasm and some to spare.

"Of course you've heard of her. Deaf people have heard of her. Do you know her reputation? She didn't make partner at the largest law firm in Boston by being a pushover. If we offer a deal now, we might as well be chum in the water. That team will just swarm in and bite the hell out of us."

"So we lose outright?"

"That's not the plan, Amy. The plan is to send the bastard to hell for as long as he still draws breath."

"And I'm telling you that best laid plans of mice and men—"

"—Often go awry. I've heard the saying."

"You're hearing, but you're not listening."

They arrived at the District Attorney's office and commandeered the first conference room in their path. Justin plopped himself in a chair and let out a deep sigh.

"I'm listening now."

"I say we try to make this go away as quietly as possible. Cut a deal for murder-two."

"And how does that play in the arena of public opinion, Amy?"

"How does Chase Bromley walking out of Suffolk Superior Court a free man? Laws for the rich don't apply? Murder-two is still a fifteen year minimum. That's hard time in a hard correctional facility."

"Fifteen years for the torture, rape, and murder of a woman who had a restraining order against the man we were supposed to protect her from? There are about a half a million women in Suffolk County that are going to take little comfort in knowing that Chase Bromley will be out on the streets again someday."

"Someday isn't next week. You have the luxury of two other major trials happening right now. Hernandez and Tsarnaev. A deal makes this one quietly go away."

"This case has made the national spotlight. Christ, Katrina Brown almost tanked this entire proceeding with that idiotic juror. No matter what we do, it makes news. This doesn't go away quietly, Amy, and you know it."

"Headlines for a day or two, then back to business as usual. Fifteen is better than nothing."

"Who do they have lined up for tomorrow?"

Amy opened up the rolling file box that she wheeled back and forth to the trial each and every day. The appendage mimicked rolling carry-on luggage. She retrieved a file, opened it, and perused the defense witness list.

"Chase Bromley. If I had to guess, I'd say the defendant. The rest of the witness list is just people who responded to Sloane's web profiles. A few character witnesses."

"Put the victim on trial."

"Right. Except they just eviscerated the victim today. No need to kick a dead corpse. Doctor wind-bag just said that she brought this thing on herself, no need to make Joe and Jane Schmo say it. Too many people denigrating the victim makes them despicable. They won't do that. So they'll put Chase on, and depending on how he does, they will either rest their case or bring some of these people up for damage control."

"He's going to be well-prepped, Amy."

"Oh - I know."

"Call Pratt. Let's see if we can meet before trial tomorrow morning."

"You're rethinking your stance on cutting a deal, aren't you?"

"I'm open to seeing what she says."

While Albright and Walsh were discussing trial strategy on Bullfinch Place, the defense team sat down to do the same on the opposite side of the city. Chase sat at the conference table inside the glass conference room at Taylor, Higgs & Pratt. A sea of lawyers moved about on the other side of the sound-proof glass. Sharks madly swimming about, busy in the work of defending various clients while the Bromley defense team did likewise inside the fishbowl at a combined rate of over $5,000 an hour.

Alex questioned her team.

"Thoughts on today?"

Kevin Bishop was all grins.

"I think we nailed it. I don't know how much we paid Elizabeth Baxter, but it wasn't enough." He looked at their client. "That woman should make your christmas card list. And I mean permanently."

"Let's not get carried away, Kevin."

"I'm with him," Max said. "I'm paid to watch the jury. I didn't take my eyes off of them. Justin Albright is his own worst enemy. And the judge tossing him? Let's just say that we are definitely glad that in the American Criminal Justice system, the prosecutor can't appeal a verdict. Wallace never should have gone to the mound and put in the rookie. If he'd done that to us, it'd be a reversible error."

"But he could appeal before a verdict," Jack Elders said. "He could argue before the appellate division that the shrink's entire testimony be stricken."

Alex looked at the young lawyer with pity.

"Who hired you? Did you even go to law school?"

The scolded puppy shriveled with his proverbial tail between his legs.

"Leave him alone, Alex." Kevin turned to the youngster. "What did I tell you about having a question? Write it down and I'll help you later. He could file a motion, but you can't unring the bell that happened today. Even if he wins the motion in appellate, which is a big if, the judge telling the jury to ignore the entire day makes it look like they're afraid of the shrink ....."

" ..... Which gives the testimony they're supposed to ignore even more weight," Elders realized out loud.

Kevin looked to Alex. "See? He can be taught, you just need to be more patient."

"He's a part of this trial as a courtesy," she said.

"And to bank more billable hours," the defendant added.

The rest of the people in the glass room gave each other sheepish grins.

Chase's father suddenly walked through the glass door at that moment without knocking.

"Kenneth. Please, have a seat," Alex said. "Can we get you anything?"

The entire defense team stood. Chase remained slumped in his seat.

"No, thank you. I'm not staying. I just came by to give my praise. I understand things went well today?"

Alex looked around the table, trying to determine how he'd heard anything about the events of the day.

"Well ..... Yes. We were just discussing how much the testimony today weighed on the jury and how to proceed tomorrow. It's been less than an hour since we adjourned for the day, how did you—"

"—I have eyes and ears everywhere my dear. Anyway, keep up the good work." He turned to his son. "And since it's *my* money that's paying those 'billable hours', I suggest you keep your trap shut."

Kenneth Bromley gave the room a once-over and walked out of the fishbowl with the same gravitas that he'd garnered upon his sudden entrance.

The dream team returned to their seats. Back to business.

"So where were we?"

Elders kept his mouth closed.

Kevin Bishop was still stunned as to what just took place.

Max picked up the slack.

"We scored big with the jury. One witness. And I think that's all we need. Juror seven is on board at the very least. I saw a lot of them with questions today. Before the break we were still toast, but after? We've got reasonable doubt in the bag."

Alex leaned in from her post at the head of the conference table.

"So you think we can rest?"

"Absolutely."

Chase stood up.

"Rest? You mean I don't take the stand? At all?"

Alex had had a long day.

"That's what 'rest' means. It means we're done. The prosecutors didn't prove their case beyond a reasonable doubt. No more witnesses. We begin closing arguments."

"But that means I don't get to tell my side of the story."

Alex looked at the ceiling and cracked her neck.

"With all due respect, Chase, your 'side of the story' doesn't mean shit. Putting you on the stand was always a last-ditch scenario. Between all of us here, the possibility was just thrown out there to keep you quiet. I can't suborn perjury as an officer of the court. If I think you're going to lie, I can't call you as a witness."

"But I wouldn't lie."

"And I can't know for sure what that pecker-wood Albright is going to ask you. If he catches you in a lie, or I know that you're going to lie, the game is over. Do you understand? Putting you on the stand is a huge risk and was never going to happen. Okay? Do you get it?"

"So I'm gonna go to prison for the rest of my life and I'm not even going to be able to tell my side of the story?"

"I can't do this with you. It's been a long day ..... Kevin, can you explain the birds and bees with him please?"

Kevin sighed.

"Chase, do you know that you don't *have* to tell your side of the story? That saying, 'innocent until proven guilty' isn't just a saying. You don't have to come up with any story whatsoever. The Commonwealth of Massachusetts has to come up with a story. And they have to be able to prove that story. The shrink today put a shotgun blast worth of holes into their story.

Max Courtland is the best jury consultant that money can buy. He just said that we, at the very least, have a hung jury. Which means that the *worst* thing that he thinks can happen at this point, is a mistrial. If that happens, worst case, the DA's office would have to decide if they want to go through this process all over again with a new trial. They would have the same evidence, the only difference would be a new jury. Trials cost money. About a half million dollars a shot. They just blew a half-mil, do they wanna do that again? Maybe. Probably not. If one jury can't decide on a verdict, maybe a second one won't. Or they may decide to acquit. If we rest tomorrow, both sides give a closing argument and the jury deliberates on the facts.

In other words, what Max is saying, is that the only way we can fuck this up, is if *WE* fuck it up. Putting you on the stand would be a huge fuck-up."

"Or I blow trial and go to prison for the rest of my life."

"In this business, you gotta play the odds, Chase."

"This isn't a business. This is my life."

"We understand. Really. But if you don't trust us by now, I don't know what to say to make you at this late juncture," Kevin said with arms open.

"Chase," Max said softly. "We have juror seven. I think we have more, but seven for sure. Guaranteed. I can further guarantee that if you take the stand tomorrow, you will die in prison. That juror, Warren Dennihan, is a professional investigator. A former cop. He can smell a lie like a horny dog can smell a bitch in heat. That juror is on your side right now. If you testi-lie on the stand tomorrow, he swings the jury to convict. Albright is on the ropes and can't wait to expose you, that too I can guarantee."

" I won't lie."

Alex stood up.

"We tried to do this nice. The answer is no. We rest tomorrow."

Chase stomped his foot like a toddler on a tantrum.

"I'm the client. You have to do what I say."

A pretty, young, bottle blonde executive assistant entered the fishbowl.

"Sorry to interrupt, Alex. But the ADA is on line six. She says it's urgent."

"*She?* Walsh?"

"Yes, Ma'am," the blonde said before leaving, closing the door behind her.

"They want to cut a deal," Bishop said.

A big grin came over her face as she pulled the phone toward her from the center of the conference room table. She stood over it watching the red light blink. Before pushing the button for line six, she looked her client straight in the eyes.

"See Chase. What did we tell you? We got'em."

28

DENI RETRIEVED THE BURNER PHONE HE HAD STASHED
behind the wide, loose floor moulding in the back of the hotel room
closet. The moment he walked through the door after leaving the
bus from court on Wednesday evening, he went straight for it. The
battery was virtually dead, the last bit of juice provided the tiny green
light to flash. He tethered the device to a power outlet in the
bathroom, sat on the john, and listened to his message.

It was Sheed. The message was three words in length.

"Call me back."

I was about to call you anyway, he thought.

He immediately did. She picked up on the second ring.

"She. Whattya got?"

"Quite a lot, actually. Are you having fun sitting on your ass
all day? Because I've been working mine off."

"No, I haven't, as a matter of fact. I'm stuck with the same
people, on the same bus, in the same seats, eating and yackin' away
in the same room ..... I haven't had a real workout since this whole
thing started. I'm stressed and I want to spar like you read about.
I'm getting fat and outta shape."

"Poor baby. You're what? One-seventy? You could use a
few pounds anyway."

"You wanted me to call you so you could give me a ration of
shit, or what?"

"Technically, you just called me, but no. I've got some really
big stuff and some interesting side-notes. I had to do some serious
digging and I owe the runner from Troop H that I used to see.
Reggie is going to love that little tid-bit. Plus the IT guy at one of the

hook-up websites Sloane Nichols used, he's going to want a favor down the line—"

"—She! You're ramblin'. Get it togetha kid."

"I've got a *possible*."

"You have my full attention."

"I'll start with the side-notes. The guys from Cornell, Katz and Needer. I looked them up and tried to talk to them, but they still work for Kenneth Bromley and are loyal. They aren't going to say boo about Chase. They each make some big coin and have wives and families."

"So whatever happened in college, is going to stay under wraps. These guys harmless?"

"They look to be. I pulled phone records and they don't even call Chase anymore."

"Dead end."

"Right."

"That wasn't that interesting, She."

"Hold your horses, I've got more. The TRO? It was filed on *behalf* of Sloane Nichols, not *by* Sloane Nichols."

"What's the difference? She had to sign it," Deni said.

"Civil lawyer filed the paperwork for her. She was going for Palimony against Chase Bromley. Which was totally an unwinnable case, but a restraining order would certainly help the cause."

"Chase did toss her," Deni said more to himself than Lisa.

"Looks like it. So she went on the offensive. She went to this third-rate lawyer who works on contingency to see if she could milk the cow for some walkaway money. Lawyer said the TRO would put them in a better position, making it look like she left versus getting kicked to the wind. It worked. Kinda. Kenneth Bromley bought his way out for an 'undisclosed sum'. No civil case and the records are sealed. I mean sphincter sealed. Gag order. I was lucky to get the info I got.

Anyway, she took her money—what was left over after the lawyer took his share—and went on to doing her thing."

"Bromley was a meal ticket. For both of them," Deni said.

"I don't follow."

"Amanda Hunt. Sloane Nichols. Both women were looking for a handout. They were into Chase for the money. The life. His lawyer is right, they put up with his shit because of his money."

"That doesn't mean he didn't do it, Deni. The domestic dispute calls to locals, he's clearly violent."

"Uh huh."

"You don't sound convinced."

"Every time I turn around, I learn somethin' new about this case, and it ain't from the lawyers. I wonder why this 'great lawyer of his' didn't dig this up?"

"Her investigators aren't as good a me, I guess. Plus the gag order, nobody is allowed to talk about it or they forfeit their dough. It got swept under the carpet and that is where it's supposed to stay. Here's some more for you to ponder," Lisa said.

"There's more? Shoot."

"I looked into Sloane's love life more extensively. One of the handles that responded to one of her more elaborate profiles on Adult Friend Finder dot com ...." Deni heard rustling of papers on the other end of the line. He assumed it was at their office, but he didn't confirm. " .... Ah. Here it is. 'I love it ruff'—which she misspelled by the way—'I want to be dominated, humiliated, sissy, cuckold, CEI, SPH, JOI, strap ons'. It goes on from there, with a profile pic of her naked with a ball-gag in her mouth for added effect. I think of myself as a fairly sexual person, but I have to admit, I don't know what half of those abbreviations mean."

"I'll bet you know what a strap on is. You and Reggie must have one in every shape, size, and color."

"You're a funny guy. Anyway, one of the profiles that responded—and I mean often—had the handle 'Dominus-Durum'. So I looked him up. When you see the expense report for all of these sex sites, you'll know why. You have to be a paying member in order to see the profiles."

"'Hard Dominator'. Subtle."

"I don't follow."

"'Dominus-Durum'. It's latin. Means hard dominator."

"I had no idea you were multi-lingual."

"I'm not. I'm Irish and I went to Catholic school. Went to church too, until I was confirmed. They used to say Mass in Latin, so it's kinda big with Catholics."

"Huh. Well, this 'hard dominator' was very taken with Sloane Nichols, whose handle was 'RavageMe44' on Adult Friend Finder by the way."

"Ravage me one thru forty-three must have been taken," Deni said.

"I know, right? So I cross-referenced 'D-D' with the other sites that Sloane frequented. He was on those as well. He uses the same handle, so it made it easy. He frequented her on those websites as well. His profile pic, if it's him, is interesting to say the least."

"How so?"

"He shaves all of his body hair."

"Big deal. So do I."

"I know you do, dummy. But you don't shave your head. And by head I mean scalp, eyebrows—no hair."

"Which means no DNA."

"Right. He could do whatever he wants to whomever he wants and as long as he uses gloves and a condom, he dominates undetected," she added.

"Gloves? Has he been fingerprinted? Got a sheet?"

"Yes, yes, and yes he does. I had my friend from Troop H pull his yellows. Dominus—Durum is one Christopher Stratton. Goes by Chris. No tats, distinguishing marks or characteristics, except for the body hair thing. The man has a long record, Deni. His juvie record is sealed, but Troop H has him in and out of the Foster Care system. He regularly beat on girls and then women as he got older, which means I'd personally like to put a bullet in his brain. Each time he got a slap on the wrist and sent to see another shrink through court diversion. But nothing since. Meek as a babe for more than a decade."

"Which is scary."

"That's what I thought, Deni. No shrink is that good. Years and years of slapping females around, then all of a sudden—nothing?"

"Agreed. I don't buy it. Great job, She. Why did you say, 'It's an interesting side-note'? This could be the guy."

"I say it's interesting because I've shown his photo to everyone in Sloane's building and no takers. He definitely had a thing for the vic, but it looks to be from afar. I can't put him in the building or having any contact with Nichols other than emails and webcams. I pulled phone records—"

"—He could'a used a burner, She."

"Probably. Because I came up blank there. So I dug deeper and listen, something about him put her off. She'd flirt and tease and do some show and tell in front of the computer, but she didn't want him to know where she lived. I printed up all the chats from the sites and their emails, Deni. She kept putting him off. And for this girl to keep someone out of her bed, you know he had to be a creeper."

"So that's it? This Chris Stratton guy never met her?"

"Not as far as I can tell. And I've dug. To the detriment of our other cases, by the way. I'm still convinced that Chase Bromley did it, Deni. The cops got it right the first time with this one. Bromley was in her apartment, and he shouldn't have been because she had a restraining order against him—trumped up bullshit to get paid or not. He beat her up on a number of occasions and never even got a rap on the knuckles. His man-juice was found in her destroyed body. His sock was shoved in her mouth. I don't know what more proof you need, Deni. That's why I say that these are all just interesting side-notes."

"I've got not love for the guy. I'm just sayin'. He kicked her out—maybe an idle threat, maybe not—and she not only takes him up on it, but takes a chunk of money with her. She was sleeping with other people with him, which wasn't enough, so she started screwing around behind his back. He's probably a woman beater, but that's not why she left. She got paid, which pissed him off, for sure. But then he waits six months before shoving a bat into her and murder? I don't know, She."

"What about the prior? The girl from Cornell who killed herself? He did that, he did this, and he isn't going to stop."

"You've liked him from the start," Deni said after a few moments of dead air.

"We've been over this.   I've been on the other end of beatings from a man I thought I loved at the time. It's probably the hardest thing to come to grips with, at least it was for me. I relate to Nichols in some ways, Deni.   She was lost and confused.   I'm fortunate enough to have finally realized that I'm a lesbian, and that I don't need to depend on a man to make me happy.   Why do you think she set up all those profiles?   Those were sexual advertisements.   She was looking for someone to take care of her because she didn't think she could do it on her own.   She had years of abuse from Bromley who kept her down.

Bromley is a scum-bag. He preys on the weak, because he's weak. He's a spoiled brat who likes to beat on women and use them as his play-thing.   Yeah, I like him for this.   And all the evidence, circumstantial though it may be, supports my hate for him. The only reason I'm looking into this is for you—"

"—Is for yourself. You want half of the business."

"Whatever. My point is that given the givens, his past and all that, none of this other stuff makes him less guilty."

"Your point has been made abundantly clear."

"Has it?"

"What is that supposed to mean?"

"I can tell from your voice that you don't agree with me."

"Did I say that, She?"

"You don't have to. I know you, and I know when you get a notion or a gut-feeling, there is no changing your mind. You're like a bruin in body-armor and everyone better get out of your way."

"I've been wrong before."

"I know that. But you can't do the wrong thing, here, Deni. This guy is a monster and you have the opportunity to stop a lot of pain and suffering."

"You don't think I know that?"

"I know you know that. I also know that no matter how much evidence is waved in front of your face, if you aren't convinced ....."

"Who said you didn't convince me?"

"Don't patronize me, convince me that you're convinced," Lisa said.

"I thought I did. What do you want to hear from me?"

"I want to hear that you know that Chase Bromley is guilty of the rape and murder of Sloane Nichols. I want to hear you say that you're going to find him guilty.   I want you to tell me that you're going to do the right thing."

"She ….. I'm gonna do the right thing."

29

THE 7:00 A.M. MEETING IN THE DISTRICT ATTORNEY'S OFFICE
was far too early for everyone involved. All interested parties were
present save for judge and jury. Both ADAs had been up most of the
night preparing for Chase Bromley's testimony in court in the event
that a deal for murder in the second degree couldn't be struck, while
the defense team burned the midnight oil crafting the closing
statement that Alex Pratt would make to the jury.

The coffee was made but hadn't fully kicked in yet. Everyone
smelled of their liberally applied brand of shampoo, deodorant, and
perfume in an effort to disguise their fatigue. The only person in the
conference room that had slept like a baby was the defendant
himself.

"No breakfast, Justin?" Alex jibed. "You called this meeting,
at this ungodly hour, the least you could have done was put out a
couple of muffins."

"My apologies for the lack of civility, Alex, but I thought it
best to get right down to business since we all have to be in court in
a couple of hours."

"Fine. We're all ears."

Each took a seat around the large table, defense on one end,
prosecutors on the other.

"I'm prepared to make a one-time offer of Murder-two, good
until we walk into that courtroom."

"Oh, you're funny, Justin. Were you in court yesterday?
Because it seems to me that we drove the commuter rail through the
reasonable doubt the shrink created yesterday. Why would we make
a deal?"

"You had a good day, I admit. But momentum is going to change today. You know as well as I do that once we go back into court, I'm going to expose your client as the liar, rapist, and murderer that he is. Pedal to the floor. Murder-one, premeditated murder during the commission of the class A felony of rape, and that's just the top count. Consecutive life terms means that he will serve the rest of his natural life in prison without the possibility of parole."

"Wow. Someone put a little extra fiber in your breakfast cereal this morning, eh Justin? Just for laughs, and so we can dot the i's, what are we talking?"

"As I said ..... Murder-two. With a sentence recommendation, all charges to run concurrent. Fifteen to life. But he allocutes in open court, and we get a preview right now."

"My client is innocent."

"If you're going to stick with the hard-line, Alex, we're wasting our time here. I was trying to understand why he did it. Maybe he went to her apartment just to talk with her. Patch things up. Maybe have sex, and things spun out of control. She said some things that made him mad and he snapped. No premeditation. But if you're going to stick with this cockamamie story of 'he had consensual sex with her and he left' ....'

Albright trailed off while shaking his head in disgust. He then turned to Bromley, speaking to him directly instead of about him in his presence.

"You have the opportunity to walk out of prison someday. Right here and now. Admit to what you did and tell us why, and you will once again breathe free air. If you don't, I promise you that I will shred every lie that you tell on the stand today, and you will never be outside of a four-by-nine for longer than one hour a day for the rest of your life."

Alex put her hand on Chase's forearm, silently communicating that he not say a word.

"I won't oppose parole when it comes up in fifteen years. Final offer," Albright added looking directly at the defendant.

A large smile formed on the lips of Chase Bromley, without a word passing from them. The two men stared at each other in silence.

Albright saw the smug satisfaction on Bromley's face.

He thinks he beat me.

"Forget it!" Albright stood. "The offer is off the table. I want you to remember this moment, Chase," he said while pointing at the defendant. "I want you to remember the moment you threw away your life while you're rotting in a cell waiting for a coffin."

He turned his gaze to Alexandria Pratt.

"I'll see you in court."

ADA Albright was more than taken aback when Alex Pratt announced to the courtroom that the defense rested. Albright certainly hoped and was expecting to disembowel not only the defendant, but the defense strategy in general when Chase Bromley testified in court on Thursday morning. The announcement came as a complete shock and disappointment.

He was still fired up from the early morning meeting where he almost made the mistake of giving the defendant a chance at freedom. The smile. The look in Bromley's eyes. Albright wanted blood. A pound of his flesh as he exposed every lie he'd tell.

But he wouldn't get the chance.

Alex Pratt was resting their entire case on one witness. The expert who, admittedly, injected some reasonable doubt on the Commonwealth's case.

Albright found it both shocking and brilliant. Leave on a high note. Quit while they're ahead. The defense had momentum and they were leaving with it. Not putting the defendant on the stand would raise some questions with the jury. Add those to the questions the expert shrink had raised, and it was enough for at least one jury member to scratch their head.

Reasonable doubt.

Albright wasn't prepared for a closing statement, and yet he would have to give one as soon as Alex Pratt was finished with her monologue.

A sick and uneasy feeling boiled in his stomach. He looked to his second chair, who was just as surprised and of no help. He hardly heard the first half of Pratt's close.

"….. And they simply haven't proven their case.

"The victim had a dangerous lifestyle, with may lovers, and many people coming in and out of her apartment for months prior to her death.

Sloane Nichols took drugs, a danger not only because of the damage that drugs have on the body, but for the possible harm stemming from the criminal element surrounding them. You heard from her their medical examiner testify to her use of Valium and many other drugs, and you heard her neighbor testify to her loud parties. People were in and out of that apartment constantly. For the sex, for the drugs ….. All that was missing was the rock 'n roll.

She placed sexually explicit profiles on craigslist and numerous other websites for the purpose of seeking out sexual partners who would dominate her.

But nobody compared to what she'd lost in her former boyfriend. She was lost in a fog of drugs and rough, casual sex.

Months of trial and error made her come to that conclusion.

So she called up my client. She wanted to reconnect.

And they had sex.

Of course he was seen in that building, he was there. We're not contending he wasn't. But he was at her apartment at Sloane's request.

Was he supposed to be there? Legally? Maybe not. But the very person who wanted the protection of that TEMPORARY restraining order, was the very person who waived it.

They had unprotected sex. Orally. Vaginally. Anally. It was consensual. It was familiar. And my client left her in her apartment alive and well.

Another man, whom has gone as of now undetected, whom we have given you a psychological profile, crafted by one of the top experts on the planet, later entered the apartment of the victim.

He bound her, beat her, and she nearly suffocated on a sock belonging to my client that was either left from the earlier sexual encounter, or taken by her accidentally when she moved out of my client's brownstone, we don't know. And neither does the prosecution. And neither do you.

This other assailant used a condom or condoms, as proven by the chemical remnants of the condom lubricant discovered inside the victim.

This other man beat and raped Sloane Nichols repeatedly. He used a bat to violate her in the most horrific of ways. He tormented her for hours.

And then, when he was through with her, he used a knife from her own kitchen to take her head off.

Does this sound like someone who loved the victim?

Does this sound like rough sex gone wrong?

No. This is someone who is psychologically damaged. Someone who hates women.

Not my client.

We've given you reasonable doubt. Any reasonable person can see that he couldn't have committed the crimes that he is accused of. Someone else did.

My client can't testify to something that he knows nothing about. The prosecutor didn't prove it, because he can't prove something that didn't occur.

For all of those reasons, you must find Chase Bromley Not-Guilty, ladies and gentlemen.

Thank you."

Alex panned the jury, looking each of them in the eye, then walked back to her seat at the defense table.

Assistant District Attorney, Justin Albright, stood up, moved around their table, buttoned one button on his suit jacket, and delivered his final remarks.

"Ladies and Gentlemen of the jury, the defendant's attorney is a very clever one. Best that money can buy. In Boston certainly, possibly even New England.

She knows that she can't put her client up in that chair to testify if she knows he is going to lie. Which is why she didn't let him sit there.

Instead, she paid a renowned psychology professor to tell you that there is no way that the defendant could have done it. The doctor used all kinds of circular reasoning to confuse us into believing that the evidence that we have, points to someone else. She did it to raise what the defense attorney called 'reasonable doubt'.

Reasonable doubt isn't *NO* doubt, folks.

The defendant wasn't caught standing over the body he'd raped and murdered and the victim isn't here to tell us that he did it. But ladies and gentlemen, there isn't any *reasonable doubt* that he did.

They're not even coming up with a plausible lie that he wasn't in the Sloane Nichols' apartment building on the day of her murder because you heard eye witness testimony that puts him there. They're not denying that he had sex with the victim, because how could they? Nor are they denying that she had a restraining order against him for having viciously beaten her in the past, which is why she left him in the first place.

They can't deny any of those things because they're all true.

So they want you to forget what you already know in your head and your heart. The defendant, a man of privilege, a man who can have whatever he wants when he wants it, was shunned. Was told by the victim that she didn't want him anymore.

And it made him mad.

So mad, that, according to the Medical Examiner's report, he raped and tortured Sloane Nichols in and out of consciousness for up to fifteen hours. Chase Bromley bound and gagged her. Her vomit was on his sock, which was shoved into her mouth to muffle the screams for help, a sock he can't explain away with one of his many excuses.

He used this bat to violate her in the most private of areas," he said while holding the weapon for the jury to see.

And he wants you to look the other way. Again.

He wants you to point the finger at some other unidentified person. A person he can't prove exists, because he doesn't, ladies and gentlemen.

If you set this man free, he will do this again."

Albright looked at individuals in the jury.

"He'll do it to your wife. Or your girlfriend. Or your daughter."

The attorney looked at juror number six, twenty-seven year old Jordan Raines, addressing her personally.

"Or he'll do it to you."

He took a step back, readdressing the entire panel.

"Chase Bromley has abused women in the past, and he was given a pass each of those times. This time he killed someone. Don't let him get away with it again.

Find him guilty, ladies and gentlemen.

Because he is."

30

JURY DELIBERATIONS LASTED THE REST OF THURSDAY,
through the night, and continued into Friday. And Saturday. The
panel wasn't bussed back to their motel rooms in the hope that they
would render a verdict. Bathroom breaks were allowed every hour—
or as needed—and meals were served in the deliberation room while
they loudly discussed their opinions.

Those opinions became more fervent, more animated as the
hours and days progressed.

Friday's breakfast, lunch, and dinner orders were handed in
to the court officer simultaneously in an effort to save time, though
the goal was not to have to provide them.

As soon as a verdict is in, they were told, they would be
bussed back to the motel to collect their things and they would be
brought home.

Home seemed so far away to each of them. A place they
hadn't seen in weeks. A place that contained loved ones that they'd
not heard from. A life they had been removed from for far too long.
Each juror feared that they would spend another weekend away
from their lives, away from the world.

Attitudes became as strong and as foul as the fetor of body
odor which clung to the air in the room.

"I say we take one more vote," Ben Post offered. It was past
lunch on Saturday and he was hoping that dinner could be had with
his boyfriend at one of the more posh establishments in the South
End.

"What would be the point? We just took a vote two hours ago and it doesn't seem like we've made much progress," Regan said. "Have we?"

Sherlie began passing out ballots again, as she had for the previous twenty votes.

"Let's give it another shot. What can it hurt?"

"My will to live," Jordan said. "I don't know how much more of this I can take."

"And you all say *I'm* dramatic," Ben mumbled.

Each member of the jury filled out the ballot, anonymously voting to convict or set free. A container was passed around the table and collected. Sherlie, as the foreperson, picked out each ballot and placed them in one of the two piles.

Eleven were in one pile, one in the other. The previous count had two ballots in the minority pile.

"Well, at least we made progress. Which is the holdout? It's either Deni or Jordan."

"I'm still not actually convinced that he did it, but I want to go home. I'm clearly in the minority, and neither Deni nor I have convinced any of you that they didn't prove their case. Because Chase Bromley isn't a good guy, and in the interest of speeding up the process, I changed my vote." Jordan Raines sat back hard in her chair as if to put an exclamation point on her statement.

"So it's Deni."

"Yeah. It's me. So what?" He looked to his left, in seat six, and said to Jordan, "We're not making a decision to convict on what he did in the past. We're not supposed to convict him because he isn't a 'good guy' or because you wanna go home. I know he's a spoiled shit-bag, but we're supposed to make a unanimous decision based on what they proved or didn't prove in court. It's about what they said he did *this* time."

Oscar rubbed his nearly bald, white head.

"Are you still hung up on the rubber? You're going to set this guy free because you can't wrap your head around the rubber? It split. Condoms break apparently."

"Yeah, that's part of it. Like I said before. Then there is the wet-work thing."

Paul Weist leaned in.

"Tell us that part again?"

"You think a guy like that is gonna break a nail doin' his own killin'? He's never worked a day in his life and you think he's gonna go through all that trouble? After he's been seen in the building?"

"He wanted to have sex with her", Renaldo added. "He had to be there to do this."

"Bromley was seen the day before," Deni said. "He just stuck around for a few hours?"

Regan Avery shook her head. "He did it over the course of fifteen hours, give or take. Maybe the neighbor saw him before he did it. Maybe he was casing the building. Who knows?"

"And that's my point. We don't know. One of the other guys that she was bangin' could have done it."

Deni had to be careful not to let on that he had more information than what was testified to and presented in court. But the information was getting jumbled in his mind. Forty-plus straight hours of deliberation was taking its toll on his sanity.

"She had a ton of people in and out of her apartment. Any one of them could have gone to her place after Chase left."

"If there was somebody to point a finger at, someone specific —not just some random profile they paid for—don't you think that high-priced legal team would have done it?" Denai Moshe stood to make his point.

"They didn't have to," Deni said. "They don't have to prove he's innocent, or prove someone else is guilty, they just have to poke enough holes in what the prosecution says to make us believe he didn't do it. I'm an ex-cop and currently an investigator in private practice. I know how these things work. I know how to read people. And I know when people are lying."

"He didn't even take the stand to lie," Evelyn added. "I'm too old for this nonsense. I don't want to argue, I just want go home. Don't you?"

"Of course I do. But you don't go to prison for the rest of your life for what you *might've* done. What you *probably* did.

Jordan, as much as you wanna go home, you have a bigger responsibility here than just throwin' in the fuckin' towel. If you feel unsure, you can't vote guilty. Period."

"It's all of us against you, buddy," Paul said. "One way or another, you're going to convict him."

"Oh, you think you're gonna intimidate me? *Guy?* Give it a try, I dare ya. But you better come correct or I'll flip your off-switch for ya."

"You touch me and they'll pull you out of here in handcuffs. Maybe then we can convict the S.O.B and go home."

Sherlie Lovett stood up.

"Maybe we can lower the level of testosterone in the room? Just a little? This is not getting us anywhere. Deni, what do you have to see or hear in order to budge?"

"Nothin'. There is nothin' that any of you can say that hasn't already been said that will change my mind. I think I've seen and heard more than you people did. He might be a scum-bag, a rich scum-bag, but I know in my gut that he didn't do this particular beating. This particular rape. And this murder. Violating the TRO? Sure. But the detectives set their sights on Bromley and never looked at any of the other randoms in and out of that apartment. If I was assigned to the case, I would have looked at each and every one of the males who responded to her profiles. I would have done more investigating."

Regan Avery stood up to get her circulation moving. She looked at the floor but spoke to Deni. "You think you have more insight into the case than we do? Why? What do you know that we don't?"

"The TRO. It was a bullshit strategy to get money. There. I said it."

Marissa Gantse looked around the table before admitting to the room, "I don't get it."

"The restraining order. She had it filed and served so she could take him for some walkaway money."

"Why didn't the defense point that out? I didn't hear anybody say that?"

Evelyn Rocher said, "Because nobody said it. How do you know that, Deni?"

"Like I said, I'm an investigator. Nobody said it because she got her payoff, but the record is sealed and a gag order was put in place. She didn't leave him, he tossed her and she got her revenge."

"So that's an even bigger motive," Marissa said.

"Then why pay it in the first place? Just kill her and not pay."

"I think we might be getting off track, people," Sherlie interjected.

A large dry erase board was brought into the room by the court officer sometime between hour five and six of deliberations. Sherlie approached it, erased all of the notes previously taken, and picked up a red and a blue marker. Two columns were made at the top of board, 'Guilty' and 'Innocent'.

"Let's go through the case point by point. Whatever testimony or piece of evidence that indicates Bromley is guilty, we'll mark in red, innocent will be in blue. Fair enough?"

"Whatever gets us there faster," Cherelle said.

"I agree. So just blurt them out, one at a time so I can jot them down."

"It was his sock," Renaldo Ramos Gomez said. Sherlie began to mark 'sock' in red, but Deni stopped her.

"How does that make him guilty? He left his sock in her place after he was done bangin' her."

"Here we go again," Paul said.

"Or she could have had it in her sock drawer as a straggler from when they lived together," Deni continued.

Paul slammed his hands down on the conference table. "But it certainly doesn't make him innocent. Just let her put in the guilty column, just for the sake of argument. We can add up all of the reds and blues and—if it's close—we can go back and talk about the sock. Okay?"

Deni remained quiet, opting instead to wave at the board, communicating for the demonstration to proceed.

"His semen was inside of her," Regan Avery added.

Sherlie put up her hand like a traffic cop to ward off any protestation before it started. She picked up a black marker and wrote the word 'semen' in between the two columns. "Happy Deni?"

"Happiness is relative. Keep going."

"He was seen in the building," Evelyn Rocher said. Sherlie marked it in red.

"She left him. That's motive." Jordan turned to Deni after injecting the comment and shrugged. "What you said wasn't presented in court. So as far as I'm concerned, she left him."

Deni shook his head in irritation as other jurors shouted out their points.

"He has a history of beating her up."

"Fingerprints."

"No alibi."

Each item was written on the board by the foreperson, Sherlie Lovett, each of them in red, none were written in blue.

When there seemed to be a lull, Deni began adding his points.

"The profiles were basically ads for group sex. 'Group' tends to mean multiple people."

It was written in blue. The only item written under the heading 'Innocent'.

"Gena Rivers. The friend and orgy partner."

Blue.

"No fingerprints on the bat or knife."

Blue.

"The shrink."

Blue.

"Condom residue."

Blue.

The two columns were looking more and more even as Deni progressed through his list of reasons to acquit. Finally, when each juror had exhausted points for either side of the equation, Sherlie proffered a thought for debate.

"I guess it all comes down to the semen.   Did it happen during the course of the rape or did it happen hours before like his lawyer said?"

31

THE HONORABLE JUDGE EMILE WALLACE TOOK TO HIS SEAT in the courtroom at 4:15 p.m. on Monday, May 26. He waved his hand downward, indicating that both sides had the green-light to sit in their seats.

When all were seated, the court officer handed Wallace a folded piece of paper, which the judge unfolded and read. He then turned to the jury, which as a group, looked war-torn. Their wrinkled clothes were the same as they'd been in on Thursday. Nobody had shaved, the facial hair on the males were far beyond a five o'clock shadow. Bags weighed down eyes, shoulders hung low. Hell had twelve faces.

Assistant District Attorneys Albright and Walsh were trying to read the faces of the jury, attempting to read non-verbal cues from each and every member, and failing. The citizens of Suffolk County that would decide the fate of the accused, the twelve people who the prosecutors were depending on to convict Chase Bromley in order for the judge to sentence him to be incarcerated for the rest of his life for the rape and murder of one of their fellow citizens, showed the body language of people who'd been beaten themselves.

Alexandria Pratt also studied the jury, and gleaned no information. She turned to her highly paid consultant. For the first time in this trial, Max Courtland looked worried. Alex nonchalantly reached behind Kevin Bishop, giving a slight tug to the right arm of Max's suit jacket. With the same slightness of gesture, he gave his boss the international shrug for 'I have no idea'.

Chase Bromley read the unspoken dialogue between the two members of his legal dream team and began to have a panic attack.

His life, as he knew it, was over. This was supposed to be a formality. It was a lock. His father was supposed to have bought him a walk-away.

I should have taken the stand.

One witness! What were they thinking?

The jury was out for five days. There's no way they're going to acquit after five days.

While these thoughts rushed through the defendant's mind, his legs began to go numb in his chair. Jack Elders leaned into his client and gave him support. The young attorney whispered into the defendant's ear to remain calm while the judge and jury were taking an infinite amount of time in the process of reading the verdict.

"Madam foreperson," Judge Wallace said.

Sherlie Lovett stood.

"I understand from your note that you have been unable to reach a verdict on the top count in this case."

"That is true, your Honor. We have reached an impasse with regard to the charge of murder in the first degree. The only charge among the many in which we have come to a consensus is the violation of a restraining order."

"A C felony. If I issue you more time to deliberate, do you think that you will be able to render a verdict on each of the more significant charges?"

"I don't believe so, your Honor. We have been hopelessly deadlocked for five days with virtually no movement."

"On the top count. How about the others? Assault? Rape? Breaking and Entering? Et cetera."

"No," Sherlie Lovett said. "We cannot agree on any of the charges other than violating the restraining order."

Max Courtland looked to Alex Pratt, giving nothing more than a wink.

Told ya.

"I received a word from my clerk on Friday and again earlier this morning that you were deadlocked, and this is the fifth day of deliberations with no result. I believe that sending you back will only postpone the inevitable. I'm forced to declare this a mistrial. Attorneys will set a short calendar date for a new trial and jury selection, this jury is free to go with the thanks of the court."

The gavel came down, the snap echoed in the courtroom like a gunshot.

Reporters were waiting at every entrance outside the courthouse to conduct interviews. They'd been camped out for days to get reactionary sound bites for their respective editors, all chomping at the bit to be the first to bring whichever verdict was handed down to their audience.

While the lack of a decision in the case was a rather large punch to the stomach after weeks and months of coverage, it also meant that each news source could milk out the commentary through another trial.

Albright stood on the front steps of the Suffolk County Superior Courthouse to convey his disappointment, and spin headlines in his favor. No decision wasn't a 'Not-Guilty'. No decision meant that he would get another bite at the apple, another opportunity to send Chase Bromley to prison.

Boston would be safe from the likes of predators like Bromley, Albright would make sure of it. In the meantime, his movements would still be monitored via his ankle bracelet, as his bail was continued pending a new trial.

Alex Pratt spoke for the defendant and the defense team. While she was likewise disappointed that the weeks spent in front of this jury were fruitless, she also spun the lack of decision, only in her client's favor. No decision meant that at least one person on that jury could see the truth and could not be convinced otherwise. No decision meant that Albright had not proven his case, and how could he? Chase Bromley was an innocent man.

By the side entrance, the jury was accosted by a gaggle of media demanding to know whom and how many had voted to acquit. How many wanted to convict?

Denai Moshe was the closest to divulging the information. He said that they had one holdout, but didn't mention that the one defiant juror was Warren Dennihan.

The court officers tried to hold off the reporters as best they could, struggling to get the jurors onto the bus and back to the motel where they'd been sequestered. It took the better part of an hour to get them safely on the bus. Microphones and recording devices and the like were shoved toward the jury. Questions rained. It took longer to get to the bus than it took for the drive to Braintree —even with the traffic.

The ride to the motel was taken in silence. Nobody spoke, since all that was needed to say had been said over the course of five days together in a cramped space. They'd been cooped up in a motel, then a deliberation room, and were now about to go home with the satiating knowledge of never having to see another person in this group ever again.

While they were happy to be getting back to their lives, each of them were bothered by their lack of success. As a group and individually. The system failed. They had failed. The jurors had a job to do and, one way or the other, it hadn't been done. They were reluctant participants in a process, a legal proceeding which necessitated finality. And they couldn't provide that finality. It was all for nothing. The disruption to their lives, the safety of their streets, the sanctity of the process, was all a waste.

All for nothing.

32

DENI COULD HEAR THE MUSIC BLARING FROM THE sidewalk outside his three-decker in South Boston. The base-line was thumping like a ghetto low-rider. The song and lyrics were unintelligible, but the muffled uptempo was unmistakeable. His two tenants above him must have been thrilled, though calling your landlord about the noise emanating from said landlord was a good way to be homeless when the lease was up.

The front door was left unlocked, which he advised his girlfriend never to do, especially at night. Repeatedly. It was after eight on Monday night, finally home from the long day and even longer trial. The music punched his chest as he opened the door, a female singer belting out how much she didn't deserve something or other. The Marantz amplifier was pumping the dance music from his multi-room Sonos system so loudly that not even the dog heard him enter.

> " .....*One ... Last ... Time,*
> *I need to be,*
> *the one,*
> *who takes you home ....*"

Ana was in the kitchen, dancing and singing into a spatula at the top of her lungs. One of his old Aerosmith t-shirts with holes in it covered her braless top, cut-off sweatpants rode high on her buttocks as she moved to the music. She turned toward him in a hopping sort of dance move, and stopped with a start.

"Aaaah. Holy shit, you scared the crap out of me," she yelled as she grabbed her chest and braced herself on the kitchen counter.

Deni started laughing, which only made Ana more angry.

Hobey ran to him, then immediately rolled onto his back on the kitchen tile. He wanted his belly rubbed, his excitement apparent from his tail wagging as fast as the beat of the loud music. Deni gave her a moment to recoup while he pet the dog. When Ana's heart fell back into time, she turned down the music with the app on her smartphone.

"I should kick your ass for scaring the hell out of me. Why didn't you let me know you were coming home? I didn't know the trial was over."

"You would have heard me call?"

She finally hugged and kissed him, he felt her heart beating into him as he lifted her and held her tight.

"The neighbors must love you right about now."

"The only time I get to play my music is when you're not around. You hate this stuff."

"That's because it sucks."

"Ariana Grande does NOT suck."

"What is she, ten? Why don't you listen to stuff more your age? And how many times have I told you to lock the doors? We're in Southie, not Mayberry. I just rebuilt this place, it stands out like a sore thumb."

"You've been home for like a minute and you want to fight?"

"No. But I do want you feisty," he said as he grabbed her barely covered ass, pulling her into him and kissing her.

"Awe, Bae, I'm gross. I've been cleaning ...."

"I told you I like the way you smell."

"You want a Redbreast? I can pour you one, it'll give me time to shower—"

"—I don't want a drink right now."

She looked worried. "Are you feeling okay?" She felt his forehead.

He kissed her again, longer this time, with more sensuality, eventually lifting her onto his waist.

Ana dropped the spatula, using the hand to grab the back of Deni's head. As they kissed, he carried her in a reverse piggy-back to the bedroom.

The rest of Hobey's belly rub would have to wait.

Deni woke up at almost four Tuesday morning, with a dry mouth and a need to piss. The dog seemed to need to perform the same function.

During the walk around the block, thoughts of the trial seeped back into his brain. And Ben Stratton. The stalker with the profile 'Dominus-Durum'.

Ben Stratton had a record and had taken an interest in Sloane Nichols. Lisa said that she couldn't prove that he and the victim had ever hooked up, that she appeared to have been putting him off, but that doesn't mean that they hadn't. Stratton was a possible suspect that hadn't been investigated by the police and one that he couldn't mention to the other jury members. A man that was still out there looking to dominate someone. His recent record had been clean, but Deni strongly doubted that Stratton had turned over a new leaf.

When deni returned to the house, Hobey waited to be unleashed and then padded to the bedroom to sleep in the bed with Ana. She was still sleeping soundly in the fetal position on her side of the bed, Hobey's return hadn't disturbed her. Deni watched her for a few moments but decided not to fight for a spot on his side of the bed. He wouldn't be able to sleep.

He needed closure to this case, a case that he wasn't being paid for but was irreversibly connect to. The truth was out there and he needed to find it. It would continue to haunt him until he did.

He thought of calling Sheed. Not on the burner, which was still in his packed luggage by the front door, but on his actual cell phone. But he didn't. She'd already left him several messages which he hadn't read, heard, or responded to. He knew what they said. She wanted him to send Bromley to hell. She wanted justice for the victim because she'd been the victim of abuse once upon a time. Lisa had probably seen the news coverage or heard about the mistrial, and she would reach out to chastise him for not doing the 'right thing' as he had promised.

Deni wanted to explain to her why he couldn't simply go with the flow. Why he couldn't vote to convict. But what could he say? What words would convey his misgivings? What would make her understand that something wasn't right?

Words wouldn't do it. He needed to prove it to her. He needed to prove it to himself. He wouldn't be able to live with himself if he was wrong. Deni wouldn't be able to look her in the eye ever again if Chase Bromley proved to have hurt Nichols and eventually hurt someone else. He would never be able to forgive himself if Bromley truly was as guilty as everyone thought he was.

The prosecutor would get another chance to convict him with another jury. But there would still be the same set of facts. The same witnesses and the same evidence. And the defense will put up the same shrink, who would sing the same song, and show the same psychological profile as proof that he couldn't be guilty.

Deni had to do something. And that something was look into this Ben Stratton character. One way or another, the truth was essential, and he felt as though he didn't have all of it.

He quietly got dressed in his usual variation of t-shirt and jeans, shoulder holster and Taurus PT 1911 semi-auto—though without a blazer—before quietly slipping out his front door. He fired up the Land Rover, heading toward his old precinct, Troop H, downtown. There was no traffic at that time of the morning, the drive took less than fifteen minutes via Summer Street.

The elderly trooper at the reception desk had little more to do than read magazines at that hour. Traffic in and out of the building mimicked the traffic out on the streets, meaning Deni didn't walk through the front door undetected. The *Guns and Ammo* magazine was tossed aside as Deni ignored the trooper's protestations and walked by the elderly watchdog.

Deni worked out of Troop H once upon a time, and that time ended in 2004 after what turned out to be an international case he'd been working blew up on him. The writing was on the wall, the politics under his then lieutenant was more than he could bear. Deni quit before he could be fired, unlike his new partner, former trooper Lisa Sheed, who was fired under the same lieutenant.

There was no love-loss between he and now Captain Manny Titanitaukis. However, Deni knew where the bodies were buried. He'd seen too much. Shady deals and back-scratching have a cost. That cost is secrecy, and Deni knew it. Whenever he needed a favor, something only the police could help with—say the address of a person of interest—Deni knew where to go. 'Tits', as he was called behind his back, would ensure that Deni got what he needed in order to keep buried information he had under a healthy amount of soil.

Tits wasn't in at five in the morning, he wouldn't arrive for a couple of hours, but was roused by a phone call from the detective on duty who had the misfortune of dealing with one former state trooper, Warren Dennihan. Captain Titanitaukis told the subordinate who sat in a desk very near where Deni used to, to give the investigator 'whatever he wanted'.

And Deni wanted the current address for one Ben Stratton.

The apartment building was still. Sunrise came and the day was in full-swing, yet nothing at the Stratton residence moved. The streets were busy, abustle with the noise of the city. Dogs barked. People yelling to one another. Car horns and car alarms. Marksdale

Street in Roxbury is a busy area. Kids going to school. Parents going to work, either to a proper job or to the corner to hustle.

Deni watched as the hours passed, and through it all— nothing at number 215 stirred. The buildings surrounding it had life, yet there was none at Stratton's.

He never took his eyes off the second story apartment, nor the others in the building. Life in Boston moved, but not that building.

His cell phone rang, probably Ana wondering where he was, but he ignored it. After almost a dozen ignored texts and calls that he let go to voicemail, Deni decided to turn the damn ringer off.

At nine o'clock, he decided to go in for a closer look. If Stratton was home, he and Deni would have a chat. If not, he'd have a look around.

A walk around the building and six raps on the apartment door produced no Stratton.

Warren Dennihan had been blessed with a finite number of talents. Some had come with practice and training, some he'd seemed to have been born with. He'd become a master at two key talents he often needed for his line of work. Fighting and getting around locks.

Fighting had come to him at an early age. When you grow up in the rough and tumble neighborhoods of South Boston, you either learn to fight or you don't grow up to be very old. Even the girls of Southie know how to fight. Not the hair-pulling kind, but the knocking fucking teeth out kind. Street fighting as a kid turned into hand-to-hand training as an adult at the academy, which fueled his desire to take up Brazilian Jiu-Jitsu, which begat Mixed Martial Arts fighting—sometimes for profit.

Picking locks also came at an early age. He was breaking into cars, stealing Alpines and Blaupunkts, before he had a full set of adult teeth. In the Southie of old, you were a crook or you knew one. Deni got out of that life and joined the state police a long time ago, but he could still pick your lock in the time it took you to get out your key.

Ben Stratton had three locks on his front door, one in the knob and two deadbolts. It took Deni less than a full minute to open the front door without drawing attention to himself. It took as long to get his titanium picks out of his wallet and replace them than it had to actually unlock the door.

He slowly pushed open the door, letting it swing wide open, and stood at the threshold for a full thirty-seconds. He watched and he listened for movement inside the tiny, filthy apartment. But there was no detectable sign that anyone was home. No pet to warn Deni that this was its domain.

Deni drew his firearm from his holster. He pushed the manual safety above the trigger to the 'off' position, while raising it. He pointed his .45 caliber ACP left and right as he slowly entered the apartment, looking down the Novak sights.

The floor creaked, each step Deni made sounded to him like a sledge hammer to the floor followed by whining. Thin, fake, hardwood floorboards have an unmistakable sound. And yet no protestations about his trespass.

Nobody was home.

He passed an open closet that was meant for a washer and dryer, yet none existed. Then the kitchen, which was not sanitary enough for food to be stored in, much less prepared. As Deni moved about the small apartment, he scanned down the barrel of his pistol in disgust. What wasn't in disrepair was covered in grease and grime. Cobwebs were in every corner.

I can't believe people live like this.

He didn't want to touch anything for evidentiary reasons, but with the level of dross, he had an additional reason for not being cross-contaminated.

A short hallway led to the one and only bedroom. A newish computer was nestled kitty-corner across and to the right. The chair, computer, and desk appeared to be the only things in the apartment that were cared for.

Deni had no talent for computers. If he had his way, people would still use typewriters or handwrite their letters. Phones would be used to call people, not send them a photo or an emoticon to keep in touch. Pornography would come in the form of smut magazines or VHS tapes, not with the swipe of your finger on an iPad.

Or a few clicks of a mouse.

He immediately regretted moving the mouse with his gun to bring Stratton's computer screen to life. The desktop photo was a picture of a naked, surgically enhanced woman, shoving a black dildo as big in diameter as a can of baked beans into her vagina.

Deni recoiled from the computer like it would burn him, and he backed away from the chair as if it were a trapdoor.

"Gaaaaahhhhh."

This is where he beats off.

He was still trying to shake off the heebie-jeebies, vigorously rubbing his left hand on his jeans though he hadn't actually touched anything, when he saw the reflected light on the computer screen change.

Deni turned around in time to catch a glimpse of a figure before he could raise his gun and felt a hard thump to his head.

Flashes and stars. The Taurus was kicked out of his hand. He tried to defend himself but he couldn't see who or what he needed to fight.

Indiscernible images came in strobes.

The muffled words, "Welcome to hell," preceded total darkness.

33

"WAKEY-WAKEY!"

Deni started to come to, hearing someone speaking to him. He further came into his whits when he was doused with what he first thought was water.

Another bucket of liquid was tossed at him, soaking him from head to toe. It wasn't water. It had a pungent, sweet aroma with a pseudo rubbing alcohol undertone.

Time to take in your surroundings, Deni.

He was in a bad spot. His feet were bound and zip-tied to a sturdy chair at the ankle. His hands were also zip-tied behind his back though not secured to the back of the chair. His head felt like it was going to explode, a not-so dull ache invaded his every thought.

Stratton's apartment.

I'm still in Stratton's apartment. Mother fucker got the jump on me.

"Warren Barra Dennihan," the hairless man presumed to be Ben Stratton said to him, reading from either his driver's license or his state issued investigator's license.

"Nobody calls me that."

"Barra. What sort of name is Barra?"

"It means 'fuck-you' in Gaelic."

"Ah. You're Irish. Temper-temper. You might not want to get too hot there, mister private investigator. Diethyl ether has a very low flash point. I don't want you to burst into flames just yet."

"You can't fight like a man, Benji? You gotta sucker me? Hairless, ball-less, Chicken-shit, mother fucker!"

"It's Ben, not Benji, and you unlawfully entered my home. You'll deserve every ounce of punishment coming your way, but first

I have to know why you're here. I know you're an investigator, says so right here on your license. But who sent you?"

"You've inherited a lot of money, Benji. I was hired to find you so I can inform you that you can move out of this shit-pile. You're rich."

"Very funny," Stratton said. "I have no family and I'm already rich."

"I can tell. Who's your decorator?"

Stratton moved closer to Deni's chair, squatting in front of him, though there was nothing to be done about it. Deni could almost see through his pasty-white skin, his blue veins could be seen meandering about his exposed head and arms.

"Ether is supposed to be an anesthetic, but you know, some pain you just can't kill. You're going to die today, Warren Barra Dennihan. You're going to burn to death and be found in the rubble of a vacant apartment building that will soon be nothing but ash. With the help of the ether to intensify the flame, you're not likely to ever be identified. How much torture you endure before suffering through the very end is completely up to you. Now, shall we try this again?"

"Why don't you untie me and we can talk about it?"

Stratton sighed. "Suit yourself. People say they don't enjoy pain, but they always choose to do things the hard way," he said as he exited the small room. He quickly returned with some rope which he then used to fasten Deni's chest to the chair. Next, Deni's already bound hands were slowly raised behind him toward the ceiling, hyperextending his shoulders.

"Have you ever heard of 'Strappado', Warren Barra Dennihan?"

"MMMMMMMMMMMMMMMMMMM - *FUCK YOU!*" The pain was excruciating.

Keep your head Deni. For Christ-sake, keep your head, he told himself through the pain.

He sparred a minimum of four times per week at his Mixed Martial Arts gym in Brookline, before the trial started anyway, and had a high tolerance for pain. All fights end up on the ground, grappling and wrestling the opponent into submission. Those are the situations you train for. When sparring with others at the gym, as the competition level of the sparring partners increase, submissions come with more difficulty, and therefore more pain. You didn't tap-out until you absolutely had to. You're never defeated.

But this was something else entirely. This wasn't sparring. The situation and the pain was real.

"I want to know why you're here. Tell me, and this can end a bit more quickly."

"If you don't want the money, I'll take it."

"Sticking with the same story?" Stratton lowered himself, still behind Deni, and whispered into his ear. "Good. I like to administer pain as much as you obviously like to receive it."

He moved around Deni, again leaving the room, returning with a surgical steel filleting knife.

"Now that you are familiar with Strappado, let's move on to flaying."

Stratton began to cut off Deni's 47 brand Red Sox t-shirt. The knife went through the cotton like it was softened butter, the torn cloth lay in shreds on the floor with just a few strokes.

"Aren't you the colorful one? Look at that tapestry of body art. Do you have any down, you know, below? I don't have any tattoos myself, never could pick out just the right thing to have permanently drawn onto my skin. Is there one that you regret? I can cut that one off of you first, if you like."

"You realize that I'm gonna fuckin' kill you, Stratton."

"That would be a neat trick. But I think not. What is going to happen, what is going to happen very slowly, is I'm going to start peeling your skin away. Peeling all of that artwork off of your body one drawing at a time. And I can't wait to see just how much of your body needs to be flayed. Once we get through with your torso, I'll cut off those jeans and see what we can do down below. Are you circumcised, Warren Barra Dennihan? If not, you will be today." Stratton paused for effect.

"Now, who sent you?"

Deni had been likened to a bruin in body armor by some of those who knew him. A dog with a bone by others. Each person trying to describe how relentless he is. There is no quit in him. He will fight until there is no more fight in him, because he's dead.

The situation was dire, but he refused to give up. He continued to scan his surroundings, looking for a way to even the score. No weapons. Just a couch that should have been thrown away with the turn of the century and a relic of a television, the kind with two large knobs—one for turning to VHF channels and one for UHF channels. On top of the ancient TV were a couple of pictures in frames. He knew the woman in one of them. She was very shapely and had red hair.

What's her name? Shit, I know her. Where do I know her from?

His head ached. His shoulders ached.

THINK!

Then it clicked.

Tired of waiting for an answer, Stratton moved to start cutting tattoos off of Deni's deltoid.

"Amanda. Amanda Hunt."

Deni struck a chord. The look on Stratton's face told him so.

The sharp knife that was in his right hand was thrown at the fake hardwood flooring like a lawn dart, the tip had plenty of purchase to hold it upright. Stratton then used that hand and all of his strength to punch Deni in the face.

Blood began to flow from Deni's mouth and cheek. Swelling began almost as instantly.

He remembered the curvy red-head testifying during the trial. She was Chase Bromley's girlfriend before Sloane Nichols.

"You had better start explaining yourself, or you are going to wish you were never born," Stratton said.

"You almost had me fooled, Benji. I thought you were poor. I came in here and I was seriously grossed out. I mean who lives like this? Nobody. Homeless people live better than this. So what is this place? Your lair? How many cases are gonna get closed when the cops comb over this shit-box for DNA? I bet you got plenty of yours for comparison by that expensive beat-off station you got back there."

Deni took another shot to the face. It hurt as badly as the first, but he laughed it off like it hadn't. The pasty, skinny fucker had a good punch, he had to hand it to him.

"You hit like a bitch. Untie me and we'll do this for real."

"You're trying to antagonize me and it won't work."

"Fight me for real you two percent milk shaded pussy."

"With your dislocated shoulders, you would pose no real threat, Warren Barra Dennihan."

"Call me that again. Call me that again and we'll see what I can and can't do."

"How do you know Amanda?" Stratton was visibly making an effort to stay calm, maintain composure.

"Amanda *Cunt*? Who doesn't know that piece of trim. More people been in and outta that twat than fuckin' Walmart."

Stratton went in to choke Deni. Dove at him. When he moved in, his face came within inches of Deni's, who head butted him with as much power he could manage with his limited range of motion. It was enough to cause damage.

Stratton's nose began to flow crimson. His hands instinctively went to his face to assess the damage and stop the bleeding as he backed away from Deni. Stitches and rhinoplasty would be needed to repair the injury. It took several moments for him to regain focus from the other side of the apartment.

"I'm going to torture you for a very long time for this," Stratton promised.

"Come on back here so we can talk about it."

"You're not short of confidence, are you Warren Barra Dennihan?"

"And why should I? Now that I've got this whole thing figured out. You're done, Stratton. You were in and out of the Foster Care system, right? One of your mommies play with your little pecker? Is that why you hate women? Except Amanda. She does whatever you want her to because you've got money, so you might actually like her. You put a big ring on that finger. Does she stick it up your asshole?"

Deni took another punch to the face. This one split the skin under his left eyebrow. But he kept on.

"You hate Chase Bromley for what he did to your girl, right? You're tired of listenin' to her bitch about how she got done dirty? So you killed Sloane Nichols as a twofer. Rape, torture, and kill her —which gets your rocks off anyways—plus you get to frame the guy who did your future wife wrong in the process. What I don't know is how many others have there been, Benji? How many others have you raped and killed you fuckin' mangy mutt? How long before you get sick of Amanda and *flay* her?"

"You'll never know. Nobody will ever know because you're not going to leave here alive. I'm going to cut off your balls and feed them to you—after I skin you alive—and then burn you. I'll find another place to rid the world of these skanks. You'll be dead and burned beyond identification and I'll be doing what I've always done. I'm not 'done', Warren Barra Dennihan. You are. The only question now, the only question now, is how and where to start?"

Stratton continued to put pressure on his nose with one hand, trying and failing to stave off the heavy blood flowing from it, and produced a rubber dildo the size of an elephant trunk from a drawer behind him with the other.

"Make no mistake. This is going to hurt."

He again crossed the room, swung the enormous phallus like a club, hitting Deni across the face with force. The sound was as loud as it was painful. The blow knocked Deni to his right, far enough to make him fall to the floor with the wooden chair still attached.

"I wonder how far we can shove this into *your* asshole?"

Deni was again seeing stars and forced himself to remain conscious. He didn't know what the sick twist would do to him if he was comatose, and he damn sure didn't want to find out.

His attacker was coming at him again. Deni was awkwardly prostrate, knees and face to the floor, chest tied to the chair with its four legs pointed toward Stratton. Deni's tied hands and seat were in the exact position he didn't want it to be in.

As Stratton moved toward him from behind, Deni pushed himself off the floor with his face, knees, and toes, driving the chair legs toward his attacker in the hopes of impaling him. He failed.

Instead he was hit on the back of the head with the enormous dildo.

Blackness creeped in.

The strobe light was turned back on.

His head was back on the floor, ear against the dirty, phony wood, eyes glazing over as he faced the front door of the apartment.

He thought he heard gunfire.

He thought he heard feet stampeding toward him, the floor vibrated against his face.

He certainly hoped help was there. But how could it be?

Nobody knew where he was.

Then everything went dark.

34

DENI WOKE TO A NURSE ADJUSTING A RACK OF FLUIDS hanging beside his bed.

"Oh good. You're awake," she said. "I tried to do it as gently as possible. Can you hear me? Do you understand where you are?"

"I hear you. What happened?"

"You're in Mass General, Mister Dennihan. You've suffered a severe concussion and we're monitoring you. You're brain-swelling is the doctor's biggest concern right now. We still need to do a follow-up MRI and wake you every few hours to ensure your condition doesn't worsen. I'll send the doctor in shortly."

"Wait. How did I get here?"

"I'll let the doctor explain—"

"—NO! Tell me. What happened? Stratton. Did that sodomite stick that thing in my ass?"

The nurse began to laugh, failing in trying to hide it.

"No. I don't believe so. You came by ambulance yesterday. You were unconscious and presented with head trauma and two dislocated arms, with severe shoulder and ligament damage. You're shoulders and arms have been reset back into their sockets and should fully heal in a few weeks. As I said, your head is the major concern right now. You have some detectives and some visitors that are waiting to see you, but I'm not sure you're allowed to have visitors yet."

"Bring them in. The visitors. The detectives can wait."

"I will need to clear that with the doctor first."

"Bring them in or I'm checking myself outta here."

"You're going to be one of my difficult patients, aren't you?"

Deni gave her a fake smile. The motion hurt despite the morphine drip.

"I'll see what I can work out," she said on her way out of the room.

A brief and painful scan of the small hospital bedroom garnered the information that he had a single, no other person was convalescing in what would be very close quarters. A vase of flowers and a few balloons festooned a table that was only a few feet away but might as well have been on the other side of the planet. A remote control for the TV also lived there.

Deni tried to rise from the bed to fetch it, but the pain immediately stopped him in his tracks, his head returned to the pillow with the same urgency it had left.

"You're probably going to be tender for a while."

Lisa Sheed entered the room, Ani all but fighting to get through the door before her. Two of the most important people in his life, both happened to be women, began to nurture in their own way simultaneously. Sheed turned on the TV and handed the patient his remote, while his girlfriend plastered his face with kisses.

"You gave us quite a scare," Lisa offered.

"I should fucking kill you for almost getting yourself killed," Ani said between pecks.

"He got the jump on me. A few weeks out of the shit and I make a rookie mistake."

"Your mistake was not calling me for backup," Lisa said. She took a seat in the only chair available, next to the small table.

Ani gently took space next to the patient in bed, lying next to him, continuing to preen.

"Or let me know where you were," Ani added. "I woke up and you were gone."

"I couldn't sleep. I had a hunch. What happened? Did he confess?"

"Stratton didn't get the chance. I put two holes in him, center mass with a .45. He didn't have the time nor the strength to say much of anything. But his prints were compared to one set that was pulled from Sloane's apartment. DNA might take a few more days but at the very least, he'd been there. The detectives who investigated the case had so many prints from the apartment that they dismissed all but Bromley's."

"How'd you find me?"

"Ani called, worried. I tracked your phone with mine to Stratton's shithole. I went up the apartment to see what was up and there you were, getting your ass handed to you."

"I had him right where I wanted him."

"Yeah, okay. The real question is how did *you* find the apartment?"

"I know people in Troop H also."

"Yeah, but that's not his real address. He lives up on Beacon Hill. Swanky area."

"That's the address I got on his last known. It was his cave."

"Look," Lisa said, pointing to the television which Deni had landed on NECN, the news covering the very story they were discussing. File footage from the original investigation and outside the courtroom during the trial flashed on the screen, though the sound had been muted.

"Everybody is trying to C-Y-A at this point," she continued. "Cops are blaming the vic for having too many lovers in and out of her place, among other things, that's why they hooked the wrong guy. They want to talk to you, by the way. Leiman and Champagne have been camped out in the waiting area to interview you. We had to pretend to go get some coffee to beat them in here. They want to know how and why you ended up in Stratton's place."

"I'll deal with it."

"Press is making you out a hero, they've been camped outside the hospital reporting updates on your condition. With the press you're getting, Albright isn't likely to want a pound of your flesh. He's telling anyone who will listen that he was just following the evidence he was provided by the cops, vigorously prosecuting the suspect at the other end of that evidence. You should hear him, Deni. He keeps going on about how he has faith in the judicial process because the jury, meaning you, refused to prosecute Bromley, who turns out to be innocent after all. Such bullshit."

"He did it, She."

"Bromley? You convinced me. He didn't do *this* thing. But he's still a piece of shit."

"No. It was Stratton. The whole thing. That sick prick gets his kicks from doing that kinda stuff, but setting up his girlfriend's enemy and former boyfriend was a bonus."

"I know. I didn't mean Bromley being innocent was bullshit, I meant Albright's 'faith in the process' is bullshit. If Bromley didn't have the legal dream team he had, or you as the holdout, he'd be sitting in a four-by-nine waiting to hear where he was going to be spending the rest of his life right now. I still say that's where he belongs, but you've heard my rant on him.

On top of all of it all, Pratt has been on all the news channels and is hitting the morning talk circuit about her client, saying how easy it is for the police and DA's office to railroad a suspect.

She's been the only good thing stemming from this trial. Because of her, Taylor, Higgs & Pratt want to hire us to conduct ad hoc investigations for their law firm. Alex Pratt has been calling me non-stop between interviews to get ahold of you."

"What did you tell her?"

"What could I tell her, Deni? You've been in a coma for four days, I've been holding her off."

"That's a lot of work that will come our way if we take it. Big money."

"I know. Between G,W & A in New Hampster and getting the T, H & P account down here, we'd have as much or more work than we could handle."

"So why didn't you tell her we'd take it?"

"Without consulting you? You'd have killed me."

"I need my partner to take initiative when it comes to the good and the welfare of our business."

Lisa stood from her chair.

"Are you saying what I think you're saying? *OUR* Business? I could kiss you."

"Please don't."

Ani did the job for her.

"We will consult each other on our cases, like we do now, only we'll split the profits from all cases, fifty-fifty. Deal?"

"Absolutely. It's what I've been asking for. Thank you, Deni."

"We'll split the expenses too," he said with a fake smile.

"Duh."

"Seriously though, you deserve it. You might have even saved my life."

"Fuck yourself. Typical male ego. You know I saved your ass."

"Get outta my room and go see Reggie before she leaves you."

Lisa moved toward Deni but gave Ani a peck on the cheek.

"Don't let him lick his wounds too long, he has a lot of work to do when he gets out of bed," she said.

Ani just laughed and pressed herself further into Deni, who winced.

When they were alone, Ani told her man that she never wanted him to scare her like that again.

"I can't promise you that I'll never be in tight spots, Ani. It comes with the job sometimes."

"But I didn't even know where you were. You just took off. If Lisa hadn't tracked you ..... "

"Yeah, I'm gonna have to talk to her about that. She needs to learn some boundaries."

She gave him a gentle slap on the cheek.

"Stop it. I'm being serious. I love you so much and yet you piss me off to the point that I want to kill you."

"What day is it?"

"Friday. Why?"

"Think we'll make it to Shōjō?"

"Really? I'm trying to have a serious conversation with you and you want to know if you'll be out of the hospital in time for duck fat fries?"

"Yeah. Chicken and waffles. Our usual."

"Warren Dennihan, I love you but I fucking hate you sometimes."

"Join the club."

35

SHŌJŌ, THE RESTAURANT ON 9 TYLER STREET, WAS A MOB scene on Sunday, as it was every Sunday. The trendy Chinatown restaurant was not normally the type of establishment that suited Deni, but it had grown on him.

The murals on every wall interested him. The varying imagery reminded him of his tapestry of tattoos. The food was innovative and yet not pretentious. The restaurant, he was told, Shōjō, was named after a spirit that had a fondness for alcohol. This was also akin to him.

Ani had taken him there early on in their relationship. An Asian woman taking him to Chinatown to an Asian establishment was a situation he thought he'd have to tolerate. But the opposite occurred. He felt instantly and weirdly connected to it.

The restaurant had been a Sunday staple since.

The crowds of people in and outside of the restaurant clearly indicated each and every week that they weren't the only ones who felt connected to it.

No reservations were taken for parties under ten people, so those that wanted to take in the culinary excellence, had to wait their turn. Not something that Deni loved about the place, but since he'd become a regular, he and his asian girlfriend would sometimes get bumped up to the front of the line.

Deni had just been released from the hospital the previous day, Saturday, which was filled with police interviews, reporter interviews, calls from Alex Pratt, and one from Kenneth Bromley on behalf of his son. The remainder of Saturday was exhausting, so much so that he barely had the energy to pet the dog before passing out in his own bed, let alone spend time with his girlfriend.

When they were sat at one of the few tables for two in the small dining room, they clinked their drinks that they had ordered and started at the bar. Ani with her usual Mizu Sunrise and Deni with his Yakuza Old Fashioned since they didn't have Redbreast.

"To freedom," Deni said.

"Finally. Listen, I don't want to sound like a nag, but the doctors said no booze for a while. You're still on meds for your headaches, are you sure you should drink, Bae?"

They ordered the Duck Fat Fries to share from the attentive server while they settled down.

"I'm fine. Don't worry. Honestly my arms hurt worse than my head. I'll be good as new in a few days. Back at the gym, back to my normal weight. I'll tell ya what I shouldn't be eating is duck fat fries. I can't believe how much weight I put on in just a few weeks."

"I love you, no matter what size you are, just as long as you're in one piece. That was quite a scare."

"I know. But this is what I do for a livin'. I don't know anything else. He got the drop on me cuz I was fat and slow."

"Fat and getting old? Jeez, what am I doing with you?"

"Hey, take it easy."

Ani laughed.

"You gain ten pounds or so and you act like you're obese."

Nobody spoke for a beat. They both pretended to look at their menus but were really looking at one another. Neither was fooling the other.

"Where do you see this going, Deni? You're going to get really hurt or worse on one of these cases, and I don't know what I'm going to do. Seriously. I'm going to end up alone."

"That's kinda what I wanted to talk to you about. I am who I am, and that's not likely to change. I guess that's what I'm trying to say. I'm not really a guy who changes."

"You don't think I know that? It took how long to convince you to get the dog? I mean, you still buy actual albums instead of just downloading them. On *vinyl*."

"You didn't convince me to get the dog, Ani, you just brought him home. What was I gonna do? Kick him out?"

"You love him and you know it."

"He's okay."

"See? You can compromise, if you have to," Ani said with a wink.

The server was back with their duck fat fries, and another round of libations which they didn't order.

"The bartender sent these over. She says you're a hero."

Deni was slightly embarrassed. "I just followed the clu—"

"—Not you. Her," the server said, pointing to Ani.

Ani turned toward the bar and realized who the female bartender was. The bartender hadn't been up there when she and Deni were ordering their drinks before they sat, or Ani hadn't seen her.

The bartender was a former client. Ani had advocated for her, helped her to get out of an abusive relationship, and out on her own two feet.

"Oh, wow. Tell her thanks and I'm glad she's doing well."

The server asked if they wanted anything else at the moment, but Deni and Ani were taking their time. The unperturbed server simply turned to attend to the other guests in the restaurant.

"We're a couple of heroes."

"I think she said that I was the hero."

Deni smiled. "Isn't that what marriage is all about? Couples? People do this, right? This is what all the damn songs are about?"

"Deni, are you drunk already? I told you mixing booze with those meds was a bad idea."

"She and I were talking. Lisa. Before all this happened. But everything that happened, everything you said, is making me rethink things. About us."

Ani leaned in, looking Deni in the eye.

"Do you talk about us with her all the time?"

"She's a lesbian, Babe. You've got nothing to—"

"—I know that, idiot. But you have all these talks with her about us, and you never talk to *me* about us."

"I think maybe you missed the point."

"Maybe you should spell it out for me."

"This might not be the best time to do this. We're in a public place."

Ani reached across the table, grabbed his chin, pointing his face directly toward hers.

"Best time to do what, Deni?"

He put a small jewelry box in the center of the small table. It was an unmistakable size and had the unmistakable, patented sea-green color.

"Before the trial. I got this ring, but it was never really the right time. Or I just lost the nerve. I mean, I'm over forty and I haven't taken the plunge yet, so why now? You're a lot younger than me ....."

Ani was about to say, "*STOP RAMBLING,*" but she didn't at first, she just let him work things out.

" ..... But I can't see myself without you. I guess I don't want to think about life without you."

"And I don't want to be without you," she said.

"I should do this when we're alone. That's the way it's supposed to be done, right?"

Ani's heart was in her throat. "That's not the part that matters. I mean, if we are talking about what you should be doing, you should be on bended knee, but you never do things the way that they're supposed to be done. That's kind of your thing."

"I really must have hit my head hard. Maybe I am drunk. I should wait."

"Just say the words, Deni. Don't make me hurt you."

They looked into each other's eyes for a time. She didn't say a word, Deni was silent while he tried to find the words she was looking for.

Ani slightly stood, leaned into him, gently kissed him on the mouth. She then whispered into his ear, "It's okay. Whenever you're ready. I'm not going anywhere."

She sat back in her seat. She didn't look at the box still in the center of the table—the big turquoise elephant in the room—nor did she comment on it. The box just lived there, unopened, in purgatory.

Instead, she picked up a fry off the sharing plate just next to it, and stuck it in her mouth. Ani was contemplating the next item on the menu she would order, when she heard the words.

"Will you marry me?"

AUTHOR'S NOTES AND ACKNOWLEDGEMENTS

The previous work is one of fiction, any resemblance to specific and true incidents is purely coincidental. The names of real places, people, music, etc. are either coincidental or simply to give the story an authentic feel. None of the events that took place in this novel are real to my knowledge.

Domestic violence is real, however, and continues to be a problem that society cannot seem to put into the rearview. Public figures, sports figures, and such will offend us with their actions toward their girlfriends or spouses, the public will be outraged, but not enough to affect change. Enough is enough. Men are supposedly the stronger of the sexes, I maintain that the opposite is true, and the men who abuse women are proof. If you or someone you know is a victim of domestic violence, there are free public services that can and will help. Please seek out those services in your area. Shelters for survivors of domestic violence in Massachusetts are available through massresources.org

On a lighter note, I would like to acknowledge that among other liberties I took with the law, my representation of the Suffolk County Superior Court building in Boston is based upon the nearby historic John Adams Courthouse. The architecture is more aesthetically pleasing, and therefore fodder for better imagery when telling a story. Those that have been in either or both courthouses can attest to my misrepresentation, though if one is on the receiving end of justice, either mightn't be appealing.

I would like to take the time to thank those that took the time to speak with me, give me tours, and/or provide their invaluable expertise. If you enjoyed this book, it is largely because of them. A character or two may have been named in lieu of payment.

Finally, thanks to you, the reader for your time. I hope you enjoyed the story.

-sw-

ABOUT THE AUTHOR

Scott Wellinger is a well-traveled writer and novelist. He has written many novels, articles, scripts, musical lyrics, and essays under pseudo-names. His more popular novels feature, among others, the fictitious private investigations of Warren Dennihan. A native of New England, he was born in Vermont and was educated in Boston, Massachusetts. He holds a Master's Degree in Applied Economics and when he is not traveling, writing, playing music, cooking or painting, he is on a golf course.

For more author information: www.WWPGroupInc.com

Also by scott wellinger:

Use It Up (2015)

Other novels in the **Warren Dennihan crime-fiction series:**

CRASH

A Warren Dennihan Novel (first of series)

Venom

A Warren Dennihan Novel (book 2)

Sinn

A Warren Dennihan Prequel (book 3)

Ebb

A Warren Dennihan Prequel (book 4)

These novels can be purchased in Ebook and print wherever books are sold.

Thank You for Reading!

If you enjoyed reading this novel, please help others appreciate it as well.

Recommend it.   Please help other readers find it by recommending it to friends, reader groups, discussion boards, or wherever you purchased the book.

Review it.   You can add your thoughts to Amazon, GooglePlay, iBooks, kobo, Barnes & Noble, at the publisher website (WWPGroup.com), reader clubs like goodreads or LibraryThing, etc., etc. If you do write a review, please share it with either my publisher at WWPGroupInc@mail.com or me directly at scottwellinger@gmail.com (or both) so that I can thank you personally.

Follow me on twitter and Instagram for updates and special offers.   @wellinger_scott , and @SCOTT_WELLINGER , respectively.

Best Wishes,

~SW~

The following is a sample of Ebb, book four in the Warren Dennihan series. The novel is available in ebook and print wherever books are sold.

PROLOGUE

RONDO CLEARLY DIDN'T KNOW WHAT to make of his newfound freedom. The early morning walk through Stage Fort Park was normal, but the release from his leash was not. The pull of the collar followed by the release of the clasp was almost too much to wish for. He gave his master a look as if asking if he was dreaming. He wouldn't offer a chance to reconsider. The chocolate lab took off for his adventure, running at full sprint to take full advantage of the many things he had so longed to do every previous day.

The rocks. The ocean. The trees and shrubs that had withstood countless years of saltwater and harsh coastal winds. The smells of late April, the last week of the month in fact. The smells of other dogs that had been to the park before him on their leashes, as per the rules. The scent of the owners that had tethered them. He proudly scouted the state park, smelling and searching. Rondo would mark new territory on this day. His brethren could eat their collective heart out.

Ivan Kadishev was feeling good on this particular morning. The tall Eastern European was in rare form. His usual bleak outlook on life, his innate pessimism, had taken the rare day off. He and his companion would do their morning constitutional a bit differently on this morning. Ivan would manage the rocky, sandless beach at his own pace — free of the pulls and tugs from Rondo. Free to think about things other than the possibility of turning an ankle.

The two had lived in Massachusetts together for as long as Rondo had been alive, just over four years. Ivan had lived elsewhere, alone in a new land for two years before their friendship began. Every morning for the past four years they took their walk on the uneven coastal terrain, along the cliffs above the jagged shoreline. Every morning an adherence to the well-posted rules regarding dogs and leashes. Rules shouldn't be broken by those who are not citizens in the strictest sense, for that was an easy way to draw unwanted attention. But that status had now changed. He and his furry friend could now both bask in true freedom.

Nobody was around anyway. The park was always abandoned at that early hour, not even the sun had risen from the wavy horizon at that time some months during the year. But that too was different on this day. While still brisk, the new sun was up and heating both the air and the ocean. The Atlantic never gets warm, rarely above sixty degrees north of Cape Cod, though the local TV weather hottie had said that it was currently the warmest in history. Probably due to global warming or climate change or whatever the media was calling it these days. Another topic that would normally have festered in Ivan's mind, adding to his usual attitude of doom and gloom.

Nobody swam from this shore at any hour, warm or not. The water deep, the current always strong against the high rocks. The undercurrents almost ensured drowning. Never a lifeguard on duty. The danger obvious even to those without the quickest of whits.

A splash could be heard from a distance over the sound of the lapping waves against the rocky shore. Rondo would not only get a rare run, it became apparent to Ivan that his dog was also in the mood for swim. He paddled his way out to sea. Toward what, only the canine knew. Probably a stick, Ivan thought. Maybe toward nothing in particular. Rondo would now need a bath, he also thought. Maybe this was not such a good idea. He also wondered how his furry friend was planning to climb back up onto shore when he was finished with his swim. It was a question the lab had undoubtedly not thought of. That was what masters were for he supposed, to manage such details.

Ivan methodically moved toward the water, negotiating rocks while facilitating his balance by grabbing a hold of tree branches and roots. He needed to bring his dog back in, never feeling that too much freedom was possible until that moment. His usual pessimism was inching back into the forefront of his thoughts. Rondo was ruining what could have been a great start to the day.

"Rondo. Come back here," Ivan called. His accent thick. But there was no response. No bark. No whimper. Kadishev followed up with a loud whistle. The dog always responded to his whistles, an almost Pavlovian response. But Rondo was still at sea and all but invisible. "ебать," he cursed to himself.

Ivan moved south along the rocky shore, leash in hand, ready to haul in his normally well-behaved dog. Maybe the dog was looking for an egress, he thought. Or maybe his pet was drowning. Pessimism had fully returned.

He called and whistled several more times, without response.

Worry began to set in, until finally he heard panting off to his left. Ivan looked out toward the horizon, spotting his cheeky lab paddling toward the shore. Rondo was dragging something, huffing and puffing as he tried to breathe around the part of the large object protruding from his mouth.

"What have you found?" Ivan stared out across the waves which pushed his dog toward the shore with swiftness, along with the haul. "Big tree?"

But even as he said it, Ivan knew it wasn't a tree. The object was too pale. Too gray and fleshy. Had his dog killed a large fish? A stronger possibility, though he doubted his lab was quite that good a swimmer. As his wet friend came ever-closer, pessimistic wonder became unbridled certainty. Rondo let the catch go as he came to shore, moving to another area to extricate himself from the drink. Ivan didn't help him as he was frozen, inanimate from shock. Without a proper shore, the catch was pushed by the waves and beaten against the rocks below Ivan's perch. Kadishev's long wingspan was just short of being able to reach down and pull it up, had he had the strength or wherewithal to do so.

Rondo had somehow made it up onto shore further down the coast, panting as he came running back to his master, as if proud of his handiwork. The wet dog shook off as much excess water as he could before looking over the ledge with Ivan.

The milky-white and gray body was floating face down in the wash, slamming against the rocks with each tide like a bag of bones. Each thrust of the water a new assault on the person three feet below. There was no way the person was alive. If the person had been alive prior to Rondo's beach drag, the battering had completed the task of ending life.

Had the macabre discovery taken place earlier in the week, there would have been no choice for Ivan. He would have simply taken his dog out of the park and hoped against all hope that he would escape unnoticed. He would have found a new place for their daily constitutional. But it hadn't. It happened in the last week of April on a monday. A great way to start said week.

Ivan Kadishev had taken an oath, made a commitment to his countrymen. He swore to 'bear true faith and allegiance' to them, even when fallen he presumed. Doing nothing was not an option, so in that way there was also no choice. He had nothing to fear in reporting it; after all, he was innocent. He had not been responsible for the death of this person, surely the authorities would know that. But was his dog responsible? Had Rondo found the body or aided in its destruction?

He decided to reattach the leash before making the call to find out. He removed his phone from his pocket, staring at the touchscreen. How would he explain the dog being off of the leash? How severe was that crime? Would reporting one crime forgive another? He second-guessed his thought. Maybe he shouldn't make the call.

Part One

The Head and the Heart
April

1

THE 2013 CHEVY IMPALA slowly made its way through the
parking area of Stage Fort Park in Gloucester, Massachusetts toward
the tumult of vehicles and personnel. The ashen gray-metallic sedan
sparkled in the hot sun, the stone and gravel crackled and popped
under the tires as they rolled over them, eventually coming to a stop.
Though the vehicle was unmarked, anyone with a lick of sense knew
it was a Massachusetts State Police car. What was less obvious was
that it was from Troop H out of Boston, a major crimes unit.

In Massachusetts, the State Police handle all major crimes
along with traffic on the interstate highway system. Although
Gloucester was outside of Boston and Suffolk County, Troop H was
the closest precinct and therefore assigned to the case.

Two detectives exited the vehicle, the male from the driver
side, the female from the passenger as any chauvinist would expect.
They made their way over the uneven terrain, over the grass and
rock, toward the gaggle of local police and personnel from the Crime
Scene Unit. A perimeter had been cordoned off, various workers
positioned both in and outside the yellow police tape.

"I'm Detective Sergeant Hobbs, this is Detective Sheed," the male said to the first of the uniformed officers they came upon. They both had their badges exposed in the event that there would be a need for validation. There wasn't one. "Who's in charge here?"

"I guess you are now," the uniform said. "The ME took control of the scene until you guys got here. He's been chomping at the bit for a couple of hours waiting for you." The officer nodded, pointing his chin toward the shore.

"We ran into traffic and we weren't at the House yet. Which examiner?"

"I think he said his name was Bowman. He's down on the ledge, they just hoisted the vic out of the soup."

"Thanks," Hobbs said. Sheed took in the surroundings, no need to speak as she was not called upon to do so. They finished the short walk down toward the water in silence; the Medical Examiner, Mark Bowman, spotted them and impatiently awaited their arrival.

"Where the hell have you two been? I got the call at a little after six," he said. "It's quarter to nine. Don't tell me you hit *that* much morning traffic."

Again, Hobbs took the lead. "We were both still in bed when we got the call."

"Together?"

"Go fuck yourself, Bowman," Sheed said.

"No need to get hostile."

"Nobody's laughing. Even Rick's wife doesn't want to sleep with him," she said.

"Very funny. Both of you. So what do we got here, Mark?"

"Floater." He pointed back up the hill toward the vehicles. "Guy walking his dog, dog hauls in the body. Female, probably early to mid-twenties judging by the bone structure."

"Drowned?" Hobbs hadn't pulled out his notepad, he let his junior female partner take the minutes of the meeting. Bowman led them over to the body-bag.

"Too early to tell. Bruising on the back of the head, but that's normal for drowned victims. Buffeting in the water commonly produces post-mortem head trauma, so it could have happened before, during, or after." Bowman unzipped the bag. "Facial bruising is normal for all corpses also."

The milky-white body was bloated and the skin bubbled like that of lepers. One eye was cloudy while the other was missing. There were holes in the body from where oceanic parasites had hosted on it. Both detectives cringed, despite having each seen an unfortunately high number of dead bodies. Sheed smelled the inside of her right wrist where a bracelet would be, smelling her perfume instead of the aroma of ocean and decomposing corpse. Hobbs was close to retirement, Sheed a seasoned veteran. Both found the scene greatly repugnant.

"Ah, Jesus. How long has it been in the water?"

"It's a she, Hobbs. Not an it. And I can't tell you that yet. This one is going to be tough. As you can see, I don't have much left to work with."

"Hedging your bets already?"

"No, Rick. Crabs and small fish and what-not have been at her. When a dead body is left to decompose in the water, especially salt water, the microbes and bacteria don't break the flesh down as they would on dry land. It's called brining, and if the water temp is under seventy degrees, the body forms a thick, soapy substance which we call 'grave wax'. It preserves the body, but as you can see it still bloats and blisters. Water temp in this area is in the low sixties, which is the warmest since they have been keeping records on such things, but I'll still have to track Atlantic temperature fluctuations to try and determine rate of decomp. That's *if* she was bobbing around this area the entire time. She could have floated here from water that was warmer or colder. That will make T. O. D. a guess at best."

"Lovely."

"I can say that adipocere, which is the process of transforming that fatty layer beneath the skin into grave wax, takes several weeks to two months."

"What about fingerprints or dental records?"

"Are you telling me how to do my job now, Hobbs? Anserina cutis, or goose-skin, loosens and shrivels the skin. Ever been in the water too long and your fingers prune? Her entire body is like that. No fingerprints, no fingernails. If she put up a fight and had DNA under her fingernails, that evidence was taken care of by the ocean. No gums and no teeth. Between washer-woman's skin and — "

" — Hey! Easy on the macho bullshit. I deal with enough of that with Hobbs, " Sheed interjected.

"No offense intended, Lisa. Washer-woman's skin is just what it's called. Swelling and wrinkling of the skin followed by the shedding of layers. I was just saying that it's going to be nearly impossible to tell you who she is, let alone how she died. Depending on how long she has been in the water and where she was put in, which I told you I probably won't be able to tell you with any certainty, she could have been killed prior to the water and died in the water due to vagal inhibition — "

" — She was raped?" It was Hobbs's turn to interrupt the examiner.

"No, Rick. Vagal not vaginal. Vagal inhibition is when the heart stops from the shock of immersion in cold water. She could have drowned in the Atlantic for all I know, or hypothermia from prolonged exposure in deeper and colder water. The one eye I do have is cloudy so I won't be able to see if there is any petechial hemorrhaging. I will check for froth or foam in the airways or foreign material in her lungs and stomach, but unless she was drowned in the ocean I'm not likely to find anything compelling in the bronchioles and alveoli."

"She was in the water, so it makes sense that she drowned in the ocean," Hobbs said.

"I don't like to presume. She could have been killed then dumped in the ocean. Or drowned in fresh water then dumped in salt water. Or she might have accidentally drowned and floated away from those that were looking for her. That's what I'm saying, folks. I don't know, and from what I have to work with there is a strong possibility that I may never know. I'm just trying to prepare you ahead of time. I've been doing this for fifteen years detectives, bodies from the ocean are always the most difficult. That's why the mob used to give their victims 'concrete sneakers'. Have you ever seen the show *Dexter*? It's effective."

"So you're suggesting that this is a mob hit? She was weighed down with concrete and somehow floated to shore?"

"No, I'm not saying that at all. There are indications of ligature marks but nothing to suggest that a weight was used. What I am saying is that if one wanted to get rid of a body, the ocean has been and continues to be a way to do it with a lesser probability of getting caught because it is exponentially more difficult to run tests. Clear enough?"

Sheed spoke up as if to somehow speak for her species. Insert a ray of optimism. "A twenty-something woman missing sometime in the last two months? Somebody has to be missing her."

Hobbs was less sanguine. "How many twenty-somethings are missing in Boston alone, Sheed? Imagine if she floated here from someplace else? Where ya wanna start?"

"You're the boss. But we gotta start someplace."

2

THERE ARE OVER 2300 WOMEN REPORTED missing annually
each day in the United States. They vary in age and circumstance,
but the statistical majority of the missing women are between the
ages of 18 and 40. Larger cities account for a higher proportion for
obvious reasons. For a city like Boston, Massachusetts, a city with
roughly four million people, with sixty or so colleges and
universities, the proportions grow to an unfortunately high number.
The average comes out to one hundred and four reported Boston area
women missing each month. Each and every year.

The two month window that the Medical Examiner, Mark
Bowman, had given the detectives might as well have been a garage
door. Two hundred and nine females had DPS-159-C forms filled out
on them in that time. The Clearinghouse, the state's central
repository of information on missing persons, spit out all two
hundred of these names to the horror of Detective Lisa Sheed. She
shook her head in disbelief as she realized the exponential pain that
was caused from these two hundred and nine missing women. How
many husbands, girlfriends, children, parents and relatives were
hurting? How many families destroyed?

The Clearinghouse holds the name and information of all missing persons as well as those who reported them. Runaways, abductions, and parental abductions are all listed with semi-equal importance. All DPS-159-C's under the age of 15 get an automatic amber alert, receiving the highest level of importance. All under the age of 21 should be reported to the NCIC, or National Crime Information Center. The NCIC avoids the waiting period and enters the missing young adult into an interstate database. Unfortunately this doesn't happen as often as is needed. State and local authorities handle these on a case-by-case basis as adults sometimes go missing on purpose, avoiding the hassles of restraining orders or goodbyes.

More than twelve thousand names go into the Clearinghouse every year in Massachusetts. Of those, more than two thousand get cancelled because the person is found alive, or comes home of their own volition. Nineteen hundred of the remaining ten thousand plus are predominantly females over the age of eighteen. Less than one half of one percent of the nineteen hundred are found either dead or alive by police. This is why private investigators are used in many instances, sometimes consulted by the very police that are tasked to find the lost sheep. To protect and serve. If an investigator is used, the chances of finding the person goes up to twenty-five percent, albeit many are no longer alive when found.

Lisa Sheed knew all of this. She was no rookie. Only she now had to reverse engineer the situation. Normally she would get a name and description which she would use to find the person. But now she had a body, needing to match it to a name and description. It was going to be her and her alone to do this, she knew that as well.

Her partner, Rick Hobbs, was the "thinker not the doer". Only he was no brain-trust. He was overweight and lazy. A self-absorbed, know-it-all, megalomanic that Sheed had inherited in 2004. He had kept his job up to this point because of her work ethic, her close-rate. Hobbs was there to drive the car, most of the time in the wrong direction.

With two hundred nine names to go through, the one thing that she could count on was the lack of help from her partner. It would be Lisa to organize any and all interviews, follow-up on any leads. Hobbs would be in-tow of course, they were attached at the hip during all working hours. He would be virtually useless, yet take the credit for any progress in the case reported to their boss, Lieutenant Manny Titanitaukis.

Massachusetts State Police Detectives are judged on their closure rate. Period. As long as they avoid excessive abuse allegations and keep an average or better closure rate, they fly under the radar. For this reason, many detectives in Troop H would play the odds with their cases. They had no control over which cases they caught, that was done by rotation. But they could control which cases to focus on and devote the majority of their attention to. The layups were always dealt with first. Close it and move on. Get a confession or hand it to the District Attorney's office. The more cases that moved off of a detective's desk, in whatever way possible, the better.

Lisa was always determined to clear the cases she and her partner caught. Every case. But this one had become different. The names and information of over two hundred women stared back at her on her computer screen. Two hundred names, all of whom could have been the bloated and blistered body decaying off the coast of Massachusetts. All of whom demanded justice. All still waiting. Lisa Sheed couldn't solve them all, but she could solve this one. And she was determined to do so.

The call came through to Sheed's desk phone three days later, more than seventy-two hours after the body was found. Mark Bowman was calling to let her know that preliminary findings were completed on the woman floating off the coast of Gloucester. She and, to a lesser extent, her partner's presence was needed at the lab. She and Hobbs would get into the Impala from the motor pool and head across town right away. Lisa tried not to get her hopes up, but try as she might she could not help but pray that something tangible would lead them in the right direction. Any direction for that matter.

Boston autopsies are conducted in the belly of Massachusetts General Hospital, which is located on Fruit Street, across from Lederman Park along the Charles River. If you could fly there in a straight line from the Troop H precinct, the trip would take six minutes. Alas, mere mortals must drive there, fighting traffic on either Washington Street or Storrow Drive. Either was a nightmare, either would take exponentially longer than six minutes.

Mass General is a teaching hospital. Both academic and pathological autopsies are conducted at the facility as well. While the forensic autopsies have the same set-up, they are located on a different and more secure floor. For chain-of-custody reasons alone it was essential to segregate the medico-legal from the medico-academic.

Mark Bowman had expected the two detectives within the hour. An hour was reasonable. He had called Sheed in the afternoon, past the time of day for lunch hours. He was not informed that there would be a delay. In fact the opposite, Sheed had told him that they would be right over. Almost two hours after making the call, the two state police detectives pushed through the basement double doors to the morgue. Bowman was in an irritable mood prior to making the call, the lax stroll through the doors escalated him to nearly irate.

"Take your time ladies," he said. "It's not like I have other things to do today. It's almost five o'clock. I called you two hours ago. What is it with you two? You're always late."

"I'm sorry, Mark." Lisa was embarrassed, her apology contrite.

"I just found out about it, I got over here as soon as I could," Hobbs said. He always passed the buck to his junior partner. He also didn't take shit from Medical Examiners.

"Wait a sec, Rick. Don't blame your bullshit on me. I told you we were needed down here as soon as I got the call. You made every excuse in the book to stall this trip," Lisa said. She turned to the ME "I'm sorry again. I'm not going to stand here and be thrown under the bus. He always does that shit and it's not my fault."

Before Mark could comment, Hobbs spoke which cut him off. The slight further agitated Bowman. "This case is a dud and everyone knows it. We got stuck with it but we don't have to put all of our other cases on the back-burner, cases that are much more likely to get solved."

"That's a great attitude, detective. I'm sure the family of the victim will be very understanding. How do you expect to solve a case that you have given up on from the start?" The ME moved closer to Hobbs, standing almost nose to nose.

"Did you find anything that could point us in the right direction or give us a lead, Mark? Do we even know who the mourning family is?" Hobbs had his arms out, palms up while staring down the examiner. The result was a deafening silence. The tension in the lab was as thick as the smell of cleaning agents. The two men stared each other down, Bowman contemplating using one of the myriad tools at his disposal to saw up another body. The Tuffier retractor was looking like the most promising choice.

Lisa looked around the room as if she had not been there countless times. The tiled walls. The stainless steel tables with the deep utility sink at the foot of them. She had many times witnessed the carnage from the table simply sprayed into the sink and sent through the plumbing via disposal. The instruments. Each tool designed to cut, pry and lever organs out of the corpses. The fluorescent lighting at virtually every level. Beyond the working area where the three people were standing in eerie silence was a three-sided bay of body lockers. On the table in front of them, a baby-blue cloth was draped over the current victim. Sheed knew that under the cloth, the victim's entire body had been further defiled in order to determine who had done so originally. The solemnity of the situation hit her while the two men carried on.

"Okay. That's enough boys. Zip-'em up. Measure them later. We need to get down to business, yes? Mark, what do we have? Anything good?"

Mark snapped out of his stare-off and spoke to Lisa. Only Lisa.

"Yes. Right. Detective Sheed, I have still not been able to identify the woman, exactly. I can tell you after examining her various organs that prior to whatever caused her death she was in very good health, caucasian, and in her early twenties."

"Meaning that you don't know what caused her death as of yet."

"I didn't say that, did I? I'm getting there," he said. "Her narrow hips indicate that she had not given birth up to the time of her passing and investigation into her womb confirms that she wasn't pregnant. What few hair samples we could obtain identify her as having blonde hair, naturally not chemically. Under a microscope, I analyzed the one cloudy eye that was intact — structurally I'm ninety percent certain that she had blue eyes."

"I thought eye color was caused by fluid in the eye," Lisa said more like a question.

"Neither light green nor blue pigments are present in the eye. Any eye. Ocular fluid sometimes tells us color, but more often than not it eliminates possible eye colors. If neither light green nor blue pigments are possible structurally, we know that the person had some shade of dark green or brown eyes. We don't often have the type of scenario that we do in this particular instance where we need to scientifically determine eye color. Nevertheless, I'm confident on blue," Bowman explained to Sheed. He was still ignoring Hobbs who listened to the conversation in a quiet fit of his own making.

"Blonde hair and blue eyed young woman. Somebody has to be missing her," Lisa said.

"I should think so, detective. Additionally, while the bloating and body resurfacing from adipocere made my job more difficult, I can say with a high degree of certainty that she was fit. No tattoos for help in identification either."

"Young piece of ass with no tramp stamp? Probably just narrowed the field a bit," Hobbs chimed in.

"Jesus, Rick. Can you give it a rest for a minute? Show some respect if not decency," Lisa said.

Hobbs raised his arms in surrender after making the motion like he was zipping his lip.

Bowman shook his head and continued. "When her body dried and I drained the soap-like substance from the skin that we talked about at the scene, with a process very much like liposuction by the way, I noted that her skin was taught and well cared for. Very good muscle-tone given the circumstances in which we found her. I am putting her weight at between 120 and 130 pounds. For a female of five-foot-eight, that would put her below average weight. I have a ten pound variance because her bowels had been voided, stomach empty."

"Meaning she was held in captivity and starved prior to death."

"That is a strong possibility, detective. Her lungs, specifically her bronchioles, were heavy with fresh water. So was her stomach." Mark let Sheed work through the implications of what he had just said. It took her a few seconds but she understood the meaning quicker than most.

"So she was shoved under fresh water, enough for her to swallow a great deal of it and eventually drown."

"Correct. The voided bowels confirm that she hadn't eaten prior to her torture and the fresh water likely flushed what little masticated food that was in her digestive tract, out of her. What little clothing fibers remained did contain feces. But the ad pestem, was the blow to the back of the head. The hemorrhaging in the brain and the skull fragmenting indicates it was a very hard hit. It was just under the skull so that's why I didn't see it at the scene. Also with the fresh water in her lungs; she was either knocked unconscious from the blow to the back of the head and drown in water other than the Atlantic, or she was tortured by drowning to the verge of death for some reason, then the hit eventually finished the job. In either case her brain was slowly bleeding which would have been excruciatingly painful if she was conscious."

"So the son-of-a-bitch that did this probably took his sweet time. He beat her and dumped the poor girl into the ocean," she said.

"Not necessarily in that order but yes, that is what I am writing in my report. I did find ligature marks. They indicate that she was tied up, but I can't tell you if it was prior to going into the ocean or to hold her below the surface. Either way she never stood a chance."

"So we sort of have an idea of how she died, we just don't have a clue as to who she is or who did it or when."

"And that most likely it was a man or someone who was strong enough to immobilize a healthy woman. I wish I could offer you more, but there is one more thing, Detective Sheed."

"I'm listening."

"Embedded into that soapy material just under the surface of the skin were traces of stained wood and some sort of plastic or hardened resin. From what is anyone's guess. If I had to guess, I would say it was from whatever hell this poor woman was locked into prior to her death. As always, I'll send all samples over to Maynard for testing. Once my voice recording of the autopsy is transposed I'll send it over to your desk as usual. Maybe something will turn up."

"Thanks Mark. It's a start. Sorry again for jamming you up."

"Clearly not *your* fault," he said loudly while eyeballing Hobbs who had silently taken a chair off in another corner of the lab. "Let's just hope there aren't too many missing five-foot-eight, blonde females in the Clearinghouse," he continued to Sheed.

"Cheers to that."

3

"**DO YOU REALLY THINK WE'RE GONNA** ID the concrete blonde?" Hobbs was still pissy from the altercation with Bowman and the general disrespect he believed he encountered as the two detectives left Mass General.

Lisa was getting into the passenger seat of the Impala. "Concrete Blonde? What are you talking about?"

"Remember at the scene? Bowman said that people who dump bodies in the ocean tie them down. Concrete sneakers. She was a blonde...."

"You should write headlines for the Globe, Rick."

"It's a gift."

"It wasn't a compliment."

They left the parking structure of the hospital, heading east on Storrow Drive toward the 93 connector. Hobbs was driving as usual. And as usual he was driving badly.

"Where are we headed?"

"North."

"I get that, Rick. *Why* are we headed north, and specifically where?"

"I wanna have another chat with this Ivan guy. The guy who found the body."

"So you went from being uninterested and content to send this to cold cases in a few months to liking the wit for the crime? How'd you get there?"

"Now that we know a little more about the vic, we can ask better questions."

"To whom? The dog?"

"Very funny, Sheed."

"Seriously? Who reports finding a body that nobody can identify if they were the one who did the killing? Uh....nobody, that's who."

"I believe that I am still the senior partner here."

"Key word being partner, Rick. You just make decisions for both us and expect that I'll sit by quietly."

"How do you figure?"

"You decided to stall on this. You made us look bad in front of Bowman — "

" — An ME? You're pissed because we rustled the feathers of a medical examiner?"

"It's *ruffled* the feathers, genius. Not rustled. And yes. We work with all the examiners regularly and it would be nice to treat them as colleagues rather than adversaries. Besides, it doesn't end there. What happens when you need a favor from him?"

"It's his job to help us. Those nerds work for us not the other way around," he said.

"Let's see how well that attitude works the next time you need an expedited autopsy."

"I do it all the time. I just get Tits to call over there."

"Whatever. The point is that you just decided that you want to investigate this case, and that you like the poor slob who just got his green card without even discussing it with me. What are we saying to the guy? 'Welcome to the United States. Thanks for signing the guestbook and doing things the right way. You are a good citizen for reporting a body floating in the ocean instead of ignoring it like ninety percent of the people born here would probably do. Most people would probably have kicked the victim back into the water and tried to forget about it, but not you. You did a good thing and we would like to thank you by fucking with you, possibly arresting you as a murder suspect.' Is that the gist? 'Cuz if so, you're a real class-act Rick."

"You don't think he did it?"

"You're not good at reading sarcasm are you?"

"So let's just re-interview him and eliminate him once and for all. Humor me."

"Just go easy," she said. She secretly hoped the dog would eat her partner.

This time the trip to Gloucester took only an hour. During evening rush hour. It is amazing what can be accomplished when an effort is put in, Lisa thought.

Ivan Kadishev and his dog Rondo lived in a small, white, two-story off of Essex Ave. It wasn't much, but it was well-maintained. The backyard was fenced in and Rondo was speaking to the entire world, letting whomever was listening know of the police presence. Ivan was home and expecting the visit as Hobbs had asked a runner from the precinct to call him. His name and address was on file from the initial interview conducted at the scene; but even if it wasn't, it could have been looked up from his driver's license.

Mr. Kadishev was a mechanical engineer who had just come home from his work day. It was still light out and he was likely more interested in grilling a burger and having a beer than speaking to the police. But he was cordial enough despite the horrible cop — good cop routine that was being played on him.

He didn't know anything more. He had to say it dozens of times and in dozens of different ways, but the point finally got across. Sheed could see that Ivan had had just about enough. They were about two steps from being thrown out of his house by her estimation. It probably would have happened sooner if Ivan had realized that he had the right to. And she wouldn't have blamed him. The guy tried to do the right thing and he was being accused and bullied. Ivan knew most of his rights better than most of the people that were born with them. He asserted them often. "No, I do not own a gun, and no you may not search my home for a non-existent gun .... No, you may not take a DNA sample, of me or my dog .... No, you may not fingerprint me, not unless you have a warrant .... " It went on like that for some time.

The interview was officially over when Rondo was let back into the house. The chocolate lab was excited and jumping around. He wanted to play. Have his belly rubbed. Hobbs wasn't interested. Lisa wasn't allowed to be.

The trip back to the precinct took forty-six minutes. The two detectives did little more than check their messages before calling it quits for the night. They left the House at 9:40 PM, fortified with no more information than when they left Bowman in the morgue at Mass General earlier that day.

The following day, friday, was dedicated to searching through missing persons. For Lisa that is. She worked on the computer at her desk while Hobbs worked at his, facing her on his computer. Only he was playing Candy Crush. Seniority has its privileges.

While Hobbs was content on waiting for the samples to be sent from the autopsy table in the morgue to the forensics lab in Maynard, Massachusetts; those subsequent findings to be relayed back to him when they were ready, Sheed was actively working the missing persons angle. While the facility in Maynard was incredibly thorough in testing ballistics, DNA, vehicles, and a slew of other types of forensic evidence, they were not timely. Maynard was the only such facility in the state, meaning that they had a backlog of cases. Due to issues in the past, the facility was uber-procedural. Those procedures took time. Sheed wondered at what level her senior partner would be at in Candy Crush by the time the results came back from Maynard.

She had narrowed the search down to 49 missing women. Age hadn't helped much. Once Blacks, Indians, Hispanics and Asians were eliminated, her list was still quite large. She couldn't rely too much on hair color. Women died their hair, usually to blonde. Presumably because they have more fun. Hair color is merely a question to be answered on the Clearinghouse survey. The person reporting the missing woman may not know her true hair color.

Weight could fluctuate as well, and often embellished. So she was left with height, and eye color. She was in the process of printing out the fifty names from their shared printer when her cell phone vibrated in her pocket.

Lisa knew who was calling, it was plain as day on her touchscreen. She also knew she couldn't take the call with her partner facing her. She walked toward the coffee machine and answered.

"Deni. To what do I owe the pleasure?" It was Warren Dennihan, a former Massachusetts State Police Detective who had gone out on his own as a Private Investigator. Lisa had been promoted to his vacant spot, with his former partner in 2004. But there were no hard feelings.

"What's up She?" Deni never called anybody by their actual name. It was one of his many 'things'. Another one was his accent. True Boston. True South Boston to be more specific. People from *Southie* almost have their own language.

"Not much. You called me, remember? So what do you need?" She looked around the precinct to see if she was being watched or listened to. She didn't seem to be.

"Wow. Like that?"

"I'm in the middle of a case, and the only time you call is when you need to be hooked up. So what is it? Yellows? Plate number?"

"I can't just call to say hey? I thought we were friends."

"With friends like you, Deni…."

"You're a hard woman." He said 'hard' with a more emphatic *haahd* than the stereotype.

"I'm hanging up now," Lisa said.

"Okay, okay. I called to see if the swimmer is mine." *Swimmah.*

"The swimmer?"

"Don't play me like that. I read the papers, see the news. Gloucester." *Pay-pahs. Glah-stah.* Lisa was used to it otherwise she might have needed him to repeat himself.

"We don't know. I've got it down to fifty possibles. Who's your girl?"

"Lara Myhre. Berklee student. Been missin' a couple months. Was datin' this hockey player that I like for her disappearance but I haven't been able to crack him."

"So who are you working for? Her parents?"

"Yeah. Yuppies from Connecticut."

"Connecticut? Wow, Deni. You really get around."

"We still talkin' about jobs?"

"Very funny."

"She went to school here. Berklee. Big-time music college, you've seen pictures. Parents wanted somebody who knew Boston, so here I am."

"Well like I said, we don't know yet. We're working on it," she said.

"You mean you're working on it. Still with the fat-fuck?"

314

"You know it. My so-called partner is playing Candy Crush right now and he thinks that I don't know."

"Let you in on a little secret, She? He don't give a shit if you do or not. He's always been a piece of shit and at this point he ain't likely to change."

"Narcissism has a name and it's H-O-B-B-S."

"I don't know that that means but he plays games like we're all dumber than him, but you'd have to be a complete fucktard to be dumber than Ricky."

"I know right? He hates being called Ricky, by the way."

"I know. That's why I do it," Deni said.

"He hates you too. He would kill me if he knew that I talked to you."

"Now or in general."

"Pick one. Anyway, I could bash him with you all day long but I gotta stuff to do. How about you give me the parent's name and number for this Lara and I'll reach out to them."

"Nice try. I get fucked outta my money? I don't think so."

"It's always about the money with you?"

"It's not about the money," Deni said.

"I've seen you get into a cage and fight those UFC animals for money, so don't try to shine me. Or is it because you like beating on people?"

"Pick one."

"Ha-ha. Just do the right thing and give me the parents."

"Nobody does the right thing, She. I just like to get paid for it."

"How very Zen of you."

"Why don't you come give me shit in person?"

"I'm in a relationship, Deni. And you are so not my type."

"I meant meet me at her apartment."

"Who's apartment?"

"His thickness is rubbin' off on ya. Lara Myhre's apartment, who else?"

"Hobbs isn't gonna like working with you again."

"Leave him out of it. If it's not her then it's not her. We can all go back to pretending we don't exist in the same city."

"Do you think that we're gonna be able to figure out if it's her just from going to her apartment?"

"Can't hurt," Deni said.

"Give me an hour. Oh, and text me her address," she said as almost an afterthought before hanging up.

"Can't you look it up from her license?"

"Yes, Deni, of course I can. But you texting it to me will save time. Oh, that's right. You don't text. Or email. Or anything else that is convenient or from this century. Jesus how old are you?"

"It's not the years it's the mileage, doll. I'll meet ya there."

"Yeah fine. I just gotta shake Ricky."

4

WARREN DENNIHAN IS A COLORFUL MAN. In the literal sense and in the figurative. Literal in that his body is an inked tapestry from his collarbone to his knees with the exception of his man-parts. Figurative in that his past and present were rife with dangerous events and acquaintances. The fabric of the man was weaved together with both physical and emotional scars, not that he let many close enough to see any of them.

He had been burned out of Southie, though he was too stubborn or stupid to leave entirely. To some extent everyone in his neighborhood was being burned out. Gentrification was proving to be a problem for the group he had grown up with. Two income couples, both gay and straight, were buying up all of the three-decker homes. Rents were on the rise, forcing the natives out of South Boston. What was once a community of crooks, gangsters and those that wanted to be, had become an up-and-coming area of Boston. Some thought that was progress. Deni didn't. Those petty criminals now expanded to other neighborhoods. The police used to know where to concentrate their presence. Now, no place was safe.

Warren had rebuilt his three-decker and his reputation in the streets from whence he came. He grew up just blocks from where he was forced to rebuild and now spent some of his time. Had he not made some very important choices many years ago, he would likely still be committing crimes in and around the neighborhood. He had abandoned the thievery, B&E's and so-called friends long ago, just not the neighborhood.

Deni was accepted into the police academy because of those connections, but the agenda backfired. He used those contacts for information instead of busts, which infuriated his supervisors with the state police. The writing was on the wall and he was forced out of Troop H. In 2004, Deni ventured out on his own, initially working part-time for a fellow private investigator.

He now also owned a house in Barstone, New Hampshire, staying there whenever he worked for the attorney he had become friends with in the town of Wayland. Or when he needed the peace and quiet away from the city, which was more often than not.

The small New Hampshire legal firm in Wayland, New Hampshire, had once represented ninety percent of Deni's investigations. Now it only comprised about a third. Deni was doing well in both reputation and finances. What was once a piece-meal existence subsisting on MMA fights and whatever investigations he could get had become a career of doing what he wanted, when he wanted. At forty-one, he was getting too old for Mixed Martial Arts though he was in remarkable shape. Unless it paid well.

He drove his 2013 Range Rover HSE to the Prudential Center parking garage, which took up a square block and multiple levels underneath the skyscraper in Back Bay. Lara Myhre's apartment wasn't located in the Pru, but it was the closest and safest place to park with respect to Berklee College of Music and where the missing woman lived.

He had also had his fair-share of mishaps with street parking and understood the need to spend money for a more secure place to store his vehicles. His Grand Am and both of his former black Escalades had been damaged beyond repair or totaled parking on the streets of Boston. He had upgraded to a Mercedes AMG, given to him for services rendered in 2013. But he had traded the new car for his Rover for reasons that had nothing to do with parking. He told people that he traded it because the small luxury sport sedan was impractical. In truth it was because the car reminded him of the case in which he had earned it. The case that had ended as badly as the would-be relationship that developed during it. His new Loire-blue SUV was worth over $140,000 and street parking was no longer a desired option. Besides, Lara's white BMW 3-series was still in the monthly parking area of the underground garage.

Lara lived on Holyoke Street, near Mass Ave and Columbus. It was a nicer apartment, in a nicer area behind both the Berklee Performing Arts Center and the Prudential Tower. The walk from the garage to the apartment took Deni eleven minutes. As he made the walk he imagined Lara walking to and from her car when she needed to leave the city. Walking to school every day. Detective Lisa Sheed was leaning against a streetlamp post in front of the apartment building, waiting for Deni as he turned the corner from Carleton Street.

Deni's daily uniform consisted of jeans, a t-shirt, and a sport jacket to cover his handgun. That day's version of the uniform as he walked toward Detective Sheed was a well-worn Led Zeppelin t-shirt, his Taurus PT1911 .45 calibre pistol bulging from a shoulder harness under his black sport-coat. His conceal and carry permit allowed him to keep the weapon on his person unless he was going into such public places like a prison or school. Since he wasn't forbidden to carry one on this particular occasion, it was nestled firmly under his armpit.

"Where have you been? I found a parking spot half a block away," Lisa said as a greeting. "And do you ever change clothes? You look like shit, what's your secret?"

"When you have a cop car, you tend to park wherever you want. I parked at the Pru, that's where her car is still parked by the way," Deni said, ignoring the jabs.

"Your missing girl didn't take her car?"

"No. Which is one of the reasons I fear the worst. She's rich but leaving a new beamer isn't something one would expect."

"She's rich or her parents are?" Lisa's head was cocked like she knew the answer despite asking the question.

"Reserve judgement for when you know what the fuck you're talkin' about, huh?"

"Fair enough. So did she have roommates or do you have a key?" She asked knowing Deni's reputation for tumblers. There wasn't a lock built that Deni couldn't pick, and fast. Another one of this 'things'.

"It's a studio and I got a key from the parents," he said with a wink. The apartment was three floors up a narrow staircase and the building was old enough to be grandfathered out of requiring an elevator. Moving in and out of these buildings, as college students tend to do with frequency, must be a bitch.

The apartment was listed as a large studio, but nobody that had ever been inside considered it to be one. High ceilings, a large kitchen for Boston standards, an open dining and living space, and a bedroom that was larger than Lisa's.

"This is nice. Nicer than my place. How the hell does a college kid afford this in Back Bay? She really is rich," she said. The furnishings did not scream college student, nothing was past-prime or from IKEA.

"Parents are money. With her talent and looks, she is gonna be money. If we can find her, that is."

"She plays guitar huh?" Lisa had noticed the five guitars on their stands lining the wall next to the sofa. It was difficult not to notice them. There was a Taylor Builder's Reserve VII acoustic, a white Gretsch electric, a Gibson Les Paul Standard, a Martin 12-string, and a vintage Stratocaster, each polished and gleaming even

320

in the owner's absence. The least expensive axe in the line-up was worth nearly $5,000.

"Yeah. Sings too. Did you see her DMV photo?"

"Very pretty. Not many people have a glam license picture."

"I saw a video with her in concert, She. With her looks and talent, she is gonna be huge. She is already makin' a name for herself on the Youtube. Nobody walks away from that."

"'*The* Youtube'? It's just Youtube."

"Whatever. Break someone else's balls."

"So you don't think she just decided to get away? You know, runaway? Get away from the pressure?"

"No. But say you're right. Why not hawk a guitar or five? Why leave the Beamer? Running away with nothing when you could have a pocket full of cash is a stretch. Plus the girl hasn't used her debit or credit cards."

"Fair enough. You said she has a college boyfriend who plays hockey?"

"Plays hockey, yeah. But they don't have NCAA sports at Berklee. Can you imagine how coordinated musicians are? The answer is they typically aren't. You follow the Bruins at all?"

"Who doesn't?"

"Gary Rennick. He gets called up and sent back down to Providence like a yo-yo. He's up right now. Has one goal so far in the playoff run."

"The name sounds familiar. Wait. *That's* your hockey player? Wow. Some girls have it all. I almost wanna find this girl just so I can hate her."

"Why the envy? I didn't even think that you dug men."

"This again, Deni?"

"Whatever. You can save the envy in any case. Rennick is a fuckin' goon. Most penalty minutes in the AHL, most fights, and he's makin' a bid for those records in the NHL even though he spends very little time in the bigs. He's a thug. Six-three, two-twenty-five."

"And you like him for her disappearance, Deni?"

"Absolutely. Just give this sitch a look, will ya. Go to Berklee with Hobbs and check out Lara Myhre. Then have a sit-down with Rennick and let me know what you think."

"Hobbs is never gonna to go for this. Especially if he knows that you turned me on to her. You are persona non grata down at Troop H, my dude. And you know it."

"I do. But you know what your Troop H told Leonard and Sorche Myhre? The parents? 'She's a college student. She missed a check-in, it happens all the time. Give it a few weeks and get back to us.' She isn't even on the Clearinghouse or the NCIC. Your friends just gave them the fuckin' runaround. These poor people have been pullin' their hair out with worry for nine weeks, She. They call every week, and every week they basically tell these poor people to fuck themselves. Just look into it, will ya?"

"I'll see what I can do."

"One more thing. Give me a ride back to the Pru."

"You're in good shape, you can walk," she said.

"Correction. I'm in excellent shape, but that's besides the point. I want you to check out her car."

"Sign of a struggle?"

"Come with me and see for yourself."

The drive two blocks up and over to the Pru took longer than if they had walked. Then as long to find the correct color code for the monthly parking area. It took a visit to the parking office on the first level to get directions to the yellow level. While in the office, Detective Sheed inquired as to the monthly rate to park in Boston's largest parking structure. $500 a month. And yes, it was paid in full and on time each month. Her hunch was confirmed. Sort of. As they reached the white Beamer, she ran the hunch by Deni.

"Her parking space is paid every month and on time. She hasn't gotten evicted from her apartment more than two months after she disappears .... someone is still paying the bills. Rennick or her parents?"

Deni had already thought about it and done the checking. "Parents. I thought the same thing. Parents are convinced that she is comin' back. And breakin' a lease in this city is expensive. Rennick pays for nothing. The same friend that I had look into her finances, looked into his. No expensive gifts that I can tell. A girl like this could have any guy she wants but she goes for a cheapskate goon."

"It's a girl thing, Deni. Eventually they outgrow it and learn to appreciate a nice guy, hopefully before a beating or a divorce."

"*They?* Are you speaking from experience?"

"You know my deal. Most men are assholes that's why I steer clear .... hey did you just break into her car?" Deni had the driver door to the BMW open, his arm open like a valet inviting her to enter the vehicle.

"Relax. Her parents gave me the key. The lease is in their name."

"What am I looking for?" Sheed made her way to the car but paused as she waited for Deni to give her some space.

"I don't want to taint your impression. Give it a once-over and tell me what you see." Deni backed away, giving her the space he sensed she needed.

Sheed knelt down just outside the car, first looking under the driver seat then at the pedals. Once she determined that those were clear, she put her knee on the driver seat and scanned the interior in its entirety.

"I assume the car is as she left it, or at least how you found it," she said out to Deni.

"Yep."

Sheed turned around and noticed a keyless fob in Deni's hand. "There's still a fob in the ignition." Another fob was in the console ready to start the car.

"Right."

"But there's no sign of a struggle, Deni. No blood. She opens the car door, puts the fob in place, maybe she starts it, maybe she doesn't but she leaves it in for some reason."

"If it's a car-jacking, she could just drive away if it's already started. Which leads me to believe that she knew whoever approached the car," Deni said.

"Mmmmm. Maybe," Lisa said. "Okay, I'll bite. She knows the person enough to have a conversation, then what? He takes her in the middle of the parking structure? With all these people around? Did you look at the CCTV footage?" She pointed toward the ceiling.

"Blind spot. Can't see a damn thing. Her parents should have gotten a reduced rate. The car wasn't secure, and it damn sure wasn't being watched. I figure if she knew the guy, she left willingly."

"But left the key in the ignition? Do BMWs even lock when it's still in the ignition? Expensive cars tend to have idiot-proofing," she said. She was shaking her head like something didn't add up.

"That's what makes it weird." *Wee-yahd.* Deni let the information sink in for a few seconds. The detective worked it through before coming to a decision. Lisa went from shaking her head to nodding.

"You've peaked my curiosity," she finally said. "Blonde, blue-eyed, and the height and weight match. Missing about the same window as our vic and her disappearance is wonky. Technically she isn't a missing person because she's not in the Clearinghouse, but I'll run it by Hobbs."

"And you'll keep me posted?"

"On the D-L, yes. But information needs to go both ways. You forget I know you."

"Yeah, yeah."

"Where are you parked?"

"In this place? Who knows?" Deni hit a button on his own keyless fob. The horn echoed from nearby, the hazards flashed and reflected off of the concrete on the ramp just fifteen yards ahead of them. "Hey, how is that for luck?"

"Irish. You have the best .... no fucking way, Deni. *That's* your ride? What did you steal it?" The Land Rover was still flashing. The shiny blue SUV looked almost black in the garage lighting, accented with silver gills and alloy wheels.

"Of course not. It's kinda flashy and way too many bells and whistles, but I fell in love with it as soon as I test-drove it."

"You're a big fish now, huh?"

"I work hard for it."

"Work hard you say. Seems like a man's version of working hard is having a woman do all the work."

"Easy with the feminist shit. I'm not Hobbs. I'm askin' for help, not askin' for you to do all the work."

"We'll see."

5

THAT NIGHT, BETWEEN HIS FIRST AND SECOND glass of
Redbreast 12 year Irish Whiskey, Deni called Leonard and Sorche
Myhre at their home in Fairfield, Connecticut. They were home,
which was usual for the last nine weeks. They had rarely left home
since learning of their daughter's disappearance. It was a friday
night and Deni had a drink in his hand, which was also usual though
he wasn't normally at home. Definitely not in South Boston.

He sat on his high-backed barstool at his bar. The bar was
built between his kitchen and parlor on the first floor of his three-
decker. Deni was watching his flatscreen behind the bar, which was
playing the Bruins highlights on NESN. And he was getting angrier
by the minute.

The Bruins were playing and losing to the rival Canadians in
a best-of-seven playoff series, but that wasn't why he was upset.
Gary Rennick flashed on the screen several times; a hit, then a fight,
another dirty hit followed by more time in the penalty box. Finally a
celebratory fist-pump and a group hug as they showed several
different angles of him scoring a much-needed goal from the blue-
line. He wore a smug grin with a full set of teeth as his teammates

congratulated him. Fans were in the background pounding on the glass. Deni wanted to pound on Rennick.

Three fingers of the amber liquor over rocks is what it took to acquire the courage to call his clients. The phone rang, picked up after just the second ring.

"Hello?" The male voice was inquisitive yet hopeful. Deni pictured him on the other end, somewhere in his large and beautiful, ocean-front home on the Connecticut coast. His missing daughter was taking a toll on the man. The once kind eyes and gentle features were becoming hardened. He was aging in years by the day. Deni was watching the degradation occur with every meeting.

"Mr. Myhre? This is Warren Dennihan. Deni."

"Yes I see that. Your name appears on the caller ID. Do you have some news?"

"Possibly."

"What does that mean? Possibly? Deni it has been nine weeks. My wife read a statistic online that stated that if missing persons are not found within the first seventy-two hours — "

" — I'm sorry to interrupt Mr. Myhre but — "

" — Call me Leonard."

"I'm sorry to interrupt you, Leonard, but getting hung up on statistics isn't very often helpful. Especially when you get those statistics off of the damned internet. I told you when we initially spoke in your home that this could be a mercifully short process or an indefinitely long one. I know it's taken a while, and I thank you for bearing with me but I assure you that I'm doin' all I can. I'm callin' because I would like to set up a time to meet. I have some news, which may mean nothing. But it could mean something. I'm leaning toward that it could."

"Well? What is it?"

"I'd rather not say over the phone. I'd much rather do it in person. As I said, I'd like to set up a time to meet with you. I would come to you, but you should probably come to Boston."

"What is it, Deni? Just come out with it."

"There is really no good way to say it, and it might not even be accurate or applicable. So you might want to come to Boston. How is monday?"

"*Monday?* Do you realize that it's friday night? How are we supposed to wait until monday for news about our missing daughter? Let me put you on speaker." The noise changed in Deni's ear. There was no way that the phone call was going to go smoothly, he knew that going in. That is why he needed the whiskey. At least that is what he told himself. But this was tougher in real life. Much more so than when he played it out in his head while watching the asshole who was responsible for it on the television.

"I'm here Deni. Please tell us what is going on with Lara." It was Sorche. Sorche is the Gaelic-Irish name for Sarah. Sarah means 'Pure Lady' or 'Happy' depending on the dialect and religion. Hebrew or Catholic, she did seem pure and elegant in the times that Deni had met her. Always pleasant. Always optimistic. Although she didn't sound very happy to Deni at the moment, not that he could blame her.

"There is no easy way to say this, and keep in mind that it isn't definite. I really wanted to speak to you in person — "

" — Oh my God, is she dead? Deni is she dead?" Sorche was in near hysterics. Through the tiny speaker on his phone, Deni could hear Leonard trying to console his wife. He imagined him embracing his beautiful wife in their parlor. The last nine weeks had taken a toll on her as well, as one would imagine. Their daughter was missing for more than two months and intelligent people realize the probable outcome. The Myhres were intelligent people. But the head and the heart are two very different things.

"I honestly don't know for sure. But the body of a young woman was found in the ocean up Gloucester," he said. The discovery was all over the news, whether that news had reached southern, affluent Connecticut he didn't know.

"Gloucester? That's north of Boston. Why would she be in Gloucester?" Sorche was trying to work through the denials, reasons why it couldn't be her daughter. Reasons for hope. "It might not be her. Her car is still parked in the garage, so it couldn't be her. You're just calling to let us know that it's not her, right?"

The emotion and vulnerability coming through the phone was getting to Deni. He had been called a heartless prick too many times to count. In truth, most times he had been. He tried to stay removed from emotion. He tried to just do his job and get paid, which often came off as heartless. But the middle-aged couple on the other end of the phone had pulled a chord. Deni wasn't a parent, nor could he completely understand what his clients were going through. But he felt for them just the same, even when his head told him not to. The head and the heart are two very different things.

"You're right Mrs. Myhre. It's probably not her. But just the same, maybe you will want to come to Boston? We should rule it out. I promised to keep you posted and that is what I'm doin'. We will know more by monday. Could you meet me in the city on monday?"

"We'll be there tomorrow morning," Leonard said. He stated it as fact. An inarguable statement. Though Deni did try to negotiate.

"Tomorrow is saturday, so the — "

Deni realized that the phone was now dead. Negotiation over. They had hung up.

"Shit."

He immediately dialed Detective Sheed. This was also going to be a tough conversation but for different reasons. Very different emotions.

"Deni you just left me like two hours ago," she said when she picked up the phone. "I have nothing more to say to you at the moment."

"Did I catch you at a bad time?"

"It's friday night and I'm not on-shift, do the math."

"I'm sorry but this is kinda urgent."

"Make it quick," she said.

"I called the parents. They're kinda freakin' out and they'll be in Boston tomorrow. My guess is early morning."

"Jesus Christmas, Deni. Why would you do that?"

"I wanted to prepare them. There are more leaks in Troop H than …. uh, things that leak. I didn't want them to learn that their daughter was dead on the six o'clock news."

"You don't know that their daughter *is* dead for one hundred percent certain, you idiot. Now they're going to be all over us first thing. Hobbs isn't even on board yet."

"Well, he better get on board."

"Godammit Deni. How do I let you get me into these messes? This is going to create a shit-storm of the highest order."

"I'll call you as soon as I hear from them tomorrow."

"Yeah fine, whatever. Thanks for fucking me big-time."

"Sorry, She. I owe you one."

"I lost count at one hundred, asshole."

6

THE FIRST THING ON THE TO-DO LIST FOR Hobbs and Sheed on saturday morning was to visit Berklee. Hobbs double-parked on Boylston Street across from the Hynes Convention Center, trying to get into the Berklee College of Music Administrative Building. Since it was saturday, the building was locked and nobody opened the doors. Most calloused citizens of Boston would just as soon step on your neck as look at you; however a kind twenty-something directed them to try the building on the corner of Boylston and Mass Ave, the performing arts building.

Boston is filled with one-way streets, Boylston is one of them. They couldn't take the first left, Gloucester Avenue, for the same reason. They took the next left on Fairfield near the marathon finish line, then the following left onto the very chic Newbury Street in order to reverse direction. The street names which alternated directions off of Boylston were in reverse alphabetical order, all the way down to the public garden and Arlington Street, though they wouldn't need to travel that far. Three blocks back and left onto Massachusetts Avenue brought them back to the Berklee Performance Center. The trip took nearly fifteen minutes even at almost nine in the morning, though they could have walked it in less than four.

Hobbs parked the unmarked Impala in the alley behind the building, where large tractor trailer trucks were being unloaded. The flashing of badges ceremony occurred; explanations from the Teamsters from the moving company informed them that they were unloading stage lighting, special effects, and sound equipment for a performance. The detectives followed the movers into the back of the building, which was backstage of the large theatre. A hipster female stage manager was barking orders to people and checking things off on her clipboard. The mover in charge pointed her out and left without introducing her.

Hobbs took the lead in approaching the young woman, again flashing his badge and again introducing himself. Sheed showed her badge as well, but kept quiet. She was currently in the doghouse, her presence more insignificant than usual.

"Detective Sergeant Rick Hobbs. I was told that you're in charge?"

"Yes, and I don't have time for this. Dress rehearsal is tonight. What do you need?" The woman with short blue hair, matching royal blue eyeglasses, and dressed in Urban Outfitter clothing was annoyed and impatient.

"What's your name miss?" Hobbs didn't take shit from women. Period.

"My name is none of your business until you tell me why you're here? Do you have a reason for being here? If not, you can show yourselves out the same way you came in. The building is closed to the public." Blue-hair was speaking to Hobbs but gave Sheed the look from head to toe to head again.

Sheed read what she needed to from the situation and interjected despite already being in deep shit with her senior partner.

"I'm sorry, maybe we got off on the wrong foot. We're major crime detectives with the state police. We are here about Lara Myhre. We understand that she goes to school here."

The fight seeped out of blue-hair. She turned away from Hobbs and spoke directly with Sheed. Hobbs realized that his partner was going to get further than he was. That realization in and of itself was a minor miracle.

"Oh geez. Yeah. Yes. Well, she used to go here. She was supposed to be performing in this show as a matter of fact. Showcase. The best that the school has to offer perform, and she was definitely the best."

"So she dropped out? I'm sorry, I didn't catch your name."

"Julie. Julie Spaulding. I'm a music business senior here. This is my final Showcase, Lara performing would have made it so much better. All the greats drop out."

"What do you mean 'all the greats drop out', Julie?"

"All the super-talented drop out. You can only learn so much music theory or harmony or whatever. Performing is performing. Recording is recording. If you can write music you can write music. You don't need people who are no longer famous teaching you things that you already know," she said. She continually took brief looks away from Lisa to take note of what was happening with her troops.

"So Lara decided to leave? You know that for a fact?"

"No, but it seems reasonable. Why else would she not show up for classes again?"

"Maybe something happened to her. Is that possible?"

"Yeah. Talent happened to her," Julie said. "She got confidence in her three years here. She's a gorgeous and talented woman who finally realized that she didn't need Berklee anymore. Charlie Colin from the band *Train*, Diana Krall, Ben McKee from *Imagine Dragons*, Susan Tedeschi, Natalie Maines from the *Dixie Chicks*, John Mayer .... all Grammy winners, all went here, and none of them actually graduated. And those are just off the top of my head. There are probably a hundred more. Lara was the female John Mayer and she was convinced that they were related."

"*Was?*"

"Is. She will be the next big thing. 'Was' because she isn't here anymore. What is this about? You said 'Major Crimes'. Did something happen to her?"

"We're not sure. We're just trying to find her. Her parents haven't heard from her, so we would like to talk with her. Do you know where we could find her?"

"Talk to her boyfriend," Julie said with a roll of her eyes.

"I take it you didn't approve? We heard that he was a famous hockey player. A girl could do worse," Lisa said.

"Listen we weren't close, okay? But it's a small school. He showed up here from time to time. His name is Gary Rennick, you might have heard of him. If you are into the tall muscle-man type, then I guess she did well for herself. But I thought she could do better."

"You liked her, didn't you Julie?"

"Who didn't?" Julie had forgotten about the movement around her, she was concentrating on her purple shoes.

"I get it, believe me I do," Lisa said. We just need to find her. So can you think of anything that might help? We'll go see Rennick, but is there anything else? Her apartment looks like she is ready to come home at any minute, all her guitars are still on the stands and her car is still in her monthly spot."

Julie looked up into Sheed's eyes, trying to see if what she had just heard was true. The detective could see that she was surprised by the new information.

"I don't know anything else. Not really. She wouldn't just leave her guitars, though. She always had one on her or within reach." Julie paused. Nobody spoke to fill the void. Workers moved around them seemingly on mute.

"You should really look at the tapes," she said after some time.

"Tapes? I don't follow."

"She's amazing. She didn't have a lot of friends here because of the jealousy. She has been in multiple performances, multiple Showcases. The school was riding her for all they could get out of her in order to recruit new students. They knew what everyone knew, that she was going to be huge. Berklee wanted to be part of that. Things can get kinda cutthroat. 'Why does she get this, or why does she get that?' I can't imagine that anybody would do anything beyond gossip and backstab, but you should really see what I'm talking about."

"Backstabbing?"

"*Verbal* backstabbing," Julie said.

"Do you have them handy? The tapes?"

"Yeah, of course. Gimme a sec to get things in order and I'll meet you up in the booth." Julie pointed toward the front of the theatre, where the sound and effects booth was dark. She ran off to deal with some things that she needed to fix with her team. Yelling and pointing ensued.

Hobbs moved back to Sheed after blue-hair went back to work. "This is bullshit. Lesbo-smurf is wastin' our time. We don't need to see her MTV videos. I'm gonna fuckin' kill Dennihan when I see him. He's got us runnin' around all over Boston on a saturday morning for nothin'. And you .... you fell for it hook, line, and sinker. You don't remember what a shit-bag he is? I was never happier than when he got fired."

"He didn't get fired and you know it. Deni may be a pain in the ass but he's a bloodhound when it comes to these things. You didn't like him when he was your partner, and you're still a little butt-hurt that he left you. Look at it this way, Rick - it's a lead. We need to figure out who the woman is, why not exhaust all leads? We never would have gotten here without Deni, she wasn't in the Clearinghouse or the NCIC. If this turns out to be her, we're way ahead of the game. We would still be scratching our heads years from now without him." Sheed let the lesbian comment slide.

Julie met them in the control booth after a short time. She had used the term 'tape', but the videos were digitized. She pulled up several performances, queueing them up on the computer. All of the videos vertically lined the right side of the screen. She told them to run down as many as the detectives cared to view. She stayed for the first minute or so of the first video, then left to return to her duties onstage.

The first video was of a gorgeous female with a blue Stratocaster and long-haired drummer far behind her. The two were alone, almost lost on the enormous stage. As the camera panned in, virtually getting closer to Lara Myhre, she began to play her guitar. It was difficult to determine which was most haunting; the sound of her guitar, her voice, or her beauty. And she was model-beautiful. She could have been twin sisters with Kate Upton, though less voluptuous and her eyes more blue. Lara's blue eyes were as bright as the lights which lit the stage, performing to the filled seats in the audience. The blue guitar accented just how piercing her eyes were. Lara's long, blonde hair spiraled down to her small chest, framing her slightly freckled face. The high definition struggled to find a flaw.

The guitar had an indescribable sound. Lara's left fingers moved about the frets, her right picking at the strings just behind the pickups. It looked effortless. She began singing a cover of the London Grammar song *Stay Awake*. If the guitar and drums didn't do the job of transporting the audience, Lara's voice did. Nothing more was needed. The theatre was as full as the attention she received. Lisa found her captivating. Lisa was far from alone in that way.

"....*Stay awake with me*," Lara sang. "*.... Take your hand and come and find me.*"

"I'm trying sweetie," Sheed said under her breath. "I'm trying."

www.ingramcontent.com/pod-product-compliance
Lightning Source LLC
Chambersburg PA
CBHW031145270326
41931CB00006B/151